LEARNING AND USING
GEOGRAPHIC INFORMATION SYSTEMS:

ARCEXPLORER EDITION

LEARNING AND USING
GEOGRAPHIC INFORMATION SYSTEMS:
ARCEXPLORER EDITION

Wilpen L. Gorr
H. John Heinz III School of Public Policy and Management at Carnegie Mellon University

Kristen S. Kurland
H. John Heinz III School of Public Policy and Management and the School of Architecture at Carnegie Mellon University

THOMSON
COURSE TECHNOLOGY

Australia • Canada • Mexico • Singapore • Spain • United Kingdom • United States

THOMSON
™
COURSE TECHNOLOGY

Learning and Using Geographic Information Systems: ArcExplorer Edition
by Wilpen L. Gorr and Kristen S. Kurland

Senior Vice President, Publisher
Kristen Duerr

Vice President, Technology Product Strategy
Mac Mendelsohn

Executive Editor
Bob Woodbury

Senior Acquisitions Editor
Maureen Martin

Senior Product Manager
Eunice Yeates

Development Editor
DeVona Dors

Senior Marketing Manager
Karen Seitz

Production Editor
Jill Klaffky

Associate Product Manager
Sarah Santoro

Editorial Assistant
Jennifer Smith

Senior Manufacturing Coordinator
Justin Palmeiro

Compositor
GEX Publishing Services

Copy Editor
Mary Kemper

Proofreader
Wendy Benedetto

Indexer
Liz Cunningham

Any additional questions about permissions can be submitted by e-mail to thomsonrights@thomson.com

Disclaimer
Thomson Course Technology reserves the right to revise this publication and make changes from time to time in its content without notice.

All photos provided by Pittsburgh, Pennsylvania CitiParks Department / © Duane Ashley

ISBN 0-619-21747-2

BRIEF CONTENTS

TABLE OF CONTENTS

PREFACE

Geographic information systems (GIS) is an amazing technology that fascinates and engages students. GIS maps have a dazzling array of purposes:

- Street maps create delivery routes, provide driving directions for the public and emergency vehicles, aid planning public transportation routes and schedules, and even pinpoint the location of fire hydrants and manhole covers.

- Maps that show geographic features help planners identify wetlands that need protection, areas at risk for flooding, and neighborhoods near or downwind from pollution sources.

- Population profile maps provide demographic analysis. At the neighborhood level, this data can reveal residents' ages, gender, ethnic background, income, educational attainment, transportation modes, and occupation. Such maps can help retailers to determine the location and size of new stores—or which customers to target for increased business. Similarly, city planners can use such maps when planning public facilities.

- Crime maps show recent criminal activity in neighborhoods, identify locations' criminal history, and highlight "at risk" areas. Every major city's police department has crime analysts that produce daily and monthly crime maps for uniformed police officers, detectives, and top management.

- Maps that track long-haul trucks using global-positioning-system receivers can show where trucks are at any point time, transmit how fast they are traveling, and provide directions to the nearest loads for return trips. The same technology can track emergency medical service, stolen vehicles, and military vehicles.

GIS maps are built layer by layer. A typical city might have more than 100 map layers, each showing a different feature type. A municipality's map layers can be combined with map layers from other sources to provide endless combinations of data that profile people, land, infrastructure, and the built environment.

Extraordinary Free Resources

This textbook would impossible without great GIS software and digital maps. The good news: (1) Great GIS materials are available, (2) this book shows students how to locate and use those resources, and (3) the resources are *free*!

The world's leading vendor of GIS, the Environmental Studies Research Institute (ESRI), produces a wide range of GIS software packages including the free *ArcExplorer—Java Edition for Education*™ that we use throughout this book. ArcExplorer is desktop software for use on a Microsoft Windows or an Apple Macintosh computer. It is downloaded easily from ESRI's Web site, *www.esri.com*, or may be obtained on CD from Thomson Course Technology. While ArcExplorer does not have the full range of capabilities of a commercial GIS, it has a remarkable set of capabilities perfect for an introductory text such as this.

Tax dollars are at work in this textbook: The Federal government used them to create digital maps for the entire United States and many spatially-referenced data sets, such as the decennial census, that can be mapped. These maps and data are free and easily downloaded from the Internet for your own city or community. In addition, many states, cities, and counties have created their own maps, which are often free for downloading. (We have taken care to select Web sites that are unlikely to change, and as this book goes to press, all are operational.)

A Unique Approach

There is no doubt that GIS is an exciting technology and career field. Unfortunately, the obstacle to entering this field is that it has a very steep learning curve—it is very hard to get a start in GIS. This textbook, however, flattens out the learning curve out and makes it easy to teach, learn, and use GIS at an introductory level. We have been teaching GIS for more than 15 years to a wide range of students, including high school juniors and seniors, GIS practitioners, undergraduates, master-degree students, and Ph.D. candidates. *Learning and Using Geographic Information Systems* brings together all the good ideas and approaches to introducing this subject that we have discovered.

Learning and Using Geographic Information Systems provides a one-stop, complete educational solution for an introduction to GIS. It has both the instructional text students need to learn GIS's underlying principles, concepts, and knowledge, **plus** step-by-step tutorials for hands-on use of ArcExplorer. This arrangement, with instructional text at the beginning of each chapter followed by computer tutorials, solves several problems. For instructors, it coordinates readings and tutorials for a good flow of study and computer lab work. For students, it means that they must buy only one book, and there is no waste in what they read—it all "bakes bread." Furthermore, the tutorials are time efficient because students already know the underlying concepts for their use before turning on their computers. This means that the tutorial portions of this book have no background reading to slow down computer learning.

This textbook's only prerequisite is basic computer literacy, including the ability to locate and open files, use a file-compression program to unzip compressed files, and create simple word-processing documents. Some experience with spreadsheet and presentation software is desirable but not essential: We provide step-by-step instructions for the tasks to be carried out in Microsoft Excel and PowerPoint. We also provide instructions on using Microsoft Paint (Win) and AppleWorks (Mac).

To the Student

ArcExplorer—Java Edition for Education requires 91 MB of free space on your c:\ drive for Windows computer installation and about the same amount for Macintosh computers. You will need an additional 177 MB of free space for installation of data files required for working through tutorials and exercises.

We want you to be able to work smoothly and quickly through the book's computer tutorials. At the same time, you need practice to internalize computer instructions. It is critically important that you do the Practice exercises that are interspersed throughout the tutorials. They make you pause long enough to rethink and reuse what you just learned—and that really helps you make the material your own.

To the Instructor

Instructors can use this book as a module in an information technology (IT) course or other field of study. It can also be used for a short, stand-alone course on GIS. For IT courses, GIS makes an attractive extension to spreadsheet or database skills: It attaches the graphic features of maps to spreadsheet and database tables. For substantive course-work areas, courses such as geography, environmental science, public policy, or sociology, GIS is an invaluable tool for student projects.

Chapters 1, 2, and 4 make a nice short course, workshop, or course module that spans two weeks at the pace of regular classes. Chapters 1–5, with exercises assigned, make a more complete introduction that can be covered in approximately three to four weeks. Adding the remaining chapters, which provide more advanced GIS capabilities and project management skills, and an independent project can easily fill a mini-semester course of seven weeks.

Supplemental Materials

The following supplemental materials are available when this book is used in a classroom setting. All of the teaching tools available with this book are provided to the instructor on a single CD-ROM. Some of these materials may also be found on the Thomson Course Technology Web site at *www.course.com*.

- *Electronic Instructor's Manual*: The Instructor's Manual assists in class preparation by providing suggestions and strategies for teaching the text, chapter outlines, technical notes, quick quizzes, discussion topics, and key terms.

- *Solutions Manual*: The Solutions Manual contains answers to end-of-chapter questions and exercises.

- *Sample Syllabi and Course Outline*: The Sample syllabi and course outlines are provided as a foundation to begin planning and organizing your course.

- *ExamView Test Bank*: ExamView allows instructors to create and administer printed, computer (LAN-based), and Internet exams. The Test Bank includes an array of questions that correspond to the topics covered in this text, enabling students to generate detailed study guides that include page references for further review. The computer-based and Internet testing components allow students to take exams at their computers, and also save the instructor time by grading each exam automatically. The Test Bank is also available in Blackboard and WebCT versions posted online at *www.course.com*.

- *PowerPoint Presentations*: Microsoft PowerPoint slides for each chapter are included as a teaching aid for classroom presentation, to make available to students on the network for chapter review, or to be printed for classroom distribution. Instructors can add their own slides for additional topics they introduce to the class.

- *Figure Files*: Figure and table files from each chapter are provided for your use in the classroom.

- *Data Files*: Data Files, containing all of the data necessary for steps within the chapters are provided in the data CD-ROM that comes with this, through the Course Technology Web site at *www.course.com*, and on the Instructor's Resources CD-ROM.

Book Organization

The goal of this book is to give students the knowledge and skills to do analytic mapping and provide information to shed light on issues in their own communities. To help students meet this goal, we use an actual project from our community as a sustained example throughout the book. The project, the Swimming Pool Case Study, provides a real-world backdrop against which students can learn the principles of GIS.

The Case Study

The Swimming Pool Case Study is examined in each chapter. Its purpose was to provide information to help city officials in Pittsburgh, Pennsylvania, determine which public swimming pools to keep open. Prior to our consultation, city officials had closed half of the city's 32 pools because of city budget problems. In the future, the city will close four more pools. A GIS was needed to determine which subset of pools best serve the needs of Pittsburgh's youth population who, in the absence of summer recreation, are at risk for delinquent behavior. Students will begin working on this project in Chapters 1–6 and then complete their analysis in Chapter 7.

Chapter Features

Each chapter contains features that present tutorial activities, provide hands-on practice that extend the teaching, reinforce concepts through short-answer questions, and extend learning through real-world exercises. A list of those features follows.

Instructional text: Each chapter begins with a section for students to read before turning on their computer. The text presents key concepts and methodologies that are supported by examples.

Step-by-step tutorials: For building students' GIS skills, we have students work through short sequences of steps on their computer. Most blocks of work contain 8 to 10 steps. Instructions are provided for both PC and Mac users. Screen captures illustrate parts of steps that are difficult or lengthy to explain in text.

Practice activities: Series of hands-on tutorial steps are periodically interrupted by Practice exercises. These brief activities have students repeat the steps they've just completed, but for slightly different situations. This additional practice moves students toward independent work and helps them to internalize the concepts and skills they've practiced.

Summary: Each chapter concludes with a summary of the chapter's content.

Key terms: Key terms are highlighted and explained within the instructional text. For easy reference, the chapter's key terms are listed and defined after the Summary.

Short-answer questions: To help students to absorb the reading materials, each chapter has short-answer questions that make students probe the principles and concepts presented. Some questions have specific answers that can be found in the instructional text; others require students to extend their knowledge by predicting outcomes and making hypotheses.

Exercises: Each chapter contains hands-on exercises that require some independent thinking on the student's part. In Chapter 7, students can choose one (or more) of four projects to complete: the Swimming Pool Case Study; a project related to Chapter 7's two examples, using the chapter examples as templates; or develop a completely new project based on the student's own interests.

References: Each chapter concludes with a list of references, both print and electronic, that the student might wish to consult for further study.

Summary of Chapter Content

A brief summary of each chapter's content follows.

Chapter 1, Introducing GIS: The instructional text defines GIS, explains its unique capabilities, discusses the fundamental nature of digital map layers, introduces map infrastructure (base maps and data) available from the Federal government, and introduces the Swimming Pool Case Study. The tutorial section is based on two GIS Web sites. The first Web site, the Greenwood County, South Carolina GIS, has GIS functionality for using detailed maps and data on all land parcels and supporting infrastructure in the county. The second Web site, San Francisco's Prospector, has advanced spatial-analysis functions that support economic development by making it easy for businesses to find and analyze buildings or sites for new businesses.

Chapter 2, Navigating GIS: The instructional text covers fundamental knowledge of latitude and longitude coordinates, map scales, and map projections. The tutorial has students open a finished map composition that we built for the Swimming Pool Case Study. Students use the GIS to zoom and pan the map, turn layers off and on, set threshold scales to automatically turn layers on and off as they change map scale, measure distances, and project the globe to transform it to common flat representations.

Chapter 3, Getting Information from a GIS: The instructional text covers vector maps and file formats, feature attribute tables of vector maps and their data dictionaries, raster maps and file formats, attribute queries including simple and compound logical conditions, and spatial selection of mapped features using buffers. The tutorial has students open a second map composition for the Swimming Pool Case Study. Students use the map to select graphic features and records directly, through map tips and the Identify tool, through a data-attribute query builder; and spatially, using circular buffers.

Chapter 4, Designing Maps: The reading material covers graphic-design principles, including graphic hierarchy; explains various properties of color and devices for choosing colors; explains how to construct numeric-variable categories needed in mapping data; provides guidelines for symbolizing graphic features on maps; and provides guidelines for designing maps for different audiences. The tutorial guides students to build their own swimming-pool map composition from base-map layers. They will use ArcExplorer's Catalog tool to study available map layers, symbolize boundaries and other context layers, symbolize the swimming-pool layer by using unique symbols, symbolize a color-coded map layer, and symbolize a point layer with size-graduated symbols.

Chapter 5, Finding GIS Resources: The instructional text summarizes two key Web sites for obtaining free map layers and associated data. The tutorial guides students to visit the Web sites, download materials, and use them in ArcExplorer. Students will need a compression program, such as PKZip or WinZip, to decompress downloaded files.

Chapter 6, Extending ArcExplorer's Capabilities: The instructional text discusses the design of map layouts for use in reports or other uses, approaches to creating new variables from existing ones in map layers, the approach of address matching to place points on maps from street address data, and the concept of table joins for attaching data tables to base maps. The tutorial instructs students in how to use ArcExplorer in tandem with Microsoft Excel and PowerPoint: Students use PowerPoint to assemble a map layout from maps exported from ArcExplorer and screen prints of map legends, use Excel to create new variables in the feature attribute table of a map layer, use ArcExplorer and Excel to address match points, and use Excel to join tables to feature attribute tables. Students will use Microsoft Paint (Win) or AppleWorks (Mac) to edit map legends exported from ArcExplorer for use in map layouts.

Chapter 7, Working on GIS Projects: The final chapter covers project management methods for carrying out independent GIS work on an issue or problem. The chapter has four projects from which to choose. They are a culmination of the Swimming Pool Case Study, a public transportation project, an environmental pollution problem, and an independent project that the student or the instructor designs. The latter three projects can be done in students' own community, with maps and data downloaded for free from the Internet.

Appendix: Downloading and Installing ArcExplorer and the LearningAndUsingGIS Data Files: This appendix has instructions for downloading and installing the ArcExplorer software in order to use this book. Instructions are given for both Microsoft Windows PCs and Apple Macintosh computers. The tutorials require map layers and other files which are also provided on the CD-ROM. The appendix has instructions for installing the data files.

ACKNOWLEDGEMENTS

We are profoundly grateful for the expert help, guidance, and work provided by Course Technology editors and staff on this book: Mac Mendelsohn, Maureen Martin, Eunice Yeates, Jill Klaffky, DeVona Dors, Mary Kemper, Chris Scriver, Serge Palladino, and Chris Carvalho. A special thanks is due to DeVona Dors, developmental editor, whose contributions to this book have been invaluable.

We also thank many others: Duane Ashley, Director of Pittsburgh's CitiParks Department, who provided the data and photographs used throughout this book and is our client for the Swimming Pool Case Study. He commissioned our GIS study, provided much valuable information on the problem and its solution, and provided funding for data input. Course Technology helped pay for the early demonstration-phase of pool data input, for which we are very grateful. In addition, Bradley Barnell kindly gave us permission to use the Greenwood County, South Carolina, GIS Web site; and Erich Seamon gave us permission to use the San Francisco Prospector GIS Web site. Matt Smith of *www. HomeTownLocator.com* gave us permission to use data on schools and Karen Florini of Environmental Defense gave us permission to use pollution data from *Scorecard.org*. We have learned much about teaching GIS from our students over the years, especially from those at Carnegie Mellon's Heinz School of Public Policy and from high school students enrolled in our InfoLink program (see *www.heinz.cmu.edu/infolink*). We thank them all.

CHAPTER **1**

INTRODUCING GIS

LEARNING OBJECTIVES

In this chapter, you will:

- Survey GIS and its unique capabilities
- Explore the basics of digital map layers
- Learn about map infrastructure
- Gain an overview of the Swimming Pool Case Study
- Use your browser to navigate maps in a Web GIS site
- Use your browser to conduct analysis on a Web GIS site

So, you're new to this?

INTRODUCTION

If you have ever used maps to find places, you know that they work pretty well. The actual streets are

shown, and they lead you to the retail store, lake, or whatever it is that you are seeking. Similarly, sailors

use nautical charts to avoid hitting reefs, and travelers use maps to find points of interest in strange lands.

Often, such needs are met even better using a **geographic information system (GIS)**, a computer-

based, dynamic mapping system. We'll explore a more thorough definition for GIS in the next section.

MapQuest is a popular GIS. If you have never used the MapQuest Web site, go to *www.mapquest.com*, click the Get Directions button, enter your address as the Starting Address, enter the White House's address (1600 Pennsylvania Avenue NW, Washington, D.C.) as the Ending Address, and click Get Directions. How many legs, door to door, does it take to travel from your house to the White House? One of the authors can make the trip in 20 legs, door to door, from his house.

Place-to-place directions, such as how to get to the White House, are an example of **reference mapping**. A GIS also offers a second kind of map use: analytical mapping, the main topic of this textbook. **Analytical mapping** involves collecting digital maps and data, creating your own map compositions, and using a GIS and its unique information-retrieval capabilities to help answer questions that involve locations. For example, in the case study that runs throughout this textbook, you'll help the director of Pittsburgh's Citiparks Department decide which public swimming pools to keep open. Recently, Pittsburgh had to close 16 of its 32 public swimming pools because of budget problems, and in the future it will close 4 more. Did the city choose the right 16 pools to close? Which additional pools should it close? It takes an analytic GIS to answer such questions.

A GIS is a tool. To use it well, you must learn certain principles and concepts. Then you need to gain experience using a GIS software package, such as ArcExplorer®, to build additional skills. Although **ArcExplorer**, a free GIS package, has some limitations, it is still a very useful tool. Chapter 6 discusses some extensions to ArcExplorer using Microsoft® Excel, Paint, and PowerPoint® that, when combined with ArcExplorer, will allow you to carry out some rather sophisticated projects.

This chapter introduces some of the unique capabilities of GISs and the fundamentals of digital map layers and provides an overview of the Swimming Pool Case Study. You will see a GIS in action by visiting two Web GIS sites. First, you will use a GIS to navigate through maps and retrieve incredibly detailed and rich information about properties in Greenwood, South Carolina. Then you will analyze commercial properties for lease, sale, or rent in San Francisco. Your market analyses will take just minutes to complete using the GIS but would take weeks without the GIS. We have included screen prints of both Web sites in case you do not have Internet access. However, if you do have Internet access, you should carry out the tutorial steps for those Web sites.

Definition of GIS

This brings us to the question: What exactly is a GIS? Clarke (2003) contends that there is no single, good definition of GIS; there are many. We have been influenced by existing definitions, but here we present our own for people like you who are interested in applying GIS. We define a GIS as *a computer-based, dynamic mapping system with spatial data processing and querying capabilities*. Let's analyze each part of this definition.

- *computer-based*: Clearly, GIS is a computer technology. You will be using the free desktop GIS package called *ArcExplorer—Java Edition for Education*® on your computer.
- *dynamic mapping system*: A GIS is not a static map, but a changeable system that you control. With a GIS, you can compose and view your own maps, change colors as you desire, zoom in to get details, turn parts of the map on and off, get recorded data by clicking on mapped features, and so forth.
- *spatial data processing*: You can put points on the map from scratch, such as the Pittsburgh swimming pools. You can symbolize map features automatically using their accompanying data values, for example, giving swimming pools that have the data value 1 (signifying open for the summer) square, blue point markers and giving those with value 0 (closed) square, red point markers.
- *data and spatial queries*: You can also conduct data queries; for example, you might find and highlight all the residences of people who intended to use a certain pool when they signed up for pool passes. In addition, you can conduct spatial queries, such as having ArcExplorer add up the number of youths living within a one-mile radius of any pool.

Unique Capabilities of a GIS

Information systems are tools that provide answers to the questions who, what, when, where, why, and how. Until the advent of GISs, however, there was no good way for an information system to answer *where* for many important uses. It is true that any information system can store street addresses, such as 4800 Forbes Ave, Pittsburgh, PA 15213 (the address of Carnegie Mellon, our university), and thus in a limited way answers *where*.

What if, however, your information needs are more sophisticated? For example, students enrolled in any Pittsburgh university can register and take a limited number of classes at any other Pittsburgh university. Suppose that several Pittsburgh universities want to combine their separate shuttle-bus services so students living off-campus can get from their housing to any number of universities—and travel between universities. How would you go about designing shuttle-bus routes? The relative locations of student residences, universities, and the street network would all come into play for a solution. You would need an analytical map with those features. In the past, our students worked on this problem using a GIS. (In Chapter 6, you will use university addresses in Pittsburgh to place universities on a street map.)

An important and unique capability of a GIS is that it represents locations in ways that we can process on a computer. To do this, a GIS stores the coordinates of **graphic features**, such as points and lines, for use in displaying maps, showing relative position on earth, calculating distances, and so forth. Instead of storing all graphic features for a map in a single folder or file, a GIS stores related graphic features in separate collections of files called **map layers**. For example, swimming pools, residences of pool users, streets, city boundaries, and so on, are all different map layers. An advantage of this arrangement is that map layers can be reused easily and assembled into any number of map compositions. What we commonly refer to as a "map" in a GIS or on paper is actually a **map composition**—several map layers symbolized and arranged in a specific way. Viewed in another way, a map composition is the final product of map design and GIS work. It provides reference information and supports analysis for the purpose at hand, such as deciding which public swimming pools to close in Pittsburgh.

In addition to providing a representation of map graphic features, a GIS has a suite of tools (computer programs or algorithms) that uniquely process locations. Next, we will discuss some of these tools.

Figure 1-1 is a screen capture from ArcExplorer showing a map of Pittsburgh with the results of using several tools displayed. Included on the map are the open and closed pools last summer and the residences of a corresponding random sample of pool tag holders. (To use any of the Pittsburgh pools, a resident must fill out a form, obtain a pool ID tag, and present the tag each time he or she visits a pool.) We did not have the resources to input all 50,000 residences of people who had pool tags; instead we captured their spatial pattern with a small random sample. A **random sample** is a relatively small part of a population, chosen as if drawn from a hat containing well-mixed paper slips. Such a sample is widely used in statistics because it is economical and represents the behavior and patterns of the entire population.

Next, we describe the GIS tools and results shown in Figure 1-1:

- *Map coordinates*: We have the mouse cursor hovering over the famous Point Park in Pittsburgh, where the Allegheny and Monongahela Rivers join to form the Ohio River. The projected map coordinates of that point in feet are (583,679.077, 4,477,065.859). Chapter 2 explains map coordinates and projections. The important thing here is to see that the map is not just a picture, but it also has a coordinate system that corresponds to locations on earth.
- *Layers turned on and off*: The check boxes to the left of layer names in the left legend panel turn map layers on and off. You can see that the layers for Pools, Pittsburgh, Rivers, Pool Tag Holders' Residences, and Allegheny County are turned on, but the other layers are off. We can change the map dramatically by clicking different layers on or off.

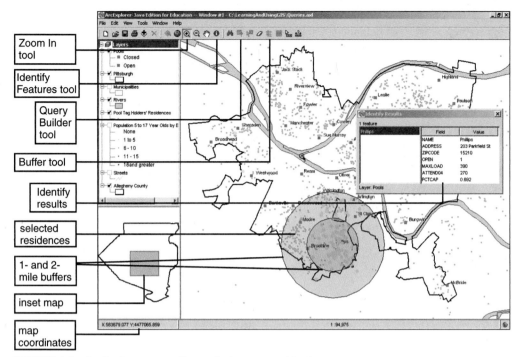

FIGURE 1-1 ArcExplorer map with results from several tools

- *Identify Features tool*: Each graphic feature in a GIS has a corresponding data record. The Identify Features tool allows you to click on a graphic feature on the map and see its record. Here, we clicked on Phillips pool, an open pool last summer, which is at the center of the concentric circular buffer areas on the map. In the Identify Results dialog box, you can see that Phillips has a rated maximum capacity (MAXLOAD) of 390 swimmers, average attendance (ATTEND04) of 270 swimmers per day, and that this amounted to over 69% usage of capacity (PCTCAP) (which is quite good).

- *Query Builder tool*: You can use standard database queries to highlight graphic features. Pool tag holders filled in a field on their application forms indicating which pool they intended to use (they could use any of the open pools, but they were to indicate their preferred pool). We used the Query Builder tool to select all pool tag holders in our sample who wrote in "Phillips" as their preferred pool. These are highlighted by the yellow circular point markers on the map. We were quite surprised to see that residents from as far away as two miles from Phillips indicated that they intended to use that pool. (Two miles is quite far because Pittsburgh has many hills and valleys causing actual travel distances to be much farther than straight-line distances, such as are measured on a map. Also, many pool users take a bus, and with stops and winding bus routes, a two-mile bus ride is far. Lastly, many youths walk to pools for distances up to about a half mile.) That is a promising result that suggests that residents may be willing to travel farther than anticipated to use the open pools.

- *Buffer tool*: This tool is used for **proximity analysis**, which answers the question, "What is near a selected feature?" We selected Phillips pool and had ArcExplorer draw one- and two-mile-radius circular buffers around it. While not shown here, you can have ArcExplorer add up the total number of pool tag holders within each of the buffers, and produce other useful statistics as well.
- *Inset map*: Before printing the map of Figure 1-1, we clicked the Zoom In button and dragged a rectangle around Pittsburgh to zoom in to the city from the larger Allegheny County. The inset map shows the outline of the county plus the rectangle we dragged, which is the current map extent. The **map extent** is the rectangle defining the window on the world presented by the GIS at any point in time. It is represented on the computer by the lower-left and upper-right coordinates of the rectangle outlining the visible map.

The previous list includes many of ArcExplorer's tools and many of the unique capabilities of GIS in general. There are additional tools built into the ArcExplorer menu system that you will use in later chapters.

MAP LAYERS

All the map layers in Figure 1-1 are **vector-based drawings**; that is, they are based geographic locations, called **points**, that have (x, y) coordinates. A second kind of map layer is a **raster image map**, which refers to a checker board of small squares, each with a solid color fill. Most of the graphic features in maps that have analytic value are vector-based, because it is this type of map layer that has data records, such as the pools example previously given. Let's take a closer look at two kinds of map layers.

Vector-based Map Layers

Vector-based maps have point, line, and polygon features. As previously noted, a point has (x, y) coordinates. A **line** has a starting and ending point and may have additional **shape vertices** (points) in between for bends in the line. Lines in an urban street network are generally one block long and share end points to form a connected network. A **polygon** has three or more lines joined to form a closed area. In maps, polygons generally share lines with adjacent polygons in a way that partitions a large area into smaller ones. Note that we have used points for swimming pools, lines for street centerlines (not displayed in Figure 1-1), and polygons for Pittsburgh's and Allegheny County's boundaries.

A vector map can display points, lines, and polygons, but a vector map *layer* has only one vector type: point, line, or polygon. Also, by convention and because of the practicality of needing a different set of attributes for each layer, each vector layer is kept homogeneous in terms of features. For example, the pools are a separate point layer as are the residences of pool users.

A **feature attribute table** stores whatever characteristics we desire, and the characteristics are available for point, line, or polygon map layers. An **attribute** is a column of data with a name, such as MAXLOAD, and a data type, such as numeric or text. Each graphic feature, such as a swimming pool, has its own record, or row, in its feature attribute table. Figure 1-2 symbolizes two points, a line, and a polygon with color, line type, outlines, and "color fill" for graphic features that might appear on a map. You do not have to paint each individual graphic feature in a GIS map. Instead, you use a GIS's automated method of symbolizing vector features based on their corresponding data values.

Vector Graphic Features

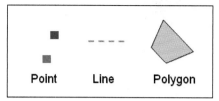

| Point | Line | Polygon |

Feature Attribute Table

POOL	CAPACITY	OPEN
Phillips	390	1
Leslie	615	0

FIGURE 1-2   Vector map feature types and attribute table

For example, for the points shown in Figures 1-1 and 1-2, we used a solid blue square point marker of a certain size for open pools, and a red point marker for closed pools. The GIS uses the *Yes* (a 1) and *No* (a 0) values for the OPEN attribute from the feature attribute table, as shown in Figure 1-2, to draw the finished map. Any pool with the value *Yes* (a 1) in the OPEN column gets the blue symbol, and so on. In the same way, some lines might get solid line types and others dashed lines, as shown in Figure 1-2, depending on the values of an attribute. Finally, the outline color and width and color fill of polygons are similarly the result of an attribute—perhaps land use categories, such as residential, commercial, and industrial.

A final note on vector-based maps: As you may have gathered, vector-based maps are not stored images which are merely retrieved and displayed. Your computer draws and symbolizes vector maps on-the-fly, from scratch, every time you display them in your GIS.

Raster Image Maps

A raster image map, by contrast, is an electronic image, such as an aerial photograph or satellite image. The electronic image is composed of a rectangular array of square cells, called **pixels**, with a number in each cell representing the solid color fill of that cell. When zoomed out far enough, all you see is a picture, and none of the individual pixels are distinguishable because they are so small. Figure 1-3 is an example of a raster map zoomed in to an individual building, a church. The second and third panels show the church spire zoomed in farther and farther until the pixels are evident.

A raster map is more than a picture, however, because it also has the same coordinates as do vector maps; otherwise, the two types of map layers would not plot together. You will work with a raster map in Chapter 2.

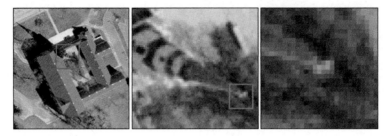

FIGURE 1-3 Raster map image zoomed in

For the most part, raster maps provide detailed spatial context for vector maps. The vector land parcels carry the data on property attributes, and the raster map provides a realistic picture. People who make vector maps for physical features use aerial photographs as their sources. They digitize them by tracing over the photos with special equipment to create vector layers for street curbs, parking lots, building outlines, and so forth.

Classification of Map Layers

So far, we have a classification of map layers based on the underlying representation of graphic features: vector or raster. Another classification is for the kind of real-world features portrayed.

- *Physical features*: This kind of map layer shows the boundaries of bodies of water, continents, street curbs, parking lots, buildings, etc. These are features that you could see from an airplane. Generally, physical features are the only map layers that have a raster image representation. All other layers are usually vector-based. Furthermore, map layers such as street curbs and parking lots are digitized from raster images.
- *Political features*: This kind of map layer displays the boundaries of countries, provinces or states, counties, and cities. Of course, these are invisible unless some physical feature, such as a street or river, happens to be used as a boundary.
- *Legal features*: For the most part, these map layers show the boundaries of deeded land parcels owned by individuals, companies, or the government. Again, these are most often invisible.
- *Statistical features*: These map layers show boundaries used by the U.S. Census Bureau and other agencies to report tabulations, such as the census. Included are polygon map layers such as census tracts—polygons used as the primary reporting areas of census variables like population—and traffic analysis zones.
- *Administrative features*: These map layers are polygons designed by governments or companies to assign responsibilities to people who will perform work by geographic territory. Examples include zip codes for delivery of the mail, school districts for delivery of public education services, police car beats for assigning patrol areas to police cars, and so on.

The work of building most information systems starts from scratch. For example, designers build databases using information collected from their company or agency. For GIS applications, however, this is not possible. A GIS depends on national and local government map layer infrastructures as the starting point. We downloaded most of the map layers used in the swimming pool case—streets, municipal boundaries, city blocks, rivers, and the county boundary—for free from government sources, and we could not have built the GIS without them. Then we built a few unique layers based on street addresses and the streets layer, namely, the swimming-pool and pool-user-residence point layers.

TIGER/Line® Maps

A major federal government map infrastructure is known as the **TIGER/Line maps** (**T**opologically **I**ntegrated **G**eographic **E**ncoding and **R**eferencing system). The original purpose of these vector-based maps was to help the Census Bureau take the census every 10 years, but the maps have found many, many more uses by organizations and individuals across the country.

Free TIGER/Line maps are available by county for all of the U.S. and its territories. There are many different layers, but some of the most useful ones include street centerlines, rivers and lakes, states, counties, cities, and census tracts. Chapter 5 covers the TIGER/Line maps in more detail; you will download some of these maps from the Census and ESRI Web sites. (ESRI is the vendor of ArcExplorer and other GIS packages.)

FIPS Codes

When using political or statistical polygon layers, you need to have a unique identification value, or code, for each polygon. The U.S. federal government's **Federal Information Processing Standards (FIPS) Codes** has assigned a code for every polygon in the world. Every country and state or province has a code. The country code for the United States is *US*, and the state code for Pennsylvania is *42*. Political and statistical areas were designed to be **coterminous**, or to share boundaries and partition areas into smaller divisions. This allows FIPS codes to be **hierarchical**, or to be subdivided into smaller areas. To continue with the example of Pennsylvania, the next smallest division under *state* is *county*. Allegheny County has FIPS Code *003*, but to uniquely identify Allegheny County among all of the state/province subdivisions throughout the world, we have to put all of the pieces together: *US42003*. For a reference on FIPS Codes see *www.census.gov/geo/www/fips/ fips.html*.

Census Data

In addition to map layers, you will need data to attach, or join to, map layers for analysis. One of the most useful kinds of data for GIS is population statistics from the U.S. Census Bureau. This data is tabulated for all political and statistical areas, from census blocks up through the entire country, and they are freely downloadable. In Chapter 2, you will see the population map of 5- to 17-year-old children by block compared to swimming pool locations in Pittsburgh. The population data is from the 2000 Census. In Chapter 5, you will learn more about the census and will download census data from the Internet.

Yellow Pages Listings

Another important kind of data is for locations and attributes on commercial land uses, such as retail stores, supermarkets, and so forth. You can download data from free sources, such as *www.smartpages.com*, that have telephone book Yellow Pages listings, but you will need to do some work in Microsoft Excel and ArcExplorer to preprocess the data and get map coordinates for them (see Chapter 6). Many public libraries have CDs from Reference USA (see *www.referenceusa.com*) that already include map coordinates for Yellow Pages listings, so you can get data ready for use on a diskette or other storage device from the CDs.

SWIMMING POOL CASE STUDY

Our purpose in writing this book is to teach you how to work on GIS projects that answer important questions. Chapter 7 provides three projects you can work on, but you can also find additional projects in your own community or area of interest. Whether you are using this textbook's projects or developing your own, you should learn to consider the "big picture" and what is needed and what is important. We include this section to step back from the details of GIS and examine the big picture for the Swimming Pool Case Study. We have completed many project phases and steps for the swimming pools problems presented to you, so we call it a case study instead of a project. A project has much less structure in the beginning than a case study and requires many decisions along the road to a solution. Many of these decisions are already made for the swimming pools study.

Costs and Benefits of Public Swimming Pools

Pittsburgh, Pennsylvania, has had a declining population for some time. Many city services were designed for a larger population than Pittsburgh now has, including its 32 public swimming pools. So, the city's recent budget crisis has been a mixed blessing. It has forced closing of many public facilities that the city no longer needs or can justify on a cost-and-benefit basis, but it, of course, also reduced access by citizens to pools.

What are the benefits of swimming pools? They are enormous for the city's youth, and especially for those living in poverty. Swimming pools, besides being fun, have many health and social benefits. They keep kids under the watchful eyes of parents, guardians, and swimming pool staff. Suppose that out of the 50,000-plus pool tag holders who use Pittsburgh pools, one child is averted from a life of crime each year because of being at the pool instead of ending up in trouble elsewhere. How much would this save society?

The leading authority on such benefits is Cohen (1998), from whom we learn that the value of saving a person from a lifetime of crime is approximately $1.3 to $1.5 million. Included are cost savings to victims (71% of the savings), the criminal justice system (24% of the savings), and foregone earnings of the criminal (5% of the savings). Roughly $1.3 to $1.5 million is how much it costs to operate all 32 pools per year! What do you think? Does it seem worthwhile to keep pools open? We think so. Nevertheless, regardless of benefits, city officials had to close pools and halt many other services to avoid bankrupting the city.

Criteria for Closing Swimming Pools

That leaves us with the question of which pools should be closed and which left open. There are many criteria to be considered in order to make such a decision. Some criteria, such as the condition and age of the pools, do not depend on a GIS. Other criteria depend on location and GIS. One criterion is equity; for example, it would be unfair to keep pools open in the wealthier parts of the city and close them in the poor areas. Other location-based criteria are based on efficiency, such as which pools draw the most youths and which are used at the largest percentages of their rated capacities. Still other criteria attempt to maximize the number of residents with good access to pools.

The purpose of the Swimming Pool Case Study is to develop or estimate a set of location-based performance measures for all 32 pools that can influence the decisions on closings. The tutorials and exercises of Chapters 2 through 6 get a good start on this analysis. You have the option of finishing up the Swimming Pool Case Study as a project in Chapter 7.

GIS EXAMPLES ON THE WEB

The two Web sites that you are about to use or examine were built with ESRI's GIS Web server product called **ArcIMS® (Internet Map Server)**. This book does not have you build ArcIMS Web sites; that is beyond the book's scope, and you probably do not have access to a Web server that has ArcIMS installed. Nevertheless, it is interesting to note that developers who build ArcIMS Web sites compose their maps using ArcExplorer! ArcExplorer is an integral part of ArcIMS.

If you have an Internet connection, follow along on these tutorial steps. If not, just read through them and look at the corresponding figures of the Web site. You will use map navigation and some advanced GIS tools and will see some amazing local government map infrastructures. Local governments contract to build their own aerial photographs, digitize their own land parcel maps, collect their own real property data, digitize their own utility lines and pipes, and maintain their own database of licensed businesses—all of which you will see and use. Both Web sites also use census data, which plays a critical role in the second Web site.

Greenwood County, South Carolina, Web GIS Site

Greenwood, South Carolina, has a great cadastral Web GIS. The term **cadastral**, or cadastre, refers to data that establishes boundaries and ownership of land parcels. County governments maintain such data records because they record the legal documents of ownership and deeds, and they collect the majority of local government taxes, the property tax, based on assessed property value. Because of an equity goal, many county governments make cadastral data public on the Internet and available on paper in government offices. County employees must assess the market value of properties from time to time for levying property taxes, a difficult task, based on the sales prices of recently sold properties. They want property owners to be able to look up properties comparable to their own and determine that the comparables' assessed values are similar to their own assessment. Having public access to such a GIS provides us with a rich learning resource.

Next, let's explore this site.

The Web Site

1. Launch a Web browser such as Internet Explorer or Netscape. Click **File**, **Open** (or similar command), type in **http://165.166.39.5/giswebsite/default.htm**, and then click **Browse** or **Enter**.

2. Click **OK** in the disclaimer window. (*These steps produce a map of the county with several map layers visible for this scale, which is 1 inch = 6.6 miles on one particular monitor.*)

3. Hover your mouse cursor over the **right-most (eastern-most) point** in the county. See Figure 1-4. (*On the lower left of the browser window, you will get a read-out of the map coordinates for the point. We get (-81.86859, 34.13325), and yours should be close to that. These are in degrees longitude and latitude, which you will learn about in Chapter 3.*)

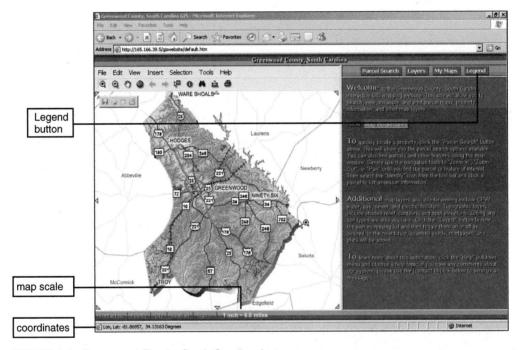

FIGURE 1-4 Greenwood County, South Carolina, home page

4. Click and drag the **right edge of the map window** to the right a bit, making more room for the map but still leaving the Legend button visible at the top right.

5. Click the **Legend** button at the top right of your screen. See Figure 1-5. (*The yellow area denotes the city of Greenwood, where you will zoom in next.*)

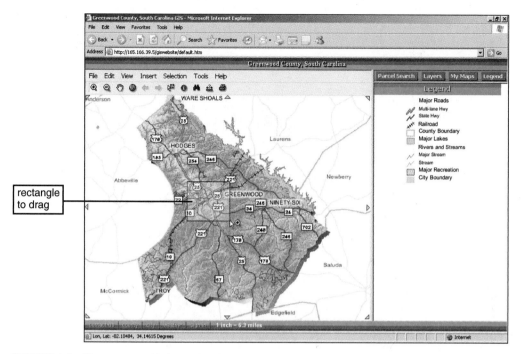

FIGURE 1-5   Home page with legend and rectangle to drag

The City of Greenwood, Zoomed In

1. You need to use the Zoom In tool to zoom in to the city of Greenwood. By default, the Zoom In tool is selected (left-most icon on top horizontal menu); drag a **rectangle** similar to the one in Figure 1-5 around the yellow Greenwood City area to zoom in to the map. Figure 1-6 shows the city zoomed in. *(If you need to try this step again, do not use your browser's Back button, but instead click the blue left-pointing arrow on the horizontal menu just above the map. The map has threshold scales that turn layers on and off, depending on the current map scale. At a scale of 1 inch = 1.1 miles, more street and stream layers are on.)*
2. Drag another **Zoom In rectangle**, as shown in Figure 1-6. Figure 1-7 shows the zoomed in area. *(Now you should be at a scale of about 1 inch = 800 feet, which displays land parcels' outlines and an aerial photo.)*
3. Drag yet another **rectangle** in the small area shown in Figure 1-7. Figure 1-8 shows the map zoomed in to several city blocks. *(The white land parcel outlines and aerial photo are looking impressive.)*

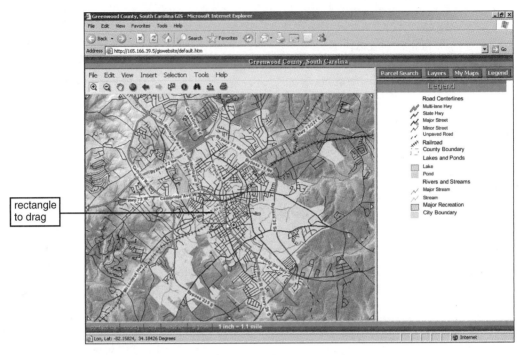

rectangle to drag

FIGURE 1-6 Map zoomed in to Greenwood City

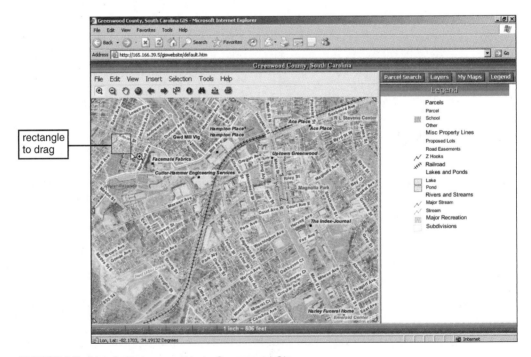

rectangle to drag

FIGURE 1-7 Map further zoomed in to Greenwood City

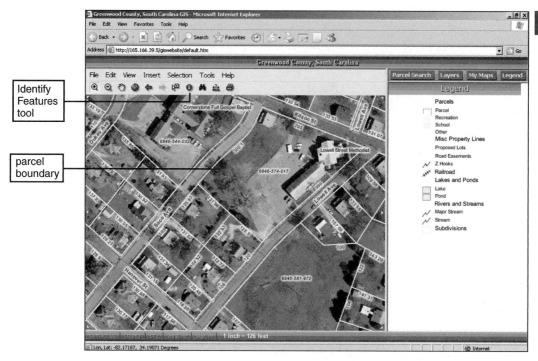

FIGURE 1-8 Map zoomed in to city blocks

Real Property Record Accessed with the Identify Features Tool

1. Click the **Identify Features** tool on the top horizontal menu. *(See Figure 1-8 for the location of the Identify Features tool.)*
2. Click inside the parcel of the **Lowell Street Methodist church**. See Figure 1-9. *(The right panel displays data from the corresponding real property data record. No assessed value is given here because the church is a non-profit organization and is therefore tax exempt. You can see, however, a few other data items such as the date purchased—December 17, 1991.)*
3. Click the **Layers** button over the right panel.
4. Click the **+** sign next to the Utility folder icon, and click **all of the utility layers**.
5. Click the **Refresh Map** button at the bottom of the layers panel. See Figure 1-10. *(When you change the map composition or anything about the map, the map server computer in Greenwood has to redraw the map, take a .jpeg format picture of the map, and then send it to your browser. That is what the Refresh button is for in this case.)*
6. Click the **Legend** button so you can interpret the utilities. *(Greenwood County is clearly in the 21st Century with this great map infrastructure and Web GIS site.)*

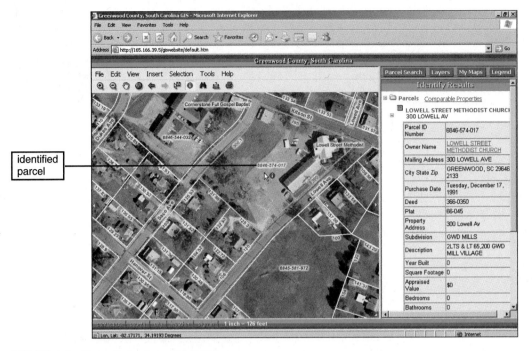

FIGURE 1-9 Map with land parcel identified

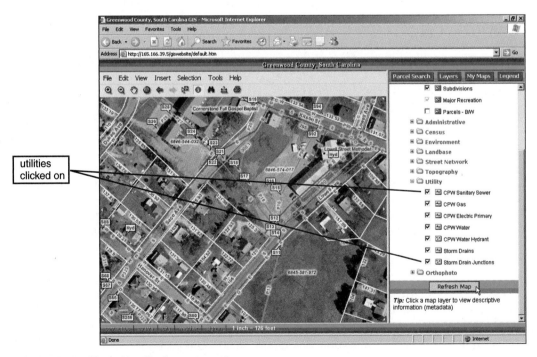

FIGURE 1-10 Map with utility layers turned on

- Use the Identify Features tool to extract a few more real property records.
- Use the Measure Distance and Area tool to get the perimeter and area of the church's land parcel.
- Use the Pan tool (the button with the white hand) to drag the map around.
- Zoom in a few times, first to a single land parcel and then to a parked car, until the pixels of the aerial photo are visible.
- Close your browser when you are done.

The San Francisco Prospector GIS Web Site

Cities attempt to attract new businesses and industry to generate more jobs, attract more residents, increase the tax base, and so forth. This is called **economic development**. The Internet is becoming a critical tool used by governments to promote economic development and make it easy for new businesses to get critical information about potential sites. You may have heard that the three most important features of a new business are "location, location, and location," and that is also true for economic development. So, clearly, there is a role for GIS here, as you will see next.

The Web Site

San Francisco's Prospector is an economic development Web site using an ArcIMS program written and sold by a company called GIS Planning. It has valuable and advanced GIS query capabilities to find and evaluate land and buildings for new businesses. Prospector is a remarkable resource for San Francisco and an incredible technology. You will use it now.

1. Launch a Web browser, such as Internet Explorer, Netscape, or Mozilla.
2. Click **File**, **Open** (or similar command), type in **http://www.ci.sf.ca.us/site/sfprospector_index.asp**, and then click **Browse** or **Go**.
3. Click the **Search for Available Commercial Sites & Buildings** link. See Figure 1-11. *(This brings up the map of San Francisco and a form in the right panel.)*

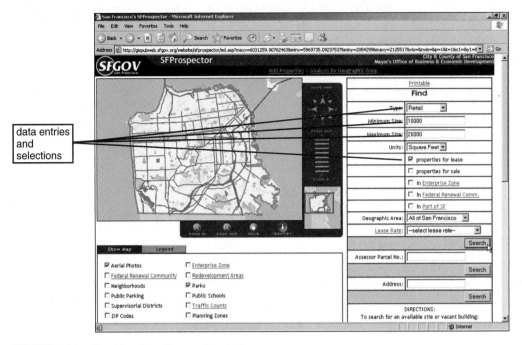

data entries
and
selections

FIGURE 1-11   San Francisco Prospector starting map

Query on Retail Properties for Lease

1. In the right panel, click the **list arrow** in the Type field, and then click **Retail**.
    (See Figure 1-11 for form entries.)
2. Type in **10000** in the Minimum Size field and **20000** in the maximum size field.
3. Click the **properties for lease** check box.
4. Click the **Search** button. See Figure 1-12. *(You will get different results than
    we have here, so you will have to use your imagination a bit and translate
    to your own results. When we ran this query, there were only two proper-
    ties available. If you did not find any properties, increase your maximum
    size from 20000 to 50000 and try again. You can see that our map zoomed in
    automatically to the extent of the two properties.)*
5. Click the link for the **first property** under Found Sites. See Figure 1-13. *(Ours
    is 111 Potrero Avenue, but yours might be different because of the passage
    of time. The result is quite nice. The map zooms in again, this time to an aerial
    photo with the building that has the available space. In the right panel is
    information about the property and who to contact for leasing information.
    You can see that the lease rate is $1.25 per square foot per year.)*

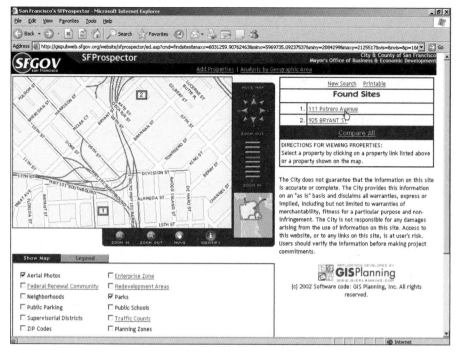

FIGURE 1-12   San Francisco zoomed in to available properties

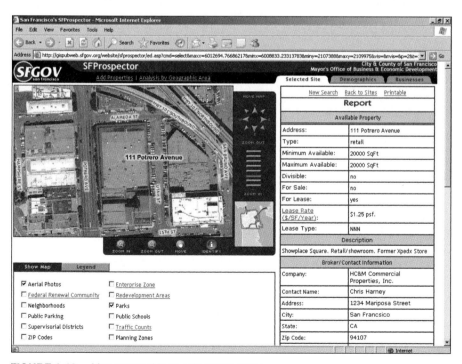

FIGURE 1-13   Map zoomed in to selected building

Introducing GIS

Demographic Analysis

1. Click the **Demographics** tab at the top of the right panel. *(The new panel is set up to calculate and report demographics for the population living within one mile of the property for lease. You could change the report to one of two other types, Consumer Expenditures or Business and Workforce, but leave the selections as is.)*

2. Click the **Calculate** button. See Figure 1-14. *(The map zooms out to an area to accommodate the resulting 1-mile-radius circular buffer, and the right panel displays demographics for the buffer.)*

FIGURE 1-14   Map with 1-mile buffer for demographics

3. Scroll down to see all of the information. *(There are age and race distributions, household income and net worth distributions, employment by industry and occupation, unemployment, number of households, educational attainment, and household size distribution. Amazing! It would take an analyst days to get the same information using non-GIS methods.)*

1. Click the **Businesses** tab at the top of the right panel. *(This form is set up to list businesses within a quarter mile of the selected property. Keep that setting.)*
2. Click the **Calculate** button. See Figure 1-15. *(This time the Web site retrieves all businesses within a quarter mile. Suppose that we want to open a restaurant at the selected site.)*

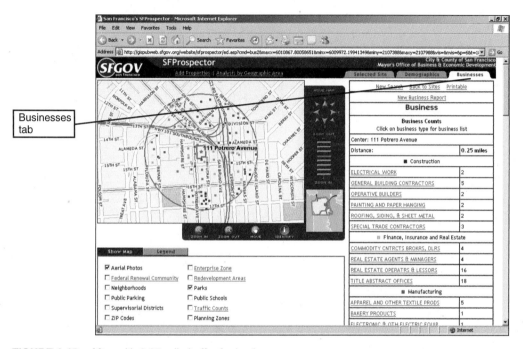

FIGURE 1-15   Map with 0.25-mile buffer for businesses

3. Scroll down to the **Retail Trade heading** in the right panel, and then click the **EATING AND DRINKING PLACES** link. See Figure 1-16. *(The result is a narrowed list of points on the map and links to them in the right panel. This is the competition for our new restaurant.)*

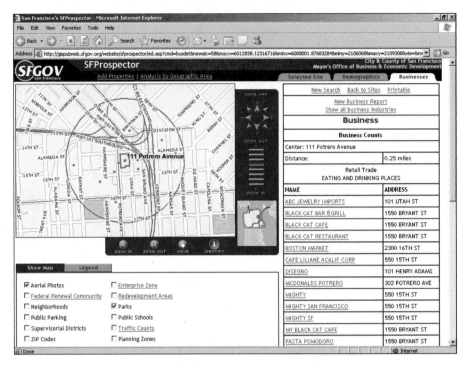

FIGURE 1-16   Map with 0.25-mile buffer for eating and drinking places

PRACTICE 1-2

- Click on some other layers of interest to you, and then click Display to refresh the map.
- Click the Demographics tab and try out the Consumer Expenditures and Business and Workforce reports. Change the distance, but do not make it larger than 2 miles or less than 0.25 miles.
- Do a new search for a property with characteristics of your own choosing.
- When you are finished, close your browser.

Chapter 1 Summary

Paper maps are used mostly for reference: to find points of interest, routes, and so forth. Such reference mapping is enhanced by a Geographic Information System (GIS). Another kind of mapping, analytic mapping, is used for analysis. For analytic mapping, a user assembles the map layers and data needed for the problem at hand, builds a corresponding GIS, and then uses the dynamic maps and tools of GIS to answer questions. In most cases, the cost of paper-based analytic mapping is prohibitive, but it is relatively easy and flexible using a GIS.

As fully defined, a GIS is a computer system that includes location coordinates for mapped features and has unique spatial processing and querying capabilities. There are many location-based questions that are impossible for textual databases to answer, but those questions are commonly answered with a GIS.

A GIS's unique capabilities include a linkage between mapped features and database records, the ability to easily symbolize maps and to add layers to a map composition, layers that can be turned on and off as needed, integration between drawn maps and images (such as aerial photos), and the ability to analyze features near other features.

GIS map layers include vector-based maps and raster maps. Vector-based maps are drawings composed of map layers having points, lines, or polygons. A GIS easily symbolizes maps, giving line features line types, widths, and colors; giving point markers shapes, sizes, and colors; and giving polygons line outline styles and color fill. A GIS uses the data attributes attached to each graphic feature to automatically symbolize maps.

Raster maps are images that a GIS stores and retrieves for viewing. Examples are aerial photographs and satellite images. In addition to the image file, a raster map also includes geographic coordinate data so the map can be displayed in its proper location.

Map layers are classified by type of real-world feature represented: physical, political, legal, statistical, and administrative. Physical maps can be vector-based or raster format, and the remaining map-layer types are vector-based.

A GIS depends on national and local map infrastructures. TIGER/Line maps are a type of map from the U.S. federal government. These free maps depict many of the real-world features of the U.S. and its possessions. Perhaps most important for analytical mapping are streets, census tracts, and political boundaries. To establish uniformity in naming and retrieving map data, the U.S. federal government has created identification codes (FIPS Codes) for most political and statistical boundaries around the world. Other useful map layers and related data are provided by the U.S. Census Bureau, Yellow Pages listings, and many other sources.

In this chapter, you used or examined two Web-based GISs to complete your introduction to GIS. ESRI's ArcIMS is the GIS Web server software implementing both Web sites. It is interesting to note that ArcIMS map designers use ArcExplorer, a component of ArcIMS and the GIS package used in this book, to build their map compositions.

Key Terms

Analytical mapping   Requires you to collect digital maps and data, create your own map compositions, and use a GIS and its unique information-retrieval capabilities to help understand behavior or make decisions in regard to locations. An example is the GIS constructed for the Swimming Pool Case Study of this textbook which has the purpose of providing information on what public swimming pools to close.

ArcExplorer   A free GIS package.

ArcIMS (Arc Internet Map Server)   GIS software provided by ESRI for building and deploying interactive GISs on the Web. An integral part of ArcIMS is ArcExplorer, which is used to build map compositions.

Attribute   A characteristic of an entity, such as a map layer, that is represented as a column of data in a table. Attributes, also known as variables and data elements, have data types such as text or numeric.

Cadastral   Refers to data or maps that have the purpose of identifying the boundaries and owners of deeded land parcels.

Coterminous   Refers to polygons that share boundaries and that partition areas into smaller areas. For example, states are made up of counties, and counties are made of census tracts. States, counties, and census tracts are coterminous.

Economic development   Initiatives taken by governments to attract new businesses and industry. For example, governments may make it easy to obtain information about potential sites and buildings available for purchase or lease, provide information on potential competitors or complementary businesses, and offer financial packages such as low-cost loans or reduced property taxes.

Feature attribute table   A table attached to the graphic features of a vector map layer. Every point, line, or polygon of a vector map layer has a record in that layer's feature attribute table.

Federal Information Processing Standards (FIPS) Codes   A set of codes provided by the U.S. federal government for identifying political and statistical areas around the world. For example, the FIPS code for Allegheny County, Pennsylvania is US42003, in which the code for Pennsylvania is 42 and that for Allegheny County is 003.

Geographic Information System (GIS)   A computer-based, dynamic mapping system with spatial data processing and querying capabilities.

Graphic feature   An element of a map that is visible on the computer screen or when printed out. For vector maps, a graphic feature is a point, line, or polygon that has been symbolized.

Hierarchical   A top-down organization with finer subdivisions at each layer. In GIS, we use *hierarchical* to refer to a classification and coding of coterminous areas that partition countries into states or provinces, states into counties, and so forth. FIPS Codes are hierarchical.

Line   An element of a line vector map. A line has two end points with geographic coordinates that locate the line on the earth's surface. They are connected with a line graphic and symbolized with a line type, width, and color.

Map composition   A collection of map layers symbolized and arranged in a GIS for a specific purpose. It is the end product of map design and GIS work.

Map extent   The rectangular window on the world provided by a GIS displaying a map. It is defined by its lower-left and upper-right coordinates on the displayed map.

Map layers   Separate files, stored by a GIS, of related geographic features. Map layers are arranged and combined to create map compositions, also called maps.

Pixels   A square area from a rectangular array of such squares that make up a digital image. Each pixel has a stored number that represents the solid color fill of the pixel.

Point   An element of a point vector map. A point has geographic coordinates locating it on the earth's surface and is displayed using a point marker graphic that has shape, area, and color.

Polygon   An element of a polygon vector map. A polygon is three or more lines joined together to form a closed boundary and area. The points comprising the lines of the polygon have geographic coordinates, locating the polygon on the earth's surface. Polygons generally share lines with neighboring polygons to partition larger areas. They are symbolized with an outline and color fill or a pattern.

Proximity analysis   Indicates features near a selected map feature

Random sample   A subset of a population drawn as if randomly selected. It provides an efficient way to estimate the distribution and behavior of the entire population (with some error, however).

Raster image map   An image file, such as for an aerial photograph, that also has geographic coordinates for location on the earth's surface.

Reference mapping   The common type of map used for travel or in atlases. Its primary purpose is to provide look-up information through visual examination.

Shape vertices   Points on a line map feature, between the line's end-point nodes, allowing the line to bend. Each pair of points, from one end-point node, through a sequence of the shape vertices, and on to the other end-point node is connected by straight-line segments. The line may not cross back over itself.

TIGER/Line maps   **T**opologically **I**ntegrated **G**eographic **E**ncoding and **R**eferencing system was created by the U.S. Census Bureau for use in conducting the census taken every 10 years. It is a very large set of line features, including political boundaries, streets, rivers, and so forth that can be compiled into separate map layers. The purpose of the line features is to create city blocks or equivalents, the smallest census tabulation unit used in the census.

Vector-based drawings   Drawings made up of points, lines, and polygons. Such drawings have no real curves, but are made up of all straight-line elements.

Vector-based maps   A map comprised of points, lines, or polygons that has geographic coordinates and a corresponding feature attribute table.

Short-Answer Questions

1. When you are using a GIS, explain what happens to vector and raster maps as you zoom in closer and closer. What happens to the vector map? The raster map?

2. Explain the difference between reference maps and analytical maps. Why is it easy to find good paper reference maps, and why do you need a GIS for analytical maps?

3. How does a vector GIS represent a circular shape or oval, such as an outdoor ice skating rink or a football stadium?

4. Do raster maps have feature attribute tables? Why or why not?

5. Map layers draw from the bottom up, as listed in the left layer panel of ArcExplorer (and most other GIS packages). See Figure 1-1. Suppose that you had the following three layers: (1) swimming pools; (2) zip code areas color coded to display the number of residents using swimming pools (0 to 499 are white, 500 to 999 are light gray, 1000 to 2000 are medium gray, 2000 and higher are dark gray); and (3) street centerlines. Which order would be best from bottom to top? Why?

6. Suppose that you have a point vector-based map layer for schools in your city, and the feature attribute table for this layer has an attribute called Type with these values: Public, Private, and Parochial. What would be a good way to symbolize the schools? Explain how symbolization works.

7. Imagine a one-street city that has its population in three various-sized clusters along a straight line. One cluster is at either end, and the third is in the center. Each cluster has its residents spread out along the street but is pretty far away from the nearest other cluster. Geographers have pretty much established that demand for goods or services declines inversely with the distance that a person must travel to make purchases. If you could locate only one swimming pool for the city, where would you best locate it? Two swimming pools? Three? Explain your rationale.

8. When creating administrative areas, it's a good idea to use census tracts as building blocks and to make each administrative area one or more contiguous census tracts. Pittsburgh police patrol districts (areas assigned a patrol car) are designed in this way. There are 42 patrol districts and 139 census tracts, so you can see that each patrol district has 3 to 4 tracts. Why are such patrol districts valuable for top police management? Assume that crime rates are roughly proportional to population levels, that the goal for designing patrol districts is to equalize work load, and that police need to study crime patterns relative to population characteristics, such as income and age distributions.

9. Greenwood County, South Carolina, has a service called "comparables" that it sells to realtors. If you subscribe to the service, you can log on, type in the address of a property for sale in Greenwood County, and the system will find similar properties that recently were sold. It provides the list of such properties and their selling price. Realtors use such information to determine the asking price of the property for sale. How do you suppose that the comparables computer program works? List the steps it must use.

10. San Francisco's Prospector Web site can retrieve census data for areas within a user-specified distance of a property that is available for lease or sale. Suppose that the census data are attached to a point file for the centers (centroids) of city blocks. How do you suppose Prospector calculates the census statistics? List the steps it must use.

Exercises

1. **Find Your House on a Map**. In this exercise, you will use the TerraServer Web site, supported by the U.S. Geological Survey, to find your house on a map. If you cannot find your house, then look for another address, such as that of your school.

    a. Launch a Web browser and open the following Web site: *http://terraserver-usa.com/*.

    b. Type in your address. If TerraServer is successful in finding the address, you will get two links, one for an aerial photo and the other for a topological map. Windows users can save just the photo and map images to their computer desktops by right-clicking and saving as *MyHouseAerial.bmp* and *MyHouseTopo.bmp*. Macintosh users can save the displayed screens that include the photo and map by control-clicking screens and then saving the images as *MyHouseAerial* and *MyHouseTopo* with image types made available (*.jpg* or *.gif*).

c. Create a Word document with the title (at the top of the page) Maps of My House. Include your name. Click **Insert**, **Picture**, **From File...**, browse to find one of your images, and insert it in the Word document. Do the same with the other image. Add some text describing some features of the maps; for example, describe something about your neighborhood from the map that you did not previously know.

d. Save your Word document as *MyHouse<YourName>.doc* (where you substitute your name for <YourName>). If you have an instructor, turn this document in as instructed.

2. **Use the MapQuest Web Site to Study Routing.** Here, we have you study the routing capabilities of the *www.mapquest.com* Web site and challenge you to find any bad directions. You can use your home address as the starting point, or another address, such as that of your school. Select three destination addresses in your own neighborhood. Look the addresses up in a telephone book or use *www.smartpages.com*.

a. Create a Word document called *Directions<YourName>.doc* (where you substitute your name for <YourName>). Type in the title: **MapQuest Routes from My House**. Include your name. List the three destination addresses that you are using.

b. Launch your Web browser, go to *www.mapquest.com*, and click the **Get Directions** button on the home page.

c. Enter the starting address and one of the three destination locations as the ending address. Click the **Get Directions** button.

d. Save a map image of each route. Right-click (Windows) or control-click (Mac), and click **Copy Image**. In your Word document, right-click (Windows) or control-click (Mac) the insertion point at the desired location for the directions, and then click **Paste**.

e. Comment on each of the sets of directions in your Word document. Do they look like the best route? Is there a better route? Are there any mistakes, such as sending you down the wrong direction on a one-way street?

f. If you have an instructor, turn the Word document in as instructed.

3. **Explore the National Geographic Map Machine.**

a. Create a Word document called *MapMachine<YourName>.doc* (where you substitute your name for <YourName>). Type the title **MapMachine Topographic Maps**. Include your name.

b. Choose a map that interests you from this Web site: *http://plasma.nationalgeographic. com/mapmachine/search.html*. Enter the name of the map type into your Word document.

c. Zoom in to an area of interest, and create a screen print of your screen by right-clicking (Windows) or control-clicking (Mac) the map and saving it to your desktop with the name *MyMap* and the image extension type made available (.*bmp*, .*jpg*, or .*gif*). In Word, click the insertion point below your map title, click **Insert**, **Picture**, **From File...**, browse to find your image, and insert it in the Word document.

d. Write a short paragraph on interesting map features.

e. Repeat Steps b–d for another map of interest.

f. If you have an instructor, turn the Word document in as instructed.

4. **Benchmark a GIS Web Site**. Benchmarking is a process that designers use to get good ideas from existing facilities, organizations, systems, or policies. You identify organizations that have good practices, study the good practices, and write a report on them to influence others.

   a. Select an ArcIMS Web site from *http://www.esri.com/software/internetmaps/visit_sites. html* that you find interesting and that has at least one advanced GIS function and one unique data set. Do not choose San Francisco Prospector, or even a similar economic development site with the same Web program. Also, do not choose the Greenwood, South Carolina, Web site.

   b. Identify a unique GIS capability used on the Web site, such as finding an address, zooming in with layers turning on and off automatically, using buffers that calculate statistics, selecting map features using data queries, and so forth.

   c. Create a Word document called *Benchmark<YourName>.doc* (where you substitute your name for <YourName>). Include a title at the top saying **Benchmark Study of http://<TheSiteURL>.** Include your name. Write a paragraph describing the purpose of the Web site.

   d. Describe the inputs to the unique GIS capability: any special databases or layers used and any inputs required of the user.

   e. Describe the output of the unique GIS capability. Get a screen printout of the output by right-clicking (Windows) or control-clicking (Mac) your screen and saving to your desktop or elsewhere with a name such as *Screenprint* and the image type extension made available (*.bmp*, *.jpg*, or *.gif*).

   f. Give each unique GIS capability a title, include your descriptions of inputs and outputs, and include your screen captures by clicking **Insert**, **Picture**, **From File...**, browse to find one of your images, and then insert it in the Word document.

   g. If you have an instructor, turn the Word document in as instructed.

References

Clarke, K. C. *Getting Started with Geographic Information Systems*, 4th Ed., Prentice Hall, Upper Saddle River, 2003, pp. 2-6.

Cohen, Mark E. "The Monetary Value of Saving a High-Risk Youth," *Journal of Quantitative Criminology*, 1998, Vol. 14, No. 1.

U.S. Census Bureau, TIGER/Line maps: Internet URL: http://www.census.gov/geo/www/tiger/index.html (accessed March 25, 2005).

CHAPTER 2

NAVIGATING GIS

LEARNING OBJECTIVES

In this chapter, you will:

- Learn how features are located on maps using coordinates
- Understand the role that geographic scale plays in map detail
- Learn about projecting the spherical world onto flat maps
- Work with map layers in ArcExplorer
- Change map scale and move around in a GIS map view
- Measure map features
- Use ArcExplorer to change map projections

Everybody, into the pool...

INTRODUCTION

The most important information that maps provide is about location. Where is something positioned? Is it

on a major street with good access? Is there a barrier to accessing it, such as a river? Is it in a certain

area? Where are similar things positioned? What or who is near it? These are some of the questions that

maps can answer about locations.

Where you are sitting right now has two unique numbers, **latitude** and **longitude**, that pinpoint your location precisely on the surface of earth. In this chapter, you will learn some useful facts about latitude and longitude coordinates and the **geographic coordinate system** that they define. You will also learn about map scale, which refers to the relative size, or proportion, that the map bears to the actual area that it represents. In essence, it shows how far above earth you appear to be when looking at a map, zoomed in or out. The closer you are, the more detail you should see. Finally, you will learn about map projections, making flat maps from the spherical earth. There must be 100 ways to project maps, and ArcExplorer has a lot of them. Sometimes, which projection you choose makes a big difference, so we give you some guidelines.

After you have learned basic concepts and facts about map navigation, you will open a GIS project file that has a map composition for the Swimming Pool Case Study used throughout this book. Then you will start navigating the map, zooming in and out, panning, and so forth, to get information. Your task is to try out several map projections for some new, simple maps that you will build.

MAP NAVIGATION

Your location on a map in a GIS is determined by the **map extent**, a rectangle on earth corresponding to the boundaries of your map (whether on a computer screen or printed). Map extent is defined by two pairs of map coordinates, the lower-left and upper-right corners of the rectangle. The **full extent** of the map is the maximum extent for the map layers in your GIS. For example, for TIGER/Line maps, it's generally a rectangle that encloses a county boundary because these maps are prepared for counties. You may be zoomed in to a small portion of the map for the **current extent**, the map on your computer screen at any moment.

Changing map extent is a form of **map navigation**, the process of changing the view of all or part of a map composition. The underlying structure for map navigation and the maps themselves is their coordinate system. In actuality, the earth is a sphere, so we need a coordinate system for locating points on a sphere. However, the maps that you view on your computer screen or on paper are flat and thus use a corresponding flat coordinate system. How do coordinates on a sphere work? How do you transform coordinates on a sphere to coordinates on flat surfaces? You will learn about these and related issues in the remainder of this chapter.

Geographic Coordinates

The planet Earth appears to be a sphere, but it is very slightly flattened at the poles and bulged out at the equator. While Earth was forming, the centrifugal force of the planet spinning on its axis threw out a little more mass at the equator at the expense of the poles. However, it is only about 77 miles shorter to go around the world passing through the poles than it is taking the 22,770-mile route around the equator (Clarke 2003, p. 37), not much of a shortcut. So for many purposes, it is safe to assume that planet Earth is a sphere. Here is the question we need to confront: How do you locate points on a sphere?

The answer is not the usual **rectangular coordinates** as used for locating an intersection on a flat sheet of graph paper or a flat map. On graph paper, the point (-80, 40) is 80 linear units measured to the left of the Y vertical axis and 40 units measured up from the X horizontal axis (see Figure 2-1). On the globe, the point (-80, 40) is 80^0 (80 degrees) west longitude and 40^0 north latitude—our hometown of Pittsburgh, Pennsylvania. Latitude and longitude are **geographic coordinates** (or **spherical coordinates**), angles of *rotation* of a radius anchored at earth's center.

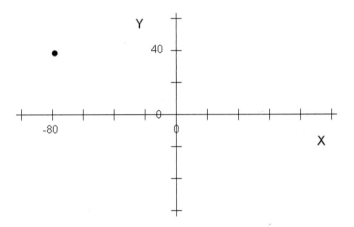

FIGURE 2-1   Rectangular coordinates

Figure 2-2 illustrates this measurement system (Demers 2005, p. 28). A **great circle** is a circle on the surface of the world that has the radius of the world. A **meridian** is a great circle that passes through the poles. The **prime meridian** is the meridian that passes through Greenwich, England. It is the line of 0^0 longitude because of historical reasons and by agreement (it is not a natural reference line). This circle establishes the reference point for measurements east and west on the globe. In the opposite direction, the natural reference circle for north and south measurements is the equator, which is at 0^0 latitude.

So, the (0, 0) point on the globe is the intersection of the prime meridian, proceeding south from Greenwich, with the equator. To get Pittsburgh's coordinates, we rotate the radius seen in Figure 2-2 through an angle of 80^0 longitude to the west along the equator, and then rotate 40^0 north along the meridian passing through 80^0 west longitude.

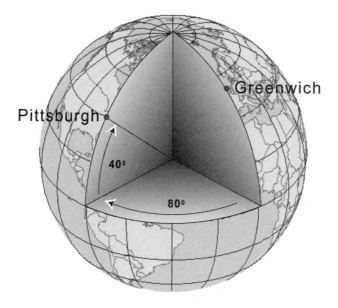

FIGURE 2-2   Latitude and longitude on the globe

Figure 2-3 plots latitude and longitude (geographic) coordinates of the world as if they were rectangular coordinates. This is a misuse of geographic coordinates, but it serves to illustrate the range of coordinate values. Longitude ranges from -180^0 to 0^0 to 180^0 for a total of 360^0 when measured around the equator. Latitude ranges from 0^0 at the equator up to 90^0 at the North Pole and from 0^0 down to -90^0 at the South Pole. The lines of constant latitude circling east to west around the globe are called **parallels** because they are parallel to each other, as you can see in Figure 2-2. So, if you are looking at a map on a GIS, which gives you readouts of map coordinates wherever your mouse pointer is hovering on a map, you can recognize geographical coordinates of latitude and longitude because they range between -180^0 to 180^0 in the first position (longitude), and -90^0 to 90^0 in the second position (latitude).

One last issue to discuss is that a degree of longitude, measured west to east between two meridians, is longest in miles (when straightened) at the equator. As we move north or south from the equator, this length decreases until approaching the poles, where longitude's length disappears. Pittsburgh, at 40^0 north latitude, is a mid-latitude area. While a degree is 63 miles long on the equator, it is roughly half this in Pittsburgh. Sometimes, we display maps with their geographic coordinates on a flat computer screen, as shown in Figure 2-3. This is not the intention nor purpose of geographic coordinates, so such maps are·distorted in the north/south direction, and more so nearest the poles. You will see this when you project maps for this chapter's tutorial.

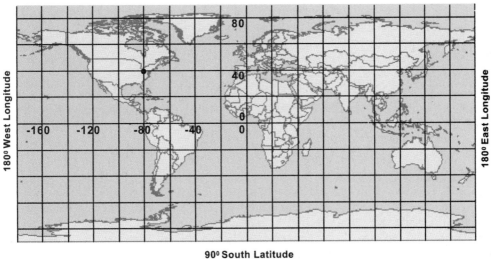

FIGURE 2-3   Latitude and longitude on a flat sheet

Map Scale

To understand map scale, consider this analogy: Model trains come in different scales. "N" is the smallest scale with a ratio of 1:160, meaning that 1 inch of model train is equivalent to 160 inches of real train. The largest model trains are "G" scale, with a ratio of 1:23. "G"-scale model trains are larger than "N"-scale trains. For example, if a real train is as long as a football field, 300 feet, then a "G"-scale model train is 300/23 = 13 feet long, but an "N"-scale model train is 300/160 = 1 foot 10 inches long. Model train manufacturers can place a lot of realistic detail on a "G"-scale model train because there is a lot of room to do so, but not so for an "N"-scale model train.

Map scale is analogous to that for model trains, except that the ratios need to be much more extreme to get sufficient reduction for maps. **Large-scale** maps, like the "G"-scale train, are relatively large, and **small-scale** maps are relatively small. Many people find these terms confusing. To make the terms "large scale" and "small scale" concrete, suppose that you have a paper map of Lake Erie. A large-scale map having a scale of 1:50,000 to 1:10,000 makes the lake look large because it is so big on paper. By contrast, a small scale map with, for example, a map scale of 1:250,000 to 1:1,000,000, makes the lake look small because it appears smaller on paper (Rosenberg, 2005).

A **map scale ratio** with the numeral "1" as its numerator, such as 1:24,000, is called a **representative fraction** by **cartographers** (mapmakers). Its beauty is that it is dimensionless, so that you can use it with any linear measurement unit, such as feet, meters, or miles.

For example, 1 inch on the map is 24,000 inches on the ground. It is possible to use two different linear measurement units, in which case the same scale is called a **verbal scale**. For example, 1 inch on the map is 2,000 feet on the ground (divide 12 inches per foot into 24,000 inches to get the 2000 feet). The graphic representation of map scale, the **graphic scale**, places a line on the map with ground distances marked, such as 10 miles, 20 miles, and so on (Demers 2005, p. 50).

Maps are created at different scales. For a fixed area on the ground, like a park, a small-scale map will have less detail than a large-scale map—in fact, the park could be a point on a small-scale map and a polygon on a large-scale map. Most of the maps that you download for free have scales appropriate for your use.

Map Projections

As discussed in Chapter 1, the five types of features that we represent on maps are physical, political, legal, statistical, and administrative. There are many ways to locate features on the globe: surveying methods, aerial photography, **global positioning system (GPS)** receivers, and so forth. GPS uses a constellation of satellites to determine the position and velocity (if moving relative to earth) of any GPS receiver on or above the earth. How do cartographers transform geographical coordinates into flat coordinates so we get good representations of earth on our flat computer screens and paper maps?

If you have ever cut a hollow rubber ball in half and tried to flatten one of the halves on a tabletop, you know what the problem is. Some parts of the ball must stretch and others must shrink. This causes distortion on the ball's surface, or variations in scale, but only for large areas of the ball, such as an entire half. Any small area, relative to itself, has no significant variation in scale. Similarly, for small areas on earth and large-scale maps—such as a city, county, or even a state—there is not much distortion. For example, the major projections used by local governments and the U.S. military, **State Plane** and **Universal Transverse Mercator (UTM)**, have no detectable distortion. For small-scale maps of the world or a continent, however, there is much distortion.

A **map projection** is a mathematical transformation that behaves as if it were projecting features of the world onto one of three surfaces: a plane, cone, or cylinder. See Figure 2-4 (Muehrcke 1986). Planes are used for projecting the areas around the North and South Poles, as if the plane were touching one of the poles. For a cone, it is as if the cone were sitting on the earth, with its point above one of the poles. For the cylinder, it is as if the earth were inside the cylinder, touching at the equator. Sometimes the cone or cylinder is rotated $90°$, resulting in **transverse projections**. Sometimes, the cone or cylinder pierce through and reemerge through the surface of the earth, resulting in **secant projections**.

Suppose that we are using a conic projection with the cone touching the $40°$ north parallel that goes through Pittsburgh. A main street in Pittsburgh is Grant Street. If we are mapping the location of a manhole (sewer line access point) in the 100 block of Grant Street, imagine a light source at the center of the earth shining up through that manhole and onto the cone. We place a dot for the manhole where the point of light shines on the cone. When we've finished projecting all the manholes in Pittsburgh, using the same approach, we cut the cone from edge to point, unroll it, and flatten it to get the projected map.

  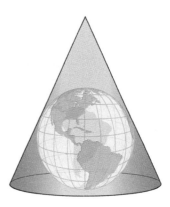

FIGURE 2-4   Map projections

Here are few guidelines for map projections:

1. *Get latitude/longitude base maps.* **Base maps** are those provided by governments or commercial firms in digital form for use in a GIS. If possible, get base map layers in unprojected, geographic coordinates of latitude and longitude. You can always project these on any flat projection surface, a capability of ArcExplorer. With advanced GIS software, such as ESRI's ArcView, you can transform from projected coordinates back to geographic coordinates.

2. *Trouble-shoot map layers that do not appear.* If you get map layers from two different sources for the same area, but when you put them in a GIS they do not all appear (or nothing appears), it is because they are in different projections. To transform all map layers to the same projection, you need a more advanced GIS, like ArcView.

3. *Use State Plane or UTM projections for local areas.* For UTM, you have to look up the zone for your area (for example, see Morton 2005 for UTM and see Mentor Software, Inc. 2005 for State Plane codes). When you project a map using either of these projections, you must supply the proper code as an input parameter. You also have to specify the **geoid**, or specific shape assumed for the world, generally either NAD 27 or NAD 83. For analytic mapping it does not matter which you choose as long as you are consistent. UTM is a more modern projection. It uses metric system measurements and applies to the entire world. State Plane projections are widely used by U.S. local governments and are defined only for Alaska and the lower 48 states.

4. *Use the Robinson projection for the entire world unless you have a better option.* Many projections of the world have enormous distortions. The Robinson projection is most accurate at the mid-latitudes in both the Northern and Southern Hemispheres where most people live. *National Geographic Magazine* often uses this projection.

5. *Use Conformal projections to preserve shape and direction.* For maps that depict areas the size of a continent or larger and that preserve local shape and direction, good projections are the Lambert Conformal conic and Mercator projections. **Conformal projections** are easy to recognize because their lines of latitude and longitude intersect at right angles (Clarke 2003, pp. 41, 42). Conformal projections distort areas. You can either preserve accurate shape or accurate area, but not both in map projections. Equivalent projections are better for analytic mapping, and they are discussed next.

6. *Use equal area or Equivalent projections to preserve area.* For maps that depict areas the size of a continent or larger and that preserve area measurements, use **Equivalent projections**, such as the Albers equal area or Lambert's equal area projections. Often when doing analytical mapping, it is necessary to use population or other densities, calculated as the number of persons or other entities per unit area. Then an Equivalent projection is needed to avoid projection-caused variations in areas and, therefore, in densities. General reference and educational maps often use equal area projections (Demers 2005).

ARCEXPLORER FOR MAP NAVIGATION

We turn now to putting the concepts you just learned to work in ArcExplorer. If you or your instructor have not already installed *ArcExplorer—Java Edition for Education* on your computer, go to the Appendix for instructions on how to do so. The Appendix also has instructions on how to install the *LearningAndUsingGIS* folder of map files on your computer's hard drive for use in this textbook. To work through the tutorial steps that follow, you must have this software and folder installed.

Swimming Pools Map Project

To get started, you will launch ArcExplorer, open the Pools **map project file**, and make a few adjustments to the application window. A map project file is analogous to a Word, Excel, or PowerPoint file because it has all the information included to render and process a map composition in ArcExplorer. *Note:* A map project file does not store copies of map layers but just points to their locations on disk and uses them where they are stored. Hence, it is important not to rename or move folders that contain map layers after corresponding map project files are built.

1. On your computer's desktop, click **Start**, **All Programs**, **AEJEE**, **AEJEE** (Win) or open **Finder** and select **Macintosh HD**, scroll down to the **ESRI** folder, open **AJEE**, and double-click on **AJEE** (Mac). *(The application window, ArcExplorer — Java Edition for Education — Window #1 opens. Note: This is the only way that you can launch ArcExplorer. In particular, you cannot double-click a map project file, such as Pools.axl in Step 3, to launch ArcExplorer and open that map file.)*

2. In the ArcExplorer window, click **File**, **Open**.... See Figure 2-5. *(The Open window opens.)*

3. In the Open window, click the down arrow in the **Look in** field, browse to **c:\LearningAndUsingGIS** (Win) or **/LearningAndUsingGIS/** (Mac) and double-click **Pools.axl** (Win) or **PoolsMac.axl** (Mac). *(The Pools project opens, displaying a view with the outline of Allegheny County, Pennsylvania, and a layer panel on the left with all available map layers and their symbolization.)*

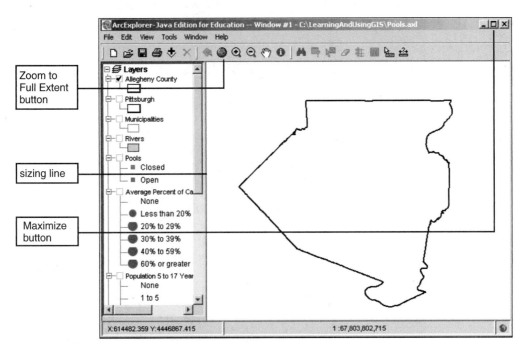

FIGURE 2-5   ArcExplorer window with map of Allegheny County

4. Click **View**, **Map Units**, and then **Meters** *(if not already selected)*. *(The map layers have meters for distance units because we projected them all permanently to UTM.)*
5. Click **View** and make sure that **Status** bar is selected.
6. Click the **Maximize** button to maximize the ArcExplorer window, and then the **Zoom to Full Extent** button to re-center the map in the window.
7. Click, hold, and drag the **sizing line** *(the line between the Layers and Map View panels)* to the right, so you can read the full legend text in the Layers panel. *(The cursor does not change shape when you hover over the sizing line, as commonly is done in other software packages.)*
8. Click the **Zoom to Full Extent** button again to center your map. *(Notice the Status bar at the bottom of the ArcExplorer window. It displays the representative-scale ratio below the map view. This value will vary depending on your screen size—an example is 1:374,615. Notice also that the Status bar displays the UTM coordinates in meters where you hover over on the*

map with your mouse. If you hover over the extreme west (left) point of Allegheny County, you should see coordinates of approximately (554,131, 4,481,037).

9. Click **File** and then click **Exit**.

Map Layers

Next, you will turn on and look at some more interesting map layers.

1. If ArcExplorer is not open to the **Pools.axl map project**, repeat Steps 1-3.
2. Click the small **check boxes** immediately to the left of legend text for the **Pittsburgh**, **Municipalities**, and **Rivers** layers in the Layers panel to turn on those layers. See Figure 2-6. *(You can see that Allegheny County has many municipalities, one of which is the City of Pittsburgh. We included a separate layer for Pittsburgh, with a wider outline than the other municipalities, to emphasize it because our case study is on Pittsburgh swimming pools.)*

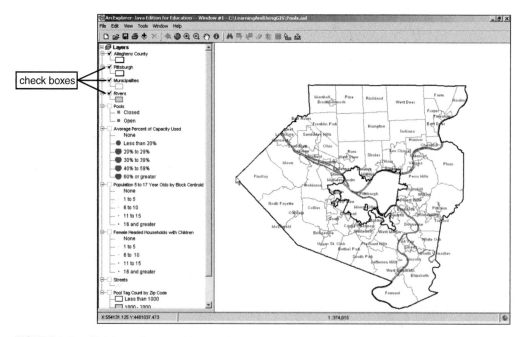

FIGURE 2-6   Allegheny County with more layers turned on

3. Click the small check box for **Municipalities** again to turn off that layer.
4. Click the check box for **Population 5 to 17 Year Olds by Block Centroid** to turn on that layer. See Figure 2-7. *(This layer represents the target population for using public swimming pools, namely, 5- to 17-year-old youths. This data is from the 2000 Census. The layer symbolizes the centroids, or center points, of city census blocks. There are 24,283 blocks in Allegheny County, and you are seeing all of the ones that have at least one youth. Clearly, there are several clusters of areas with high densities of youths, inside and outside of Pittsburgh's boundaries.)*

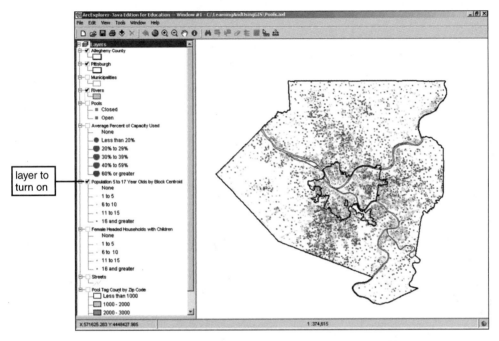

layer to turn on

FIGURE 2-7 Allegheny County with 5 to 17 Year Olds by Block Centroid layer turned on

5. Click the check box for **Pools** to turn that layer on. See Figure 2-8. *(Here, you get your first look at the supply of swimming pool services for youths, although at this zoomed-out scale the map is difficult to read. You will zoom in for a better look later. The 16 pools open in the summer of 2004 have blue squares as point markers, and the 16 closed pools are designated by the red squares.)*
6. Use your right mouse button and right-click (Win) or control-click (Mac) the word **Pools** in the legend for the Pools layer in the Layers panel. *(This opens a context menu.)*
7. In the context menu, move your mouse down to the **Move Layer** option to open a submenu and then *left*-click **Move Down** on the submenu. See Figure 2-9. *(This moves the Pools layer down below the Average Capacity Used layer.)*

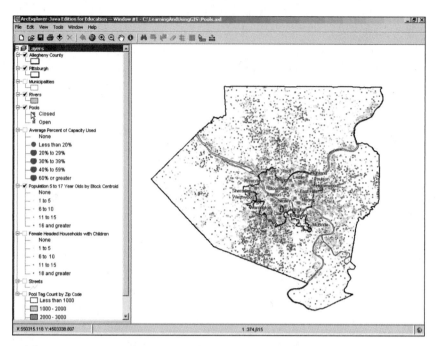

FIGURE 2-8　Allegheny County with Pools layer turned on

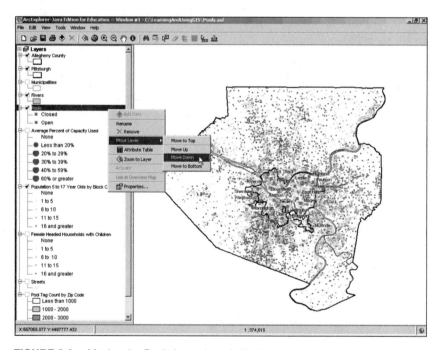

FIGURE 2-9　Moving the Pools layer down in the Layers panel

8. Repeat **Step 6** to move Pools down below the Population 5 to 17 Year Olds by Block Centroid layer. *(Look at the map and see that now you have created a problem. Map layers in GIS packages draw from the bottom up, so now the Pools layer draws before the Population of 5 to 17 Year Olds by Block Centroid layer, so the latter covers up much of the pool point markers. The lesson here is to place layers with big areas that are color-coded under layers with smaller features, such as the pools, so that valuable parts of the map are not covered up.)*

9. Right-click (Win) or control-click (Mac) the **Pools legend**, hover your mouse over the **Move Layer** menu option, and click **Move Up**.

10. Repeat **Step 9**. *(Now the map layers should be in their original order, with the Pools layer just above the Average Capacity Used layer.)*

Before working through Practice 2-2, review the following list of layers in the Pools map project file. For reference, they are listed from top to bottom of the Layer panel.

- *Allegheny County*—the boundary of Allegheny County. It has no fill color (it's transparent) and thus does not hide the rest of the layers.
- *Pittsburgh*—the boundary of Pittsburgh, also with no fill color.
- *Municipalities*—the boundaries of all the municipalities in Allegheny County, again with no fill color.
- *Pools*—all 32 public pools in Pittsburgh.
- *Average Percent of Capacity Used*—the average number of visitors per day in summer 2004 to a pool, divided by the maximum capacity of the pool, all times 100 to yield percentages.
- *Population 5 to 17 Year Olds by Block Centroid*—the 2000 block-level population of the age group plotted at block center points.
- *Female Headed Households with Children*—the number of such households for each city block's center point. This is a measure of poverty and of need for public services (such as public swimming pools).
- *Streets*—street centerlines for all streets, roads, and highways in Allegheny County. It has 81,646 one-block-long street segments. This is an amazing map layer, available for free, by county, for the entire country.
- *Pool Tag Count by Zip Code*—the number of pool tags (identification tag needed by each person using any Pittsburgh pool) for summer 2004, tabulated by zip code.
- *Aerial Photograph*—an aerial photograph produced by the U.S. Geological Survey, in UTM coordinates.
- *USGS Topographic Map*—a mosaic of maps scanned from paper U.S. Geological Survey topographic maps.

Next, practice working with all of the previously listed layers of the Pools map project.

- Turn layers on and off, one by one, and look for patterns in the layers.
- Turn several combinations of layers on for different purposes.
- Try moving some layers up or down to see the effect.
- What problem can you find with the Aerial Photograph and USGS Topographic maps? (*Hint:* Compare them to the Streets and River layers.)
- When you are finished, place all layers in their original order, according to the previous list. Also, leave on just the following five layers: Allegheny County, Pittsburgh, Rivers, Pools, and Population 5 to 17 Year Olds by Block Centroid.

Zooming and Panning

ArcExplorer, like most GIS packages, has tools you can use to change the displayed map's scale. A great thing about GIS is that you can look at a map to decide where to drill down, or zoom in, for more detail.

The Pools map project needs to have layers ordered and turned on, as described in Practice 2-2. Be sure to check that you are at the right starting place.

Your first step is to zoom in to Pittsburgh to get a better look at the pools.

1. Click **Pittsburgh** in that layer's legend in the layers panel. *(This makes "Pittsburgh" the* **active layer**, *the layer currently selected, with reverse white font and a dark background. Many ArcExplorer tools need to "know" which layer to process, and the active layer is the target of such tools.)*

2. Click the **Zoom to Active Layer** button. See Figure 2-10. *(This zooms the map view in to Pittsburgh. Now there is a lot of detail that you can distinguish clearly. For example, look at all of the youths that live around the closed Warrington, Fowler, and Brookline pools. Are those youths too far from open pools to get to them? That is a question that we hope to answer eventually.)*

3. See the screen capture in Figure 2-11. Click the **Zoom-In** button, click and hold your **mouse** button down at the upper left side of Mount Oliver, drag a **rectangle** down and to the lower right of Mount Oliver, and release your mouse button. *(This action zooms the map view in to Mount Oliver, a land-locked municipality that lies totally inside of Pittsburgh's boundaries. At this scale, approximately 1:10,000 in Figure 2-11, we could use more details, which you will get next.)*

4. Click the **Streets** check box to turn that layer on. See Figure 2-12. *(Now you can see that the block centroid points indeed are center points of blocks.)*

5. Click the **Pan** button, click and hold down your **mouse** button anywhere on the **map**, drag an **inch or two in any direction**, and release your mouse button. *(That pans, or moves, the map while maintaining the existing scale.)*

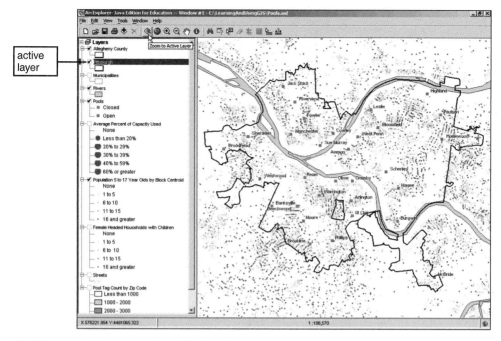

active layer

FIGURE 2-10 Map zoomed in to Pittsburgh

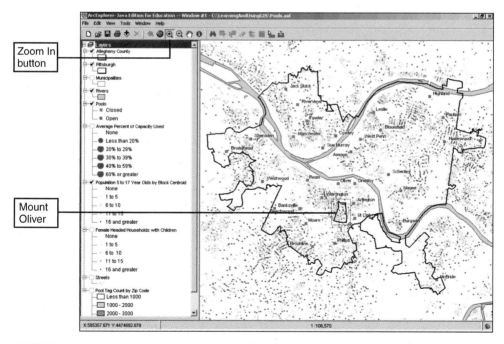

Zoom In button

Mount Oliver

FIGURE 2-11 Rectangle to drag to zoom in to Mount Oliver

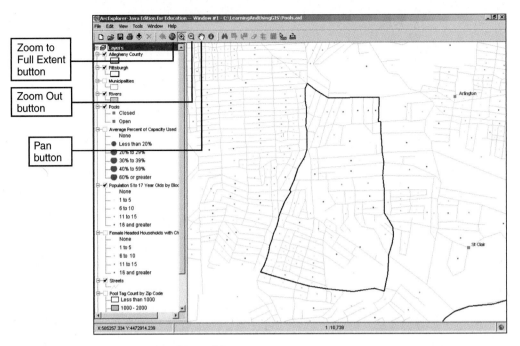

Zoom to Full Extent button

Zoom Out button

Pan button

FIGURE 2-12 Map zoomed in to Mount Oliver

6. Click the **Zoom Out** button and then click on the center of **Mount Oliver** a few times. *(Each time you click, the map zooms out a fixed amount.)*

7. Make sure that Pittsburgh is the active layer, click the **Zoom to Active Layer** button, and click the **Streets** check box to turn that layer off.

8. Click **View** and then click **Overview Map**. *(This adds a new component, a sub-panel of the Layers panel that is devoted to an overview map for use as context in zooming and panning.)*

9. Right-click (Win) or control-click (Mac) **Allegheny County** in the layer panel, and in the resulting context menu, click **Use in Overview Map**. *(This action makes Allegheny County the context for panning, as seen next.)*

10. Click and drag the **red rectangle** in the overview sub-panel of the layer panel to a new position and release. *(This is another way of panning the map view.)*

11. Click the **Zoom to Full Extent** button. *(The view reverts back to all of Allegheny County.)*

- Click the check box for the Female Headed Households with Children layer to turn that layer on, and click the check box for the Population of 5 to 17 Year Olds to turn that layer off.
- Find areas of Allegheny County and Pittsburgh that have clusters of blocks with high numbers of such households. Zoom in to and pan around in those areas.
- To make this interesting, and to give you a small preview of the kind of work you will do in Chapter 4, right-click (Win) or control-click (Mac) **Streets** in the Layers panel, click **Properties** and the **Labels** tab, click the **list arrow** in the **Label features using** field, click **FENAME**, and then click **OK**. This adds street name labels to streets for use when zoomed in.

Threshold Scales

When zoomed far in to a map, it is a good idea to turn on some detailed map layers, like street centerlines, and then to turn them off when zoomed out too far to see details clearly. Instead of turning layers on and off manually, you can automate this process using **threshold scales**. For a given map layer, you can set a threshold scale so that the map appears only when zoomed in far enough, or the opposite, when zoomed out far enough. Threshold scales are a very valuable feature of GIS for map designers and users.

1. Click the **Zoom to Full Extent** button.
2. Click **Streets** to turn that layer on, but click to turn off **Female Headed Households with Children**. *(You can leave a variety of other layers turned on, but certainly leave Allegheny County, Rivers, and Pittsburgh on. It is desirable to leave Population 5 to 17 Year Olds by Block Centroid on when zoomed out, and off when zoomed in. The opposite is true for the Streets layer. It is desirable to turn off Streets when zoomed out, but to turn it on when zoomed in.)*
3. Click the **Zoom In** button, and use it to zoom in to the top part of **Pittsburgh**. See Figure 2-13.
4. Right-click (Win) or control-click (Mac) the **Streets** layer in the layers panel, and then click **Properties**. *(The Streets Properties window opens.)*
5. In the **Streets Properties** window, click the **General** tab.
6. Note the representative scale ratio at the bottom of your screen *(the scale shown in Figure 2-14 is 35,838, but yours might be different)*, click the radio button in the **Streets Property** window for **Only show layer in the following scale range**, enter that value in the **Never above 1:** field, and then click **OK**. See Figure 2-14.
7. Right-click (Win) or control-click (Mac) the **Population 5 to 17 Year Olds by Block Centroid** layer and then click Properties on the shortcut menu *(and wait while the Population 5 to 17 Year Olds properties window slowly opens)*, and repeat Steps 5 and 6, except enter same value into the **Never below 1:** field, and then click **OK**.

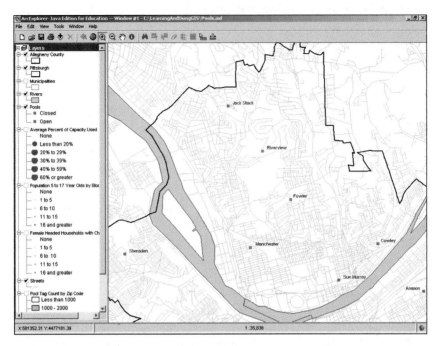

FIGURE 2-13   Map zoomed in to top part of Pittsburgh

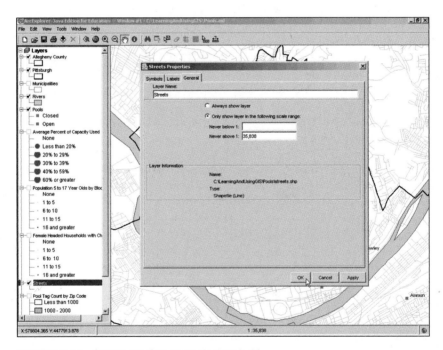

FIGURE 2-14   Setting the Streets scale threshold

8. Click the **Zoom to Full Extent** button. *(The Streets layer turns off, and the Population 5 to 17 Year Olds by Block Centroid layer turns on.)*
9. Zoom in to a **small area of Pittsburgh**. *(The Streets layer turns on, and the Population 5 to 17 Year Olds by Block Centroid layer turns off.)*

PRACTICE 2-4

Set the scale threshold for Female Headed Households with Children to be the same as Population of 5 to 17 Year Olds.

Measuring Map Features

You will use ArcExplorer's measurement tool to verify our use of map layers. The **measurement tool** measures straight-line distances in a map composition. For a source of independent information we used *www.hometownlocator.com* to get basic data on Allegheny County and Pittsburgh. See Table 2-1.

TABLE 2-1 Basic Statistics on Allegheny County and Pittsburgh

	Allegheny County	Pittsburgh
Population (2000 Census)	1,281,666	334,563
Area (square miles)	730.17	55.58
Water Area (square miles)	14.54	2.77
Population Density (persons per square mile)	1,755	6,019

1. Turn off all layers **except Allegheny County**, zoom to the **full extent**, and turn off the **overview map**.
2. Click **View**, then click **Map Units**, and make sure that **Meters** is selected.
3. Click the **Measure** button and **Miles**. *(With this selection, ArcExplorer will automatically convert meters, the units of our map coordinates, into miles when making measurements.)*
4. Click and hold down your **mouse** button at the **extreme left point of Allegheny County**, drag horizontally across to the **extreme right point of the county**, and release your mouse. See Figure 2-15. *(The resulting measurement should be about 34.6 miles. Next, estimate the perimeter of the county with a series of connected straight lines.)*
5. Click the **Measure** button and then click **Clear Measure Totals**.
6. Start at the **left most point of the county**, click and hold down your **mouse** button, drag **a straight line segment** along the border up and to the right, and release it (*but do not move your cursor from the ending point, and do not double-click at any time*).

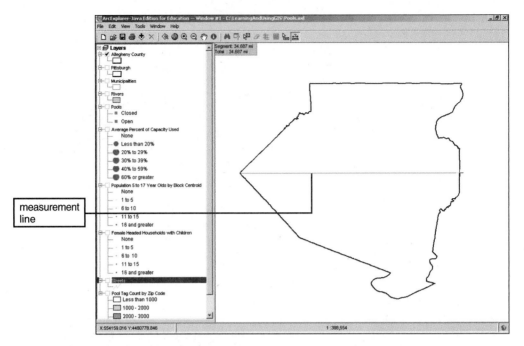

measurement line

FIGURE 2-15 Measuring the width of Allegheny County

7. Click and hold down your **mouse** button, and drag another **straight line segment** along the perimeter, until the line no longer fits the boundary well and release it (*but, again, do not move your cursor*).

8. Repeat this process until you have gone entirely around and back to the starting point. See Figure 2-16. (*Note that ArcExplorer keeps a running total of the lengths of all of your lines, which is a perimeter of approximately 122.7 miles.*)

9. Click the **Measure** button and then **Clear Measure Totals**.

PRACTICE 2-5

- Measure the width and estimate the perimeter of Pittsburgh.
- Approximate the area of Allegheny County by measuring the length and width of one or more rectangles that approximate Allegheny County. Multiply the length and width of each rectangle to get area, and add the areas up. Compare your estimated area with that in Table 2-1.
- Click **File** and then click **Exit** when you are done. If you are asked whether you want to save the project, click **No**.

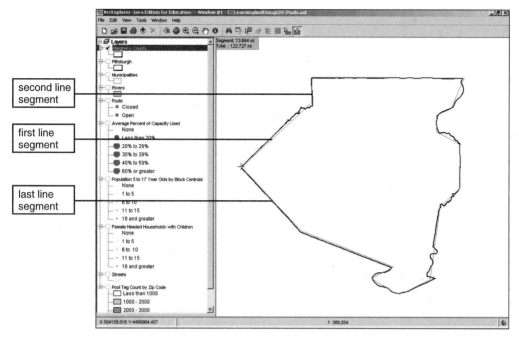

second line segment

first line segment

last line segment

FIGURE 2-16   Tracing the perimeter of Allegheny County

Map Projections

The purpose of this last section is to provide you with some experience with map projections. You will branch out a bit, away from Pittsburgh, and use some of the sample map layers that were copied to your computer when you or your instructor installed ArcExplorer.

We assume that you or your instructor took the default path for installation, so if the sample map files are elsewhere on your computer, you will have to find out where they are and browse to them as needed.

ArcExplorer cannot make permanent projections, but just makes projections on-the-fly and must have latitude/longitude maps as an input. By **permanent projections**, we mean new versions of map files that have features in projected coordinates.

Map Projections of the World

1. Start **ArcExplorer**.
2. Click the **Add Data** button and browse to **c:\ESRI\AEJEE\Data\World** (Win) or **/ESRI/AEJEE/Data/World** (Mac) folder.
3. In the **Content Chooser** window, press and hold down your keyboard's **Ctrl** button (Win) or **Command** button (Mac) while clicking on **country.shp** and **latlong.shp** to select them, and then click **OK** to add these two layers to your map view. (*The map files of this folder are in the common format called a*

"shapefile" with the .shp file extension. Make sure that latlong.shp *is above* country.shp *in the Layers panel. The next step is a precaution so that you start from the intended projection.)*

4. Click **Tools**, **Projection**, the **+** sign expander to the left of Geographic Latitude / Longitude, click the now exposed **Latitude / Longitude** icon, click **Apply**, and and then click **OK**. See Figure 2-17. *(Now, you have geographic coordinates and no projection. Hover over various parts of the map to refresh yourself on the values that latitude/longitude coordinates take.)*

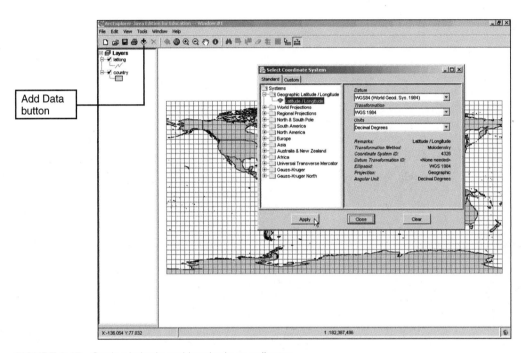

FIGURE 2-17 Setting latitude and longitude coordinates

5. Click **Tools**, **Projection**, the **+** sign expander to the left of World Projections, and then **World Projections (Sphere)**. Scroll down, click the icon for **Robinson**, and then click **Apply**. See Figure 2-18. *(Leave the Select Coordinate System window open. The last action yielded the very attractive Robinson projection. Let's see what the Mercator projection does to Greenland.)*

6. Click the icon for **Mercator** and then click **Apply**. See Figure 2-19. *(There is the famous distortion of Greenland that you might remember from wall maps in elementary school. Antarctica has an even more obvious distortion than Greenland.)*

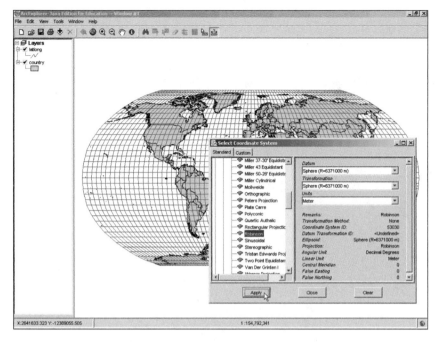

FIGURE 2-18 Setting the Robinson projection

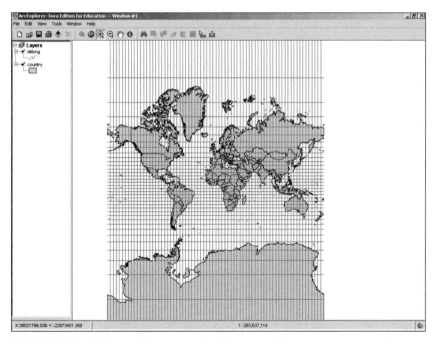

FIGURE 2-19 Setting the Mercator projection

7. Click the icon for **Orthographic** (the world as seen from outer space), and then click **Apply**. See Figure 2-20. *(This representation is not really a projection because it preserves the spherical shape of the world.)*

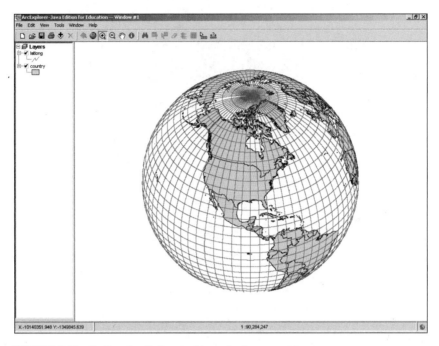

FIGURE 2-20   Setting the Orthographic projection

PRACTICE 2-6

Try several other world projections. See which ones you think are the best or strangest.

Map Projections of a County

We are back to Pittsburgh and Allegheny County.

Often it is a good idea to close ArcExplorer and re-start the package when starting something new, rather than using the File, New commands while ArcExplorer is already open.

1. Close **ArcExplorer** and re-start it.
2. Click the **Add Data** button and browse to **c:\LearningAndUsingGIS\Maps** (Win) or **LearningAndUsingGIS\Maps** (Mac), and in the Content Chooser window, click **countyunprojected.shp**, and then click **OK** to add this layer to your map view. See Figure 2-21. *(While the other maps you have seen of Allegheny County were projected to UTM, this file is in original latitude/longitude coordinates. Notice how flattened it appears. This is characteristic of latitude/longitude maps at mid-latitudes, such as Allegheny County.)*

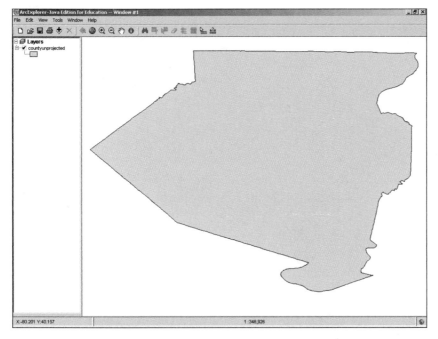

FIGURE 2-21 Allegheny County in latitude and longitude coordinates

3. Click **Tools, Projection, North America, United States, UTM (NAD27/US & Canada), UTM Zone 17N**, and then click **Apply**. See Figure 2-22. *(This is the UTM projection that we used to permanently project the map layers of the pools project.)*

4. Click **North America, United States, US State Plane 1983 (US feet), Pennsylvania Southern Zone, Apply**, and then click **OK**. See Figure 2-23. *(This is the other popular projection for local government maps.)*

PRACTICE 2-7

Repeat the steps of this section, but this time use North America, United States, US State Plane 1983, and Pennsylvania Southern Zone.

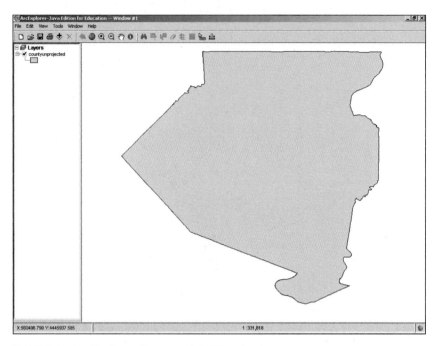

FIGURE 2-22 Allegheny County with UTM projection

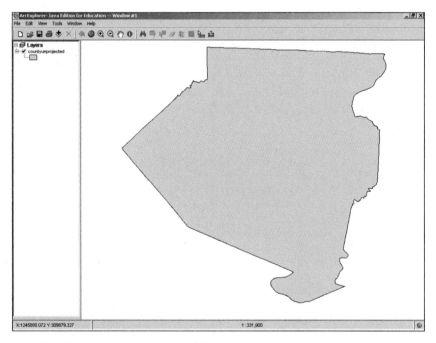

FIGURE 2-23 Allegheny County with State Plane projection

Chapter 2 Summary

Geographic coordinates locate features on the earth's surface. These coordinates are angles of rotation of the earth's radius, measured east or west from the prime meridian, which goes through Greenwich, England (longitude), and north or south from the equator (latitude). Longitude ranges from -180° to 180°, and latitude ranges from -90° (South Pole) to 90° (North Pole). The more-common rectangular coordinates are based on straight-line distances, rather than angles of rotation.

Map navigation refers to methods of changing the current extent in a GIS. The current extent is the rectangle framing a map composition on the computer screen and is denoted by the map coordinates of its lower-left and upper-right corners. A GIS user can navigate by zooming in, zooming out, and panning, or dragging, the map in any direction.

Map scale is the reduction in length of features on earth so that they can fit on a map. Map scale is often stated as a representative ratio; for example, 1:24,000 means that 1 inch on the map is equivalent to 24,000 inches on the ground. Lake Erie on a small-scale map (such as 1:1,000,000) appears to be small in size, whereas on a large-scale map (such as 1:10,000), it appears to be large.

Features on earth, located with latitude and longitude coordinates, can be projected to flat maps by any one of several mathematical transformations. Projected maps have rectangular coordinates. A point on earth, such as the western tip of Allegheny County, has unique latitude and longitude coordinates, but it has different projected coordinates for every individual projection. As a result, map layers for the same area will not appear in a GIS if they have different projections.

ArcExplorer uses map project files that it can display and process. A map project file has one or more map layers, each symbolized to be part of a map composition. Map layers draw from the bottom up in ArcExplorer's layer panel, so it is necessary to place map layers with large features that have color fill on the bottom so they do not cover up other features.

You can use ArcExplorer to navigate a map, to zoom in to areas of interest, and to investigate detailed map layers. Once zoomed in, you can pan or move the map within the view window.

ArcExplorer has a measurement tool for measuring lengths and estimating areas. It is always a good idea to check map layers and measurement units by measuring some feature having known dimensions, such as the width of the United States. If you specify the wrong map measurement units, such as feet instead of meters, you will get incorrect measurements.

An ArcExplorer user can project base maps on-the-fly, but ArcExplorer cannot store the results permanently as new map layers with projected coordinates. The latter requires a more advanced GIS package, such as ArcView. Map layers used in ArcExplorer must be in longitude/latitude coordinates in order to be projected. More-advanced GIS packages can use map layers with projected coordinates as the input and project to other projections or back to longitude/latitude. If you have map files with projected coordinates, it is possible to use them in an ArcExplorer project, but all map layers must have the same projection.

Key Terms

Active layer   The map layer selected in the Layers panel of ArcExplorer. Many GIS tools operate on the active layer, such as zooming to the extent of the active layer, so the GIS user must designate that layer by clicking on it in the Layers panel.

Base maps   Map layers available from governments or GIS vendors which provide an infrastructure, or costly-but-shared resources, for GIS applications. These map layers commonly include street centerlines, boundaries (political, legal, administrative, physical), and so forth.

Cartographers   People who design maps using associated principles and standards. Historically, cartographers were among the earliest graphic designers, and many of the graphic principles in use today derived from map making.

Conformal projections   A kind of map projection that preserves shape and direction in local areas, at the expense of distorting areas.

Current extent   The map extent at any moment in a GIS. It is the current window on a map composition, as zoomed in or out.

Equivalent projections   A kind of projection that preserves area on maps. These projections show all polygon features with their correct areas as calculated from map measurements and scale, but at the expense of distorting shape and direction.

Full extent   The rectangle that encloses an entire map composition. Maps are usually available for parts of the world, such as a country, state, or smaller area. Each such map has its own full extent.

Geographic coordinate system   Latitude and longitude coordinates that locate points on earth. They represent angles of rotation of earth's radius along the equator and a meridian.

Geoid   A mathematical representation of the shape of earth, often an ellipsoid that is nearly spherical. The user of a GIS must choose which geoid to use when projecting maps. While it's important to be consistent when projecting multiple map layers for the same map composition, it's not so important to use any particular geoid.

Global Positioning System (GPS)   A constellation of satellites that triangulate location and velocity (if they are moving) at points on earth with GPS receivers. Positional accuracy within a meter or less is commonly available.

Graphic scale   A horizontal line on a map with tick marks for corresponding ground distances, such as 1 mile, 2 miles, and so on.

Great circle   A circle on earth's surface that is the earth's radius and, thus, is of the largest possible size. A great circle's plane includes earth's center.

Large scale   A reduction of features on earth's surface for mapping that results in relatively large sizes on the map. Large-scale maps are zoomed in so the user sees only a relatively small area, but in much detail.

Latitude   The number of degrees rotation of a point on earth north or south from the equator and along a meridian. A point on the equator has 0° latitude, the North Pole has 90° latitude, and the South Pole has -90° latitude.

Longitude   The number degrees rotation east or west of the prime meridian of a point on earth along the point's parallel.

Map extent   A rectangle in map coordinates corresponding to boundaries on your computer screen's map or a printed map.

Map navigation   The methods or processes for changing map extent on a GIS. Map extent behaves like a window on the world that can be made larger, smaller, and moved around to change your view.

Map project file   The file that a GIS user saves on a computer to store a map composition. This file does not store copies of map layers, but rather just points to their existing locations on disk.

Map projection   A mathematical transformation for creating flat maps in rectangular coordinates from geographic coordinates (latitude and longitude) on the spherical world.

Map scale ratio   Two numbers that represent the reduction in size of a real-world object to a reduced-size mode, drawing, or other representation. Examples for the same level of reduction are 1 to 1,000 or 20 to 20,000, which correspond to a thousand-fold reduction.

Measurement tool   A GIS tool for measuring straight-line distances in a map composition.

Meridian   A great circle that passes through earth's North and South Poles.

Parallels   Circles of latitude on a globe. They define planes which are parallel to one another.

Permanent projection   A map layer with feature coordinates saved in projected coordinates.

Prime meridian   The meridian that passes through Greenwich, England. It is the line of 0° longitude as measured east or west from it.

Rectangular coordinates   Common coordinates as seen on regular graph paper that can be used to measure distances.

Representative fraction   Expression of map scale as a dimensionless ratio such as 1:24,000, meaning that a unit length on the map is equivalent to 24,000 of the same units on the ground. The units can be any linear measurement, such as inches, centimeters, and so on.

Secant projection   A projection of world features onto a cone or cylinder that pierces the world.

Small scale   A reduction of features on earth's surface for mapping that results in relatively small sizes on the map. Small-scale maps are zoomed out so that the user sees relatively large areas, but not in much detail.

Spherical coordinates   Coordinates that locate points on any sphere, using angles of rotation for position. These are also known as *geographic coordinates*.

State Plane   A collection of map projections for use by local governments in Alaska and the contiguous 48 states.

Threshold scales   Map scales at which map layers turn on or off automatically as a GIS user zooms in or out of a map composition.

Transverse projections   A projection in which the projection surface, a cone or cylinder, is rotated so that its central axis is parallel to the east and west direction, as opposed to the usual north and south direction.

Universal Transverse Mercator (UTM)   A collection of map projections for use in small- to medium-scale regions of the world, based on the metric system.

Verbal scale   A map scale ratio that uses two different linear measurement units; for example, 1 inch equals 2,000 feet.

Short-Answer Questions

1.   How are geographic coordinates different from rectangular coordinates? What distortion do you expect for northern Canada when plotting geographic coordinates on graph paper?

2.   Two sets of geographic coordinates are $(180^\circ, 0^\circ)$ and $(-180^\circ, 0^\circ)$. What do these two points have in common, and why?

3. Express the representative scale 1:10,000 as a verbal scale in inches to feet.

4. Explain how threshold scales are useful to GIS map designers and users.

5. Express the verbal scale 1 inch = 1 mile as a representative scale.

6. What are the major tradeoffs (i.e., you can have one aspect accurate at the expense of the other) in distortions for projections of the continental U.S. or other similarly large area of the world?

7. What is the "active layer" in ArcExplorer, and why is it needed?

8. What is the difference between panning and zooming?

9. What is different about zip code boundaries from other sets of boundaries, such as municipalities?

10. In a GIS, what is "map extent"?

Exercises

1. **Quantifying a Map Mismatch Problem.** Recall that the topographic raster map image of Pittsburgh did not fit the rivers or streets layers very well. It is moved too far north. Your task here is to estimate the average distance discrepancy between the two maps. Then in Exercise 2, you can use this distance to correct the problem, so the raster map aligns with the vector map layers much better! To get started on this exercise, perform the following steps:

   a. Start ArcExplorer and open the **c:\LearningAndUsingGIS\Pools.axl** (Win) or **/LearningAndUsingGIS/Poolsmac.axl** (Mac) map project file.

   b. Click the **Add Data** button, navigate to **c:\LearningAndUsingGIS\Maps** (Win) or **/LearningAndUsingGIS/Maps** (Mac) and add the raster map image **pittsburgh_east_pa.tif** to your map composition.

   c. Turn on the **pittsburgh_east_pa.tif**, **Rivers**, **Pittsburgh**, and **Streets** layers, but leave the rest of the layers off.

   d. Zoom in to **part of Pittsburgh** along the northern large river (the Allegheny).

   Here is your task:

   e. Carefully identify a street intersection that you can find on both the raster map image and the vector streets map.

   f. Make sure that the Map Units are set to meters, and use the measurement tool, also set to meters, to measure the vertical distance between the two versions of the same intersection. Write down the measured distance.

   g. Pick out four additional areas of the raster map, in much different parts of the map, so you get a representative sample. Repeat the above three steps so you have a small sample of five distance measurements.

   h. Save and close ArcExplorer.

   If you have an instructor, turn in a document or paper with the five sampled values and the average of them. You will use the average to fix the mismatch problem in Exercise 2.

2. **Fixing the Map Mismatch Problem**. A GIS figures out where and how to display a raster map image by getting information from the raster map's world file. Among other things, the world file includes projected map coordinates of the *upper-left corner* of the image. Our raster map image, *pittsburgh_east_pa.tif*, has *pittsburgh_east_pa.tfw* as its world file (*.tfw* identifies it as a world file). To fix the mismatch problem pursued in Exercise 1, all that you have to do is edit the y-coordinate of the map's upper-left corner in its world file by subtracting the average discrepancy of Exercise 1.

   a. Close **ArcExplorer** if it is open.

   b. Start **My Computer** (Win) or **Finder** (Mac), and navigate to **c:\LearningAndUsingGIS\Maps** (Win) or **/LearningAndUsingGIS/Maps** (Mac).

   c. Windows users can right-click **pittsburgh_east_pa.tfw**, click **Copy**, right-click **any white area** inside the My Computer window, and then click **Paste.** Macintosh users can control-click **pittsburg_east_pa_tfw** and then click **Duplicate**. This makes a backup copy, called *Copy of pittsburgh_east_pa.tfw*, in case something goes wrong, you can recover the file.

   d. Right-click (Win) or control-click (Mac) **pittsburgh_east_pa.tfw**, and then click **Open**. (If Open is not an option, use Open With... and choose Notepad (Win) or TextEdit (Mac) from the resulting list of programs.) This very simple text editor will open the world file. The last value in the file, 4483651.51200000010431, is the y-coordinate of the upper-left point of the map (and the second-to-last value is its x-coordinate, but it is accurate enough in this case).

   e. The raster map image is too high, so you need to reduce its y-coordinate. Subtract the average distance that you found in Exercise 1 from 4483651.51200000010431, edit this value in the file to make it the new reduced value, and click **Save**.

   f. Start **ArcExplorer** and open the **Pool.axl** (Win) or **Poolsmac.axl** (Mac) file. Zoom in to see if your correction worked.

   Assuming that the same correction will work for the aerial photograph, *pittsburgh_east_pa_sw.tif*, correct its world file too. If you have an instructor, submit electronic copies of the two corrected world files.

3. **Setting Some Threshold Scales**. If **ArcExplorer** is open, close it and start it again. Click **File**, **Open...**, browse to **c:\ESRI\AEJEE\data** (Win) or **/ESRI/AEJEE/Data/** (Mac), and open **3_dc_hd.axl** (be sure to get the right map project). This is a map project for Washington, D.C., that comes pre-built with the ArcExplorer installation. Click **tgr11001cty00** in the layers panel to make it the active layer, and then click the **Zoom to Active Layer** button. For the *tgr11001lkH* and *tgr1101wat* layers, set the **Never above scale** to the zoomed in map scale. If you have an instructor, submit an electronic copy of *3_dc_hd.axl*, which you should resave (using Save As...) with the name *Washington<YourLastName>.axl*, where you substitute your actual name for <YourLastName>. Try zooming out and back in to turn the two layers off and on.

4. **Setting Some Threshold Scales and Projection.** If **ArcExplorer** is open, close it and then start it again. Click **File**, **Open...**, browse to **c:\ESRI\AEJEE\Data** (Win) or **/ESRI/AEJEE/Data/** (Mac), and open **1_World_hd2.axl** (be sure to get the right map project). Make the following changes:

   a. Choose a new projection.

   b. Apply a threshold for cities.

   c. Label cities and country.

   If you have an instructor, submit an electronic copy of *1_World_hd2.axl*, which you should resave (using Save As...) with the name *World<YourLastName>.axl*, where you substitute your last name for <YourLastName>.

References

Clarke, K. C. *Getting Started with Geographic Information Systems*, 4th ed. Upper Saddle River: Prentice Hall, 2003.

Complete Electric Toy Train Sets. Internet URL: http://www.discounttrainsonline.com/electric-toy-train-sets.html (accessed on February 19, 2005).

Demers, M. N. *Fundamentals of Geographic Information Systems*, 3rd ed. Hoboken: Wiley, 2002.

Mentor Software, Inc., "State Place Codes." Internet URL: http://www.mentorsoftwareinc.com/resource/stplane.htm (accessed on February 21, 2005).

Morton, A., "UTM Grid Zones of the World." Internet URL: http://www.dmap.co.uk/utmworld.htm (accessed on February 21, 2005).

Muehrcke, P.C. *Map Use: Reading, Analysis, and Interpretations*, 2nd ed. Madison: JP Publications, 1986.

Rosenberg, M., Map Scale. Internet URL: http://geography.about.com/cs/maps/a/mapscale.htm (accessed on February 19, 2005).

CHAPTER 3

GETTING INFORMATION FROM A GIS

LEARNING OBJECTIVES

In this chapter, you will:

- Get an introduction to vector and raster map file formats
- Learn how data records are attached to map graphics in feature attribute tables
- Understand database attribute queries that select map features
- Understand spatial queries that select map features by location
- View feature attribute tables and data in ArcExplorer
- Make feature attribute queries in ArcExplorer
- Carry out direct and buffered spatial queries in ArcExplorer

Into the deep end of the pool!

INTRODUCTION

After completing Chapter 2, you should be feeling like you know how to navigate in a GIS and how to get

some information from a GIS. You can learn a lot by just navigating, studying patterns in graphic features,

and reading attribute data of graphic features. However, that is not all. Deeper-level information is available by running queries on one or more map layers of a map composition. A **query** is a means of selecting records or graphic features from one or more map layers in a map composition that meet specific criteria. This is an example query: *Select all pool-tag-holder residences within one mile of open swimming pools.* The criteria here are (1) a distance of one mile or less, and (2) swimming pools that are open. The result of the query is twofold: a list of all pool-tag-holder residences meeting the criteria, *and* corresponding point markers in a special color (generally yellow) that distinguish those residences from non-selected residences.

To extract information from an information system, you must understand that system's underlying data. So, in this chapter, you will begin by learning more about vector and raster map formats. In Chapter 1, you learned that vector maps are made up of point, line, and polygon graphic features and that each graphic feature has an attached data record with one or more attributes. Here you will learn that there are several file formats for vector maps, that there are several data types for attribute data, and that a data dictionary is essential if you need to query graphic features by using attribute values. You will also learn more about raster maps and file formats for digital images.

Anybody who uses computers is already familiar with using attribute data for making queries. For example, when you are searching for a book or other item to buy at a site such as *www.amazon.com*, you click on a category such as Books or Electronics. The Web site then uses your selected criterion value to navigate to a new Web page and show you some useful information for a next step, including recently published books or sale items that match your past purchases. You will learn how to do this kind of data searching or querying in general, and how to apply it to GIS in particular.

GIS has the unique capability to use locations and distances for record and graphic feature selection. You can simply study a map and directly select the features you want to analyze with a GIS tool designed for this purpose. With features selected and displayed in a special color on the map, you can export those features' attribute records for further analysis in Excel.

An important kind of spatial query is **proximity analysis**: finding out what is near certain graphic features on a map, such as swimming pools. Are there many 5- to 17-year-old youths living near a pool? If so, that would make it a good pool location. GIS uses circular buffers as one approach to making spatial queries.

Building on the concepts previously covered, you will use ArcExplorer in this chapter's tutorial to start an analysis of the Swimming Pool Case Study. You will answer some of the same questions asked of us by the Director of Pittsburgh's Citiparks Department.

MAP FORMATS

To extract information from GIS, you need an in-depth understanding of digital maps and how they represent data. In this section, you will build on what you learned in Chapter 1 about the two kinds of map layers, vector and raster.

Vector-Based Maps

The workhorses of analytical GIS are vector-based map layers. Besides their graphic features that we can see, they also have rich feature attribute tables that provide much of the information that analysts seek.

Vector maps have several alternative computer file formats. Some common ones originated by ESRI are as follows:

- ArcView **Shapefile**: This is a simple and widely used format. Each shapefile map layer has three or more files, all with the same file name, but with different file extensions. For example, the Pools shapefile has five files: *pools.shp* stores the pools' point, graphic-feature coordinates; *pools.dbf* stores each pool's feature attribute table; and the remaining files (*pools.sbn, pools.sbx,* and *pools.shx*) have various indices for speeding up processing. *Note*: Of the possible formats for vector-based map layers, ArcExplorer can display only shapefile maps.
- ArcInfo **Coverage**: This is an obsolete format that has a folder for each map layer and about 12 or more files (with file names such as *arc, tol, pat, dbf, lab,* and so forth) within the folder. In coverage format, the Pools layer would have a folder named *Pools* containing 12 or more files. Many of the files in a coverage have the purpose of speeding up advanced GIS processing, which was

more necessary years ago when computers had less capacity and speed than they do now.

- ArcInfo **E00 export format**: This is a single file that includes all of the data files of a coverage for easy export and interchange of map files. You need a utility program to transform E00 export files into a coverage before you can use them in a GIS.

ArcExplorer does not have any functions that transform from one map file format to another, but full-featured GIS packages, such as ArcView, can transform several map formats. Besides shapefiles, ArcExplorer can display a second kind of map format, an **event theme**, which is simply a data table that includes map coordinates, such as latitude and longitude or projected coordinates. In Chapter 6, you will create event themes and display them in ArcExplorer.

Each attribute of a shapefile's feature attribute table can be one of several data types. Some of the common data types are as follows:

- **Text** (or String): data such as names, addresses, and so on
- **Date**: dates such as 12/31/2007
- **Integer**: numbers without decimal places such as 100 or 213
- **Decimal** (or Real): numbers with decimal places such as 3.141592
- **Boolean**: one of two values, such as true or false and 1 or 0

Table 3-1 is a **data dictionary** for the Pools GIS. A data dictionary provides documentation for feature attribute tables, which is necessary when querying a GIS. A data dictionary lists all feature attribute tables, all of their attributes, and their definitions and data types. While we have trimmed down the number of attributes in the Pools GIS to keep it simple, there is no practical limit to the number of attributes that can be included in feature attribute tables. Sometimes, you need to modify, add, or delete attributes in a feature attribute table. For example, we created the PCTCAP attribute in Table 3-1 (percent of pool maximum capacity used on average) by dividing ATTEND04 by MAXLOAD and then multiplying the result by 100. While ArcExplorer does not have those capabilities, in Chapter 6 you will learn how to use Microsoft Excel for such tasks.

TABLE 3-1   Data Dictionary for Pools GIS

Map Layer	Attribute Name	Attribute Definition or Map Layer Description	Attribute Data Type or Layer Type
BlockCentroids		**24,283 center points of census blocks in Allegheny County**	Point
	STFID	Unique census ID of each block	Integer
	AGE_5_17	Population of 5 to 17 year olds	Integer

TABLE 3-1   **Data Dictionary for Pools GIS** (continued)

Map Layer	Attribute Name	Attribute Definition or Map Layer Description	Attribute Data Type or Layer Type
	FHH_CHILD	Number of female-headed households with children	Integer
County		**Boundary of Allegheny County**	Polygon
	FIPSSTCO	FIPS code for state (42) and county (003)	Integer
	STATE	State name	Text
	COUNTY	County name	Text
MinorCivilDivisions		**130 minor civil divisions (cities, towns, boroughs)**	Polygon
	COUNTY	FIPS code for state and county	Integer
	MCD2000	FIPS code for municipality	Integer
	NAME	Name of minor civil division	Text
Neighborhoods		**Boundaries of Pittsburgh's 89 neighborhoods**	Polygon
	NEIGHBORHOOD	Name of neighborhood	Text
Pittsburgh		**Minor civil divisions of Pittsburgh**	Polygon
	COUNTY	FIPS code for state and county	Integer
	MCD2000	FIPS code for municipality	Integer
	NAME	Name of minor civil division	Text
Pools		**32 public swimming pools in Pittsburgh**	Point
	NAME	Swimming pool name	Text
	ADDRESS	Street address	Text

TABLE 3-1 Data Dictionary for Pools GIS (continued)

Map Layer	Attribute Name	Attribute Definition or Map Layer Description	Attribute Data Type or Layer Type
	ZIPCODE	5-digit zip code	Integer
	OPEN	Whether the pool was open in 2004: 1=open, 0=closed	Boolean
	MAXLOAD	Maximum pool capacity in terms of number of swimmers	Integer
	ATTEND04	Average daily attendance in summer 2004	Integer
	PCTCAP	100 x ATTEND04/ MAXLOAD	Decimal
PoolBuffers1		**1-mile radius pool buffers**	Polygon
	POOL	Pool name	Text
	BUFFERDIS	Buffer distance (0.5 and 1.0 miles)	Decimal
	OPEN	Whether the pool was open in summer 2004 (1=yes, 0=no)	Boolean
PoolBuffers15		**1.5-mile radius pool buffers**	Polygon
	POOL	Pool name	Text
	BUFFERDIS	Buffer distance (0.5, 1.0, and 1.5 miles)	Decimal
	OPEN	Whether the pool was open in summer 2004 (1=yes, 0=no)	Boolean
PoolTags		**Random sample of 2,680 pool tag holder residences**	Point
	TAGNO	Serial number on pool tag	Integer

TABLE 3-1   **Data Dictionary for Pools GIS** (continued)

Map Layer	Attribute Name	Attribute Definition or Map Layer Description	Attribute Data Type or Layer Type
	POOL	Pool that the pool tag holder intended to use when he/she obtained the pool tag	Text
	AV_STATUS	Code from ArcView's address matcher where M=matched (point is on map) and U=unmatched (point is not on map)	Text
Rivers		**Rivers**	Polygon
	LANDNAME	River Name	Text
Streets		**65,535 TIGER/Line 2000 street centerline segments in Allegheny County**	Line
	LENGTH	Length of street segment (m)	Decimal
	FEDIRP	Street direction prefix (N, E, S, W)	Text
	FENAME	Street name	Text
	FETYPE	Street type (St, Ave, Rd, etc.)	Text
	DEDIRS	Street direction suffix (N, E, S, W)	Text
	CFCC	Census code for street type	Text
	FRADDL	House number at the start of the block on the left	Integer
	TOADDL	House number at the end of the block on the left	Integer
	FRADDR	House number at the start of the block on the right	Integer

TABLE 3-1   **Data Dictionary for Pools GIS** (continued)

Map Layer	Attribute Name	Attribute Definition or Map Layer Description	Attribute Data Type or Layer Type
	TOADDR	House number at the end of the block on the right	Integer
	ZIPL	5-digit zip code on the left side of the street	Integer
	ZIPR	5-digit zip code on the right side of the street	Integer
ZipCodes		**117 5-digit zip code boundaries**	Polygon
	AREA_METER	Area (m)	Integer
	PERIMETER_	Perimeter (m)	Integer
	ZIPCODE	Zip code	Integer
	NUMTAGS	Number of pool tags in summer 2004	Integer

Raster Maps

In Chapter 1, you learned that raster image maps are digital images that have map coordinates, and that a digital image is a rectangular array of pixels (short for "picture elements"). When considered as a mathematical object, a digital image is a rectangular array, or grid, of numbers. Each number signifies a unique color. The maximum size number that can be stored in each grid cell determines **color depth**, or the number of different colors possible. Each storage location in a computer's memory is a **bit**, an on/off location. One character on your keyboard requires 8 bits, called a **byte**, to be stored. Typically, black-and-white images use 8 bits (1 byte) per pixel, and color images use 24 bits (3 bytes) per pixel (Koren 2005).

A digital image has many possible file formats. Many of the formats use **file compression**, a method for making files smaller, to reduce storage requirements and speed up transmission across networks. Some image file formats are as follows (Koren 2005):

- **TIFF (Tagged Image File Format)**: This has *.tif* as its file extension. It yields very high quality images and is commonly used in publishing. Its file sizes are large because it is uncompressed.
- **GIF (Graphic Interchange Format)**: This has *.gif* as its file extension. It is at the opposite end of the spectrum from TIFF format images. It is ideal for schematic drawings that have relatively large areas with solid color fill and few color variations. Its advantage is that it has small file sizes.

- **JPEG (Joint Photographic Experts Group)**: This has *.jpg* as its file extension. It is the most widely used format for photographs and other images that have a lot of color variations. It uses file compression at the expense of picture detail, if you specify a lot of compression.

Unlike other images, raster maps have map coordinates referenced in accompanying world files (ESRI, 2005). The world file for the raster map *pittsburgh_east_pa_sw.tif*—used in the Pools GIS—is *pittsburgh_east_pa_sw.tfw*, where the *.tfw* extension signifies that it is a world file for a *.tif* image. Table 3-2 displays the contents of this world file. Line 1 denotes that each pixel is one meter on a side (because the map units of the UTM projected coordinates of the raster map are in meters, and the image has one-meter pixels). Lines 2–4 are of no importance to us. Lines 5 and 6 are the x- and y-coordinates of the upper-left corner of the image for the UTM zone of the projection (which is 17 North for Pittsburgh) in projected coordinates. If you hover your mouse over the upper-left corner of the image in ArcExplorer, you can read the coordinates in Table 3-2.

TABLE 3-2   World file for *pittsburgh_east_pa_sw.tif*

Line	Example values from *pittsburgh_east_pa_sw.tfw*
Line 1: x-dimension of a pixel in map units	1
Line 2: rotation parameter	0
Line 3: rotation parameter	0
Line 4: NEGATIVE of y-dimension of a pixel in map units	-1
Line 5: x-coordinate of center of upper-left pixel	584510
Line 6: y-coordinate of center of upper-left pixel	4477170

Here are a few additional notes on raster map images.

- Raster maps can portray only one attribute: a color for a picture, a decimal number for an elevation, a code for land use, or other value.
- Raster maps have enormous file sizes. The black-and-white aerial photo for one small portion of Pittsburgh, *pittsburgh_east_pa_sw.tif*, is 44.8 MB. This is more than half of the total storage of the Pools GIS!
- Technicians **digitize** aerial photographs to create vector-based map layers for various physical features. Using a process similar to the measurement work you did in Chapter 2 (clicking along the boundary of Pittsburgh to estimate its perimeter), technicians or automated line-following software traces out street curbs, parking lots, building rooftops, and so on, and put them in vector format.
- Satellite remote sensing yields images outside the visible range, but they are given **"false colors"** so we can see them. Every material, type of plant, and so forth has a signature reflection of electromagnetic radiation and thus can be identified (Wall, 2005).

GIS QUERIES

The partnership between database tables and vector-based graphics in a GIS is very powerful. Each vector-graphic feature on a map has a data record and visa versa. These two kinds of data are linked in a GIS: You can select records from a feature attribute table by using query criteria, and this action will automatically highlight the corresponding graphic features. The opposite is true as well: You can select graphic features on a GIS map, using your mouse directly, or shapes such as circular buffers, to automatically highlight corresponding data records. These capabilities are unique to GIS.

Attribute Queries

If you want to select all the Pittsburgh swimming pools that were closed in summer 2004 from the Pools feature attribute table, you would use the following query criterion: (OPEN = 0). This criterion says: *Select all pool records with attribute named Open that have their value equal to 0.* Another example is (PCTCAP >=.5), meaning: *Select all records with average percent capacity used in summer 2004 that equals or exceeds 50%.* This query yields the 4 pools out of 32 that had good average attendance relative to their capacity.

Each example above is a **simple query criterion**, or simple condition, and has the general form (<data attribute><logical operator><value>). For values, use numerals without any special characters, but include single quotes around text and date values. An example of a text-value criterion is (NAME ='Riverview') and that of a date-value criterion is (DATE >= 'Jun 1, 2005 12:00:00 AM'). Query data attributes are case insensitive in ArcExplorer, thus NAME and DATE could be written Name, name, Date, date, or any other combination of uppercase and lowercase letters. We use all capital letters in our queries to be consistent with the data dictionary in Table 3-1. In contrast, query values *are* case sensitive in ArcExplorer, so *a* is different from *A*.

Table 3-3 lists several logical operators available for use in query criteria, along with their meanings and examples of their use. Most are self-explanatory; however, the *like* operator is a bit complicated. It compares text attributes to text values where the text values include the % **wild card**. The % symbol stands for zero, one, or more characters of any kind. So, for example, the simple query criterion (NAME like ' We%') selects any pools with names starting with the letters *We*, including West Penn and Westwood. Another example is (NAME like '%r%') which finds any name that contains at least one *r* whether at the start, imbedded anywhere, or at the end of a value. The names Riverview, Sue Murray, and Fowler and others meet this criterion.

TABLE 3-3 Logical Operators for Query Criteria

Logical Operator	Meaning	Examples
=	equal to	(OPEN=0) retrieves closed pools (NAME='McBride') retrieves McBride pool
<	less than	(PCTCAP<0.5) retrieves pools using less than 50% capacity (NAME<'McBride') retrieves pools before McBride alphabetically

TABLE 3-3 **Logical Operators for Query Criteria** (continued)

Logical Operator	Meaning	Examples
>	greater than	`(PCTCAP>0.5)` retrieves pools using greater than 50% capacity `(NAME>'McBride')` retrieves pools after McBride alphabetically
<=	less than or equal to	`(PCTCAP<=0.5)` retrieves pools using less than or equal to 50% capacity `(NAME<='McBride')` retrieves McBride and pools before it alphabetically
>=	greater than or equal to	`(PCTCAP>=0.5)` retrieves pools using greater than or equal to 50% capacity `(NAME>='McBride')` retrieves McBride and pools after it alphabetically
<>	not equal to	`(NAME<>'McBride')` retrieves all pools except McBride
like	wild-card query with text value including the % wild card	`(NAME like 'We%')` retrieves all pools with names starting with *We*, West Penn, and Westwood

For queries with text data type attributes, results of queries depend on the order in which text values sort. Suppose you have a text attribute named ODDSANDENDS with four values: the numbers 7 and *223* and the words *zebra* and *apple*. If you were to sort ODDS-ANDENDS in ascending order, the result is numbers in order analogous to alphabetical order and then words alphabetically: *223, 7, apple,* and *zebra*. In this case, the number of digits in a number—its magnitude—does not determine sort order; instead, the number with the smallest first digit on the left is first, and if there are any ties, they are broken using the second digit and so forth. So, the query criterion (ODDSANDENDS >= `'300'`) yields *7, apple,* and *zebra*. The criterion (ODDSANDENDS >= `'lion'`) yields *zebra*.

Compound query criteria, or a compound condition, combine two or more simple queries with the **logical connectives** AND or OR. For example, (OPEN = 0) AND (MAXLOAD > 500) selects records that satisfy both criteria simultaneously. The result is a closed pool AND it has MAXLOAD (capacity) greater than 500. The open pools and the small-capacity pools are excluded. The connector AND is restrictive.

The connector OR is the opposite; it is inclusive: (OPEN = 1) OR (MAXLOAD > 500) selects any pool that satisfies either condition—or both. It selects any pool that is open or that has large capacity, *or* any pool that is both open and has large capacity. The OR connector for two simple conditions will select the same number or more records than an AND connector for the same two simple conditions.

Spatial Queries

Instead of using the values of attributes to select records, a **spatial query** uses location on the map to select spatial features and their records. Direct spatial queries depend on you being able to see what you want to select on a displayed map layer. For example, you can select graphic features by dragging a rectangle around them. You can use other mapped features as guides for selection. For example, you can select all the block centroids for 5- to 17-year-old youths that lie within the municipality of Mount Oliver. You can make several selections, adding to previous selections. An example is to drag several rectangles around different parts of Mount Oliver. See Figure 3-1.

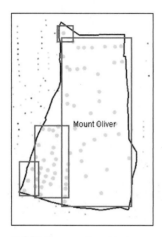

FIGURE 3-1   Graphic feature selection using a series of rectangles

An indirect spatial query method uses buffers to select features. See Figure 3-2. For example, the general question may be this: How many 5 to 17 year olds live near each swimming pool? With buffers, you would translate this question as: *How many youths live within a one-mile radius, circular buffer of each swimming pool?* Pools with large numbers of youths living nearby are better located, in most cases, than those with smaller numbers of youths. Buffers can be made for line features too, for example: *How many 5- to 17-year-old youths live within one-tenth mile of a bus route that has a pool as one of its stops?* Perhaps the better-located pools are on bus routes that pass through residential neighborhoods. Lastly, as you might have suspected, you can make buffers for polygons, for example: *How many pool tag holders live outside of Pittsburgh, but within one mile of the border?* Pittsburgh would like surrounding municipalities to help pay for the pools that their non-Pittsburgh residents use.

 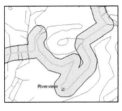 

| Point Buffer | Line Buffer | Polygon Buffer |

FIGURE 3-2   Examples of point, line, and polygon buffers

QUERIES IN ARCEXPLORER

Next, you will use ArcExplorer to see queries at work in detail. The map composition used in the tutorial has some familiar map layers, plus one new one: Pool Tag Holders' Residences. This is a random sample of 2,680 pool tag holders' residences out of 56,162 that had street address data in summer 2004. We selected data and input them from scanned paper forms into an Excel file, as if we were pulling them randomly out of a hat. While the resulting sample size is small, it nevertheless represents the spatial patterns of the entire population.

A random sample has some nice features, besides keeping the cost of data entry low for us. For example, if you find that there are 100 sampled pool tag residences in a specific geographic area, you can scale this number up to get a reasonable estimate of the actual population of pool tag residences in the same area. You would use the factor of the total population divided by the sample size: 56,162/2,680 = 20. Thus, the 100 sampled residences represent approximately 2,000 (20*100) total residences with pool tags in the same area.

A final note before we begin: The Pool Tag Holders' Residences map layer represents the *intentions* of youth and their parents or guardians to use swimming pools. Pool tags were free during summer 2004, but they had cost $60 for a family of four in previous years. So perhaps people got pool tags but did not use them. We would need to input pool visits by tag holder data to get actual pool use, but that remains a future task. We do not have that data as yet.

The Queries Map Project File

To begin, you will start ArcExplorer, open the map project file, and make a few adjustments to the application program window.

1. On your computer's desktop, click **Start, All Programs, AEJEE, AEJEE** (Win) or **Finder, Macintosh HD, ESRI, AEJEE, AEJEE** (Mac).
2. In the ArcExplorer window, click **File, Open...**.
3. In the Open window, click the **list arrow** in the Look in field, browse to **c:\LearningAndUsingGIS** (Win) or **/learningAndUsingGIS/(Mac)** and double-click **Queries.axl** (Win) or **QueriesMac.axl** (Mac).
4. Click **Pittsburgh** in the layers panel to make it the active layer and then click the **Zoom to Active Layer** button.

Direct Record Selection

1. Click off the **Pool Tag Holders' Residences** layer for now, if it's not already off.
2. Right-click (Win) or control-click (Mac) the **Pools** layer, and in the context window that opens, click **Attribute Table**. *(The Attribute of Pools window opens.)*
3. Scroll to the right in the Attributes of Pools window until you can see the **MAXLOAD** column.
4. Right-click (Win) or control-click (Mac) the **column heading** containing the name MAXLOAD, and in the context window that opens, click **Sort Descending**. See Figure 3-3. *(ArcExplorer sorts the records in descending order by MAXLOAD.)*

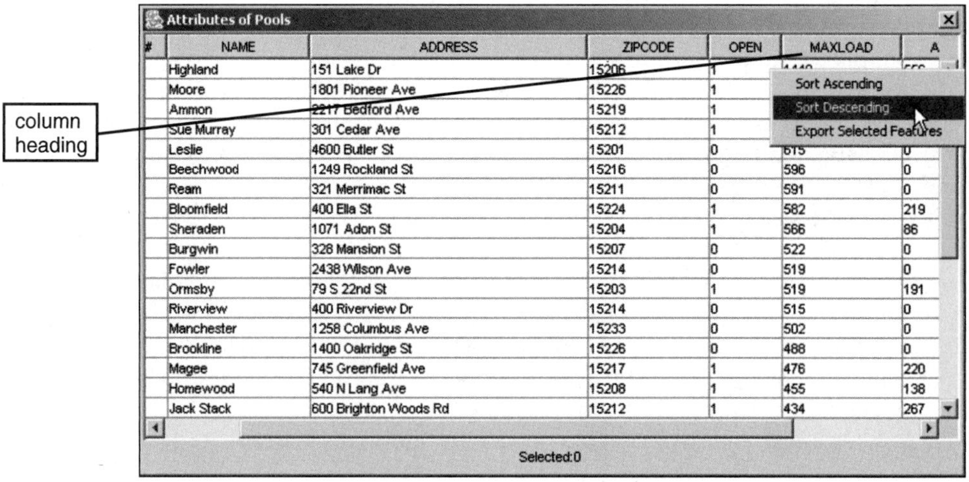

#	NAME	ADDRESS	ZIPCODE	OPEN	MAXLOAD	A
	Highland	151 Lake Dr	15206	1		
	Moore	1801 Pioneer Ave	15226	1		
	Ammon	2217 Bedford Ave	15219	1		
	Sue Murray	301 Cedar Ave	15212	1		
	Leslie	4600 Butler St	15201	0		0
	Beechwood	1249 Rockland St	15216	0	596	0
	Ream	321 Merrimac St	15211	0	591	0
	Bloomfield	400 Ella St	15224	1	582	219
	Sheraden	1071 Adon St	15204	1	566	86
	Burgwin	328 Mansion St	15207	0	522	0
	Fowler	2438 Wilson Ave	15214	0	519	0
	Ormsby	79 S 22nd St	15203	1	519	191
	Riverview	400 Riverview Dr	15214	0	515	0
	Manchester	1258 Columbus Ave	15233	0	502	0
	Brookline	1400 Oakridge St	15226	0	488	0
	Magee	745 Greenfield Ave	15217	1	476	220
	Homewood	540 N Lang Ave	15208	1	455	138
	Jack Stack	600 Brighton Woods Rd	15212	1	434	267

FIGURE 3-3 Attributes of Pools table sorted by MAXLOAD in descending order

5. Click in the **first row**, with MAXLOAD equal to 1448, highlighting the row.
6. Hold down the **Shift** key on your keyboard, click in the **second row**, with MAXLOAD equal to 1282, hold down your **mouse** button, and drag down to the row with MAXLOAD equal to 502 to select a total of 14 pools. See Figure 3-4. *(The selected records are the larger pools.)*
7. Examine your map and see the locations of these pools indicated by the yellow selection point markers. *(The large pools appear to be evenly distributed around Pittsburgh, with a few exceptions.)*
8. Close the Attributes of Pools window and then click the **Clear All Selection** button. *(Now all of the pools are again unselected.)*

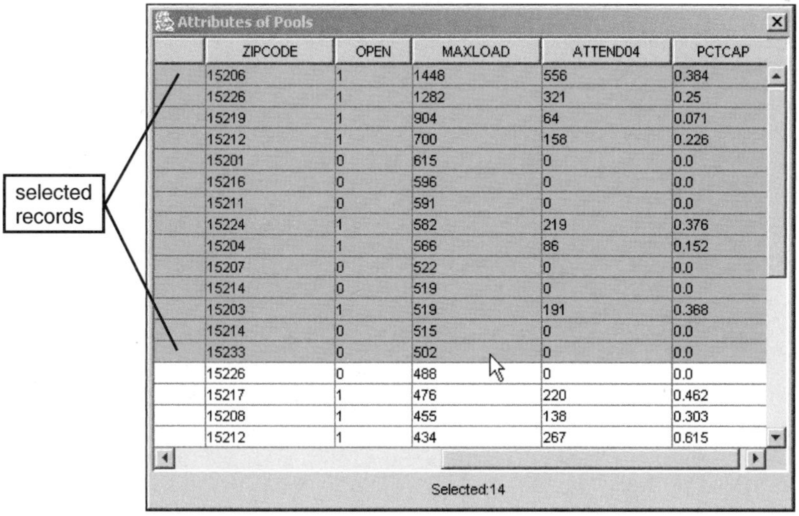

FIGURE 3-4 Attributes of Pools table with selected records

PRACTICE 3-1

- Directly select records in the Attributes of Pools table for the pools that had 200 or greater average daily attendance in summer 2004.
- When you are finished, close the table and clear the selection.

Direct Graphic Feature Selection

1. Make sure that Pools is the active layer, click the **Select Features** button, and in the menu that opens, click **Rectangle**. *(You are now ready to select pools by dragging a rectangle around them.)*
2. Drag a rectangle around the **Riverview** and **Fowler** closed pools, but do not include any open pools in your rectangle, and then release your mouse button. See Figure 3-5. *(The pools enclosed within the rectangle are now selected, as indicated by the yellow-selection point markers.)*
3. Now hold down the **Shift** key while you drag rectangles around the remaining closed pools, being careful not to include any open pools.
4. Right-click (Win) or control-click (Mac) the **Pools** layer in the layers panel, and in the context window that opens, click **Attribute Table**. See Figure 3-6. *(The Attributes of Pools window opens with the 16 records for closed pools selected.)*
5. In the Attributes of Pools window, right-click (Win) or control-click (Mac) the **FID column heading** and then click **Export Selected Features**.

Getting Information from a GIS

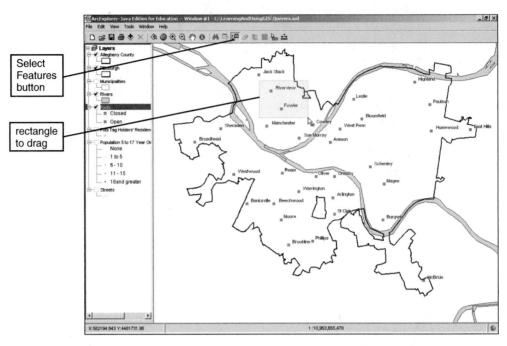

Select Features button

rectangle to drag

FIGURE 3-5 Rectangle to drag to select pools

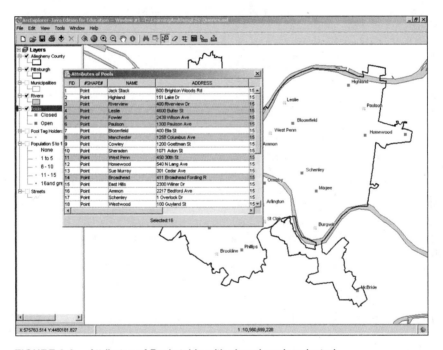

FIGURE 3-6 Attributes of Pools table with closed pools selected

6. In the resulting Save window, browse to **c:\LearningAndUsingGIS\Outputs** (Win) or **/LearningAndUsingGIS/Outputs/** (Mac), enter **ClosedPools** in the File name field (Win) or the Save As field (Mac), click **Save**, and then click **OK** in the resulting information window indicating success. See Figure 3-7.

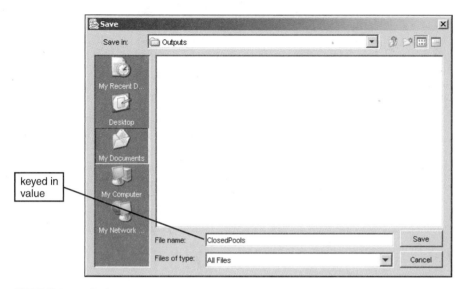

keyed in value

FIGURE 3-7   Saving exported pools data

7. Close the Attributes of Pools window and click the **Clear All Selection** button.
8. Windows users: Start **Excel**, click **File**, click **Open...**, click the list arrow in the **Files of type** field, click **All Files (*.*)**, browse to **c:\LearningAndUsingGIS\Outputs**, and then double-click **ClosedPools.dbf**. Mac users: Start **Excel**, click **File**, click **Open**, click the list arrow in the **Enable** list, scroll to the bottom of the list, and select **All Documents**, browse to **/LearningAndUsingGIS/Outputs/**, select **ClosePools.dbf**, and click **Open**.
9. Click in the **empty cell** at the foot of the MAXLOAD column, just under the 488, enter **=average(E2:E17)**, and then press the **Enter** key. See Figure 3-8. *(You have just found the average capacity of closed pools, 420 persons.)*
10. Close Excel and do not save changes.

PRACTICE 3-2

- Graphically select all of the open pools in summer 2004.
- Calculate the average capacity for open pools.
- When you are finished, clear the selected pools in the map.

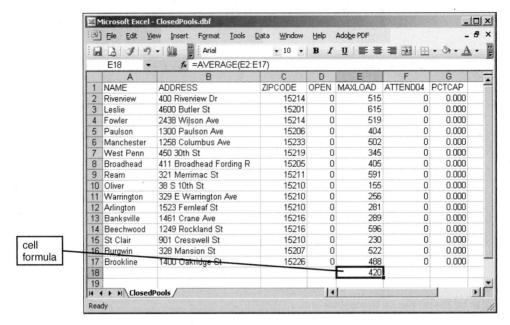

cell
formula

FIGURE 3-8   Analyzing exported pools data in Excel

Identify Tool

Now that you have a good idea of what feature attribute tables are and how they are linked to mapped graphic features, you can experiment with ArcExplorer's Identify tool.

1. Right-click (Win) or control-click (Mac) the **Pools** layer in the Layers panel. In the resulting context menu, slide your mouse cursor down to **Move Layer**, and then in the resulting submenu, click **Move to Top**. *(This moves the Pools layer to the top of the Layers panel. The Identity tool works with the top layer in this panel.)*

2. Click the **Identity Tool** button, and then click the **red square point marker** for the Riverview pool. See Figure 3-9. *(The Identify Results window opens with a nice display of the feature attribute record for Riverview. Leave this window open.)*

3. Click on another pool's **point marker**. *(The Identify Results window displays the record for the newly identified pool.)*

4. Close the Identify Results window.

5. Right-click (Win) or Control-click (Mac) the **Pools** layer, slide over **Move Layer**, and then click **Move Down**.

6. Repeat **Step 5** until Pools is just below Rivers, where it was before.

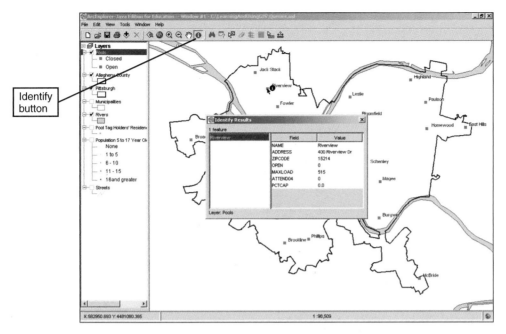

Identify button

FIGURE 3-9 Identifying Riverview pool

PRACTICE 3-3

- Click on the Pool Tag Holders' Residences layer.
- Use the Identify tool for points in that layer. The pool attribute is the pool that tag holders stated that they planned to use when they signed up for their pool tags.
- When you are finished, return layers to their original order with Pool Tag Holders' Residences just below Pools.

Map Tips

You can quickly get a data value, or map tip, for a feature when you hover your mouse cursor over it. ArcExplorer, however, does not store map tips settings, so you have to reset them every time you open a map project file.

1. Click the **Map Tips** button.
2. In the resulting Map Tips window, click **Pools** in the Layers panel, click **MAXLOAD** in the Fields panel, and then click the **Set Map Tips** button. See Figure 3-10. *(The lower-left MapTips field shows that MAXLOAD is selected to be displayed as the map tip for Pools.)*
3. In the Map Tips window, click **Rivers** in the Fields panel, click **LANDNAME** in the Fields panel, click the **Set Map Tips** button, click **OK**, and then close the Map Tips window.
4. Hover your mouse over any pool. See Figure 3-11. *(After a short pause, the capacity of the pool is displayed as a map tip.)*

5. Hover your mouse over a river. *(This time the river's name appears.)*

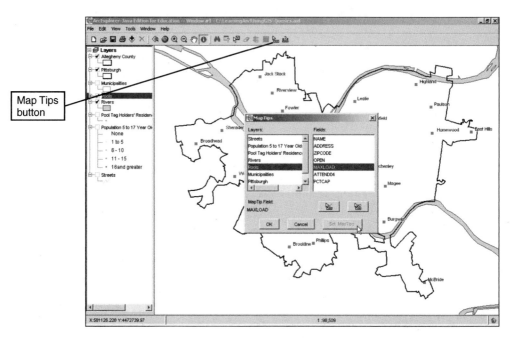

Map Tips
button

FIGURE 3-10   Setting map tips

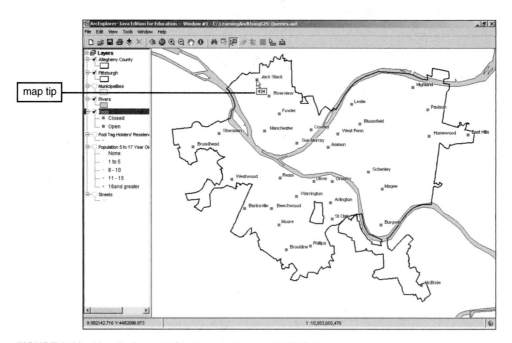

map tip

FIGURE 3-11   Map tip for Jack Stack pool showing MAXLOAD

Chapter 3

- Set Map Tips for Pool Tag Holders' Residences to Pool.
- Turn on the Pool Tag Holders' Residences layer and hover over several of that layer's points. When you are finished, click this layer off.

Simple Attribute Query Using Query Builder

1. Make sure that Pools is the active layer and then click the **Query Builder...** button. *(The Query Builder window opens.)*
2. Click **MAXLOAD** in the Select a field panel; click the **>=** button; in the field with the partially-built query expression, click to the right of >= but inside the right parenthesis, and enter **500**; and then click the **Execute** button. See Figure 3-12. *(The query executes, selecting the 14 pools with large capacity.)*

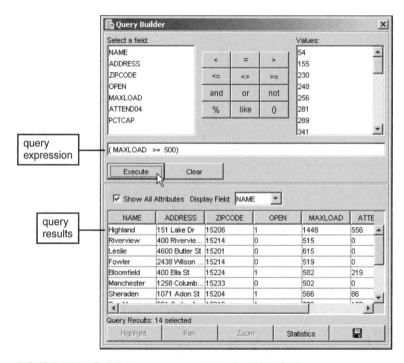

FIGURE 3-12 Building a query expression for MAXLOAD

3. In the bottom of the Query Builder window, click the **Statistics** button.
4. In the resulting Select a field to get statistics window, click the **Use Query Results** check box, select **MAXLOAD**, and then click **OK**. See Figures 3-13 and 3-14. *(The very nice Statistics Results for field:MAXLOAD window opens with several useful statistics.)*

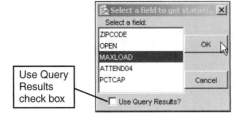

Use Query
Results
check box

FIGURE 3-13 Selecting a field to get statistics

Statistics Results for field:MAXLOAD	
Count	14
Max	1448.0
Min	502.0
Mean	704.3571428571429
Std Dev	300.25824965105704
Total	9861.0

Close

FIGURE 3-14 Statistics for MAXLOAD

5. Click the **Close** button in the Statistics Results for field:MAXLOAD window. *(Note that you could click the Save button to save the selected records as a text file without attribute names. Better, though, is to open the Pools' feature attribute table and export a .dbf file as you did in the previous Select Graphic Features Directly section.)*

6. In the Query Builder window, click the **Clear** button, and then close the window.

PRACTICE 3-5

- Build a query to select all pools with average attendance of 200 or greater in summer 2004.
- Get statistics for these pools.

Compound Attribute Queries Using Query Builder

The next query uses the AND connector to find pools that simultaneously satisfy two conditions: (1) Pools that were used at a relatively large percent of their capacity in summer 2004, and (2) the pools that are in zip code 15212. This would be a good query for a family in zip code 15212 that uses Pittsburgh pools and that might be worried about future pool closures. Open pools that used high percentages of their capacity are efficient and thus stand a good chance of staying open.

1. Make sure that Pools is the active layer and then click the **Query Builder...** button.
2. Click **PCTCAP** in the Select a field panel; click the **>=** button; in the field with the partially-built query expression, click to the right of >= but inside the right parenthesis and enter **0.5**; then click the **Execute** button.
3. Click to the right of the **right parenthesis**, click the **and** button, click to the right of the **and** and enter a **left parenthesis**, click **ZIPCODE** in the Select a field panel, click the **=** button, click to the right of the right of the **=** sign and enter **15212)**, and then click the **Execute** button. See Figure 3-15. *(That produces only one record, the Jack Stack swimming pool.)*

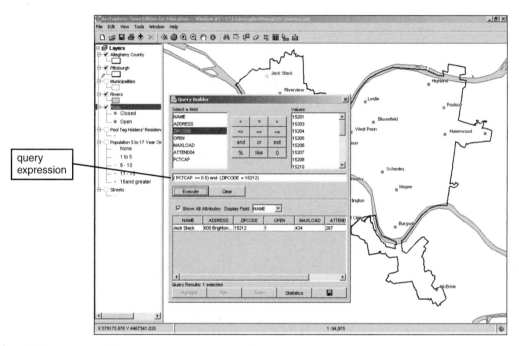

query expression

FIGURE 3-15   Building a compound query condition

4. Close the Query Builder window.
5. Click the **Clear All Selection** button.

PRACTICE 3-6

Get the list of all pools with names that start with 'B' and were closed in summer 2004.

Feature Selection Using the Buffer Tool

A good performance measure for the locations of swimming pools is the population of youths living near pools—the higher the better. Buffers provide a powerful tool for obtaining these statistics, as you will now see.

1. Click the **Population 5 to 17 Year Olds by Block Centroid** layer on.
2. Click **View, Map Units**, and make sure that **Meters** is selected.
3. Make sure that Pools is the active layer, click the **Select Features** button and **Rectangle**, and then click and drag a small rectangle around the **Phillips pool** to select it. See Figure 3-16.

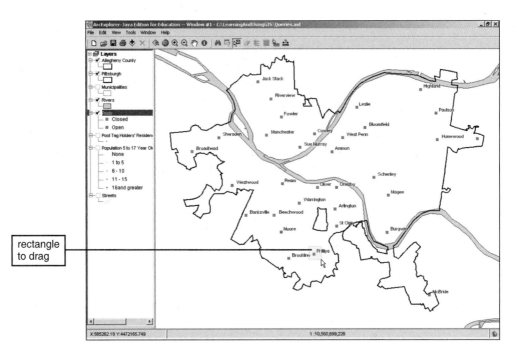

rectangle to drag

FIGURE 3-16 Selecting Phillips pool

4. Click the **Buffer** button, leave the **Buffer Distance** at **1** and **Buffer Units** at **Miles,** click the **check box** for **Use buffer to select features from this layer,** click the **list arrow** below the check box in the layers field, click **Population 5 to 17 Year Olds by Block Centroid**, and then click **OK**. See Figure 3-17.

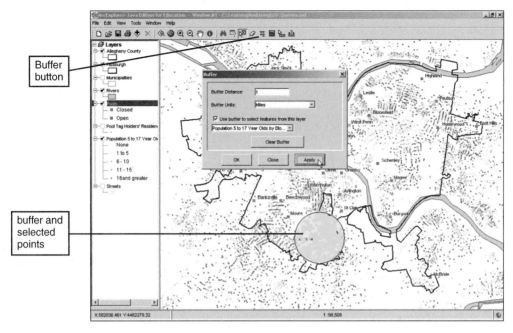

Buffer button

buffer and selected points

FIGURE 3-17   Buffer for Phillips pool and selected block centroids

5. Right-click (Win) or Control-click (Mac) the **Population 5 to 17 Year Olds by Block Centroid** layer, click **Attribute Table**, and *WAIT* until the table opens. *(It takes awhile for the table to open because it is so large.)*

6. In the Attributes of Population table right-click (Win) or control-click (Mac) the **FID** column heading, and then click **Export Selected Features**.

7. In the resulting Save Window, browse to the **c:\LearningAndUsingGIS\Outputs** (Win) or **/LearningAndUsingGIS/Outputs/** (Mac) folder, enter **Buf1PhillipsYouth** in the File name field, click **Save**, click **OK**, and then close the Attributes of Population 5 to 17 Year Olds by Block Centroid window.

8. Start Microsoft Excel, click **File**, click **Open**, click the **list arrow** in the **Files of type field**, click **All Files (*.*)**, browse to **c:\LearningAndUsingGIS\Outputs** (Win) or **/LearningAndUsingGIS/Outputs/** (Mac), and then double-click **Buf1PhillipsYouth.dbf**. *(Microsoft Excel opens with the Buf1PhillipsYouth data.)*

9. In the Excel window, scroll to the right until you see the AGE_5_17 column, click on that **column's heading** (with letter **R**) to select the column, scroll down to the bottom of that column, click in the **empty cell** beneath the last value (4), enter **=sum(R2:R397)**, and then press the **Enter** key. *(Make note of the resulting total number of 5 to 17 year olds living within a mile of Phillips: 2,532.)*

10. Close Excel without saving changes.

11. Click the **Buffer** button and close the Buffer window. *(This action deletes the buffer and corresponding selections.)*

12. Click the **Clear All Selection** button. *(This deselects the Phillips pool.)*

PRACTICE 3-7

Determine the number of 5 to 17 year olds living within 1 mile of Homewood pool, another pool that is in a densely populated area. Make note of the answer. You will need it for the exercises in this chapter.

Visualization of Proximity Using Buffers

The next query produces very interesting results. When individuals signed up for pool tags, they indicated which pool they intended to use. You will use the resulting data to study patterns of where those individuals live in relation to their intended pool. Are they mostly close to intended pools? Did some intend to travel far? Are some nearby populations excluded by barriers such as limited-access highways? Let's get some answers.

1. Click off the **Population 5 to 17 Year Olds by Block Centroid** layer and click on the **Pool Tag Holders' Residences**.
2. Make Pools the active layer, click the **Select Features** button and **Rectangle**, and click and drag a small rectangle around the **Phillips pool** to select it.
3. Make **Pool Tag Holders' Residences** the active layer and click the **Query Builder** button.
4. In the Query Builder window, click **POOL** in the Select a field panel, click the = button, scroll down in the Values panel and click **Phillips**, click the **Execute** button, and then click **No** in the Loading Query Results window. See Figure 3-18. *(It is quite interesting to see that many individuals intended to travel quite far. Next, you will see how far away the selected residences are from Phillips pool.)*
5. Close the Query Builder Window.
6. Make **Pools** the active layer.
7. Click the **Buffer** button.
8. Change the 1 to **0.5** in the Buffer Distance field, and then click **Apply**. *(Do not click OK. If you do, start this step over.)*
9. Change the 0.5 to **1** in the Buffer Distance field, and then click **Apply**. *(Now you should have two buffers on your map, 0.5- and 1-mile radius buffers.)*
10. Change the 1 to **1.5** in the Buffer Distance field and then click **Apply**.
11. Change the 1.5 to **2** in the Buffer Distance field and then click **Apply**.
12. Click **OK** in the Buffer window. See Figure 3-19. *(Do not click Close; if you do, repeat Steps 6 through 11.)*
13. Click the **Buffer** button and then close the Buffer window.
14. Click the **Clear All Selection** button.

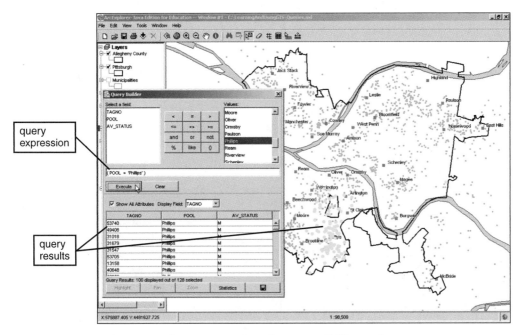

FIGURE 3-18   Attribute query for residences intending to use Phillips pool

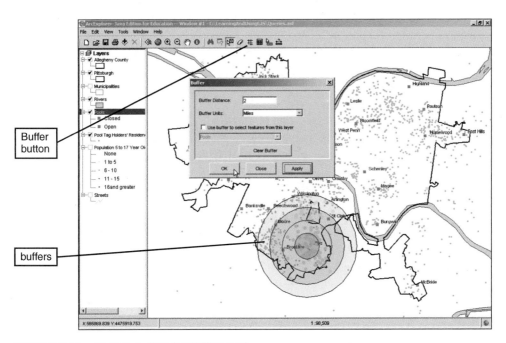

FIGURE 3-19   Multiple buffers for Phillips pool

The end result is a set of buffers that help you see the patterns of selected residences at different distances from Phillips pool. In the area between the 0.5-mile and 1-mile buffers, selected residences are quite concentrated and evenly distributed. However, in the area between the 1.5-mile and 2-mile buffers, residences only to the north of Phillips pool are selected. It is reasonable that residences to the south and east are not included, because they are outside Pittsburgh city limits. But what about all of the residences in Pittsburgh to the west of Phillips pool? Many may have intended to use Moore pool, but some are closer to Phillips. There must be a physical or social barrier about a mile west of Phillips pool that keeps individuals living on the other side of the barrier from using the pool. You'll investigate this issue in Exercise 3-1.

PRACTICE 3-8

- Do the same analysis for Homewood pool that you just did for Phillips pool.
- How does the pattern of pool tag holder residences for Homewood differ from that of Phillips?
- When you are finished, click the Buffer button and close the Buffer window to clear the buffers and selection.

Feature Selection by Polygon Using the Buffer Tool

Next, you will use the Mount Oliver polygon of the Municipalities layer to select the residences of pool tag holders within it. You have to "trick" ArcExplorer to select features of a layer using a polygon or polygons of an existing layer; you build a buffer for Mount Oliver that has a *very tiny* buffer radius, so the buffer is almost indistinguishable from the Mount Oliver polygon. This is easier than using the direct selection approach as was done earlier in this chapter.

1. Click the **Municipalities** layer on.
2. Right-click (Win) or control-click (Mac) **Municipalities**, click **Attribute Table**, scroll down in the Attributes of Municipalities table, click on the **Mount Oliver** row to select it, and then close the Attributes of Municipalities table.
3. Zoom into the **Mount Oliver** area for a better look.
4. Make sure that Municipalities is the active layer and then click the **Buffer** button.
5. In the Buffer window, enter **0.000001** for the Buffer Distance *(that is less than a tenth of an inch on the ground!)*, keep the Buffer Units as **Miles**, click the **Use buffer to select features from this layer** check box, click **Pool Tag Holder's Residences**, and then click **OK**. See Figure 3-20. *(There you have it: a very easy way to select features by polygon.)*

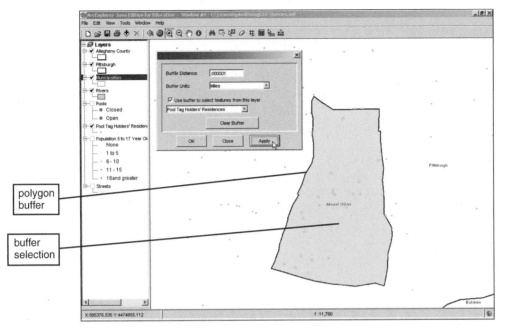

polygon
buffer

buffer
selection

89

FIGURE 3-20   Selecting residences by polygon

6. Click the **Buffer** button and then close the Buffer window.
7. Click the **Clear All Selection** button.

PRACTICE 3-9

Repeat the steps above for the Municipality of Munhall.

Getting Information from a GIS

Chapter 3 Summary

Vector-based map layers have graphic features consisting of points, lines, and polygons. Attached to each such graphic feature is a data record with attributes describing the graphic feature. A vector map can have one of many file formats. Three from ESRI include the shapefile, coverage, and E00 export formats. Attributes can be of many data types (such as integer, decimal, text, date, and Boolean). The records of a map layer make up its feature attribute table. A data dictionary provides essential documentation for feature attribute tables. It lists all tables, their attributes, data types, and definitions.

Raster maps, by contrast, are images stored using digital-image formats—often as TIFF files—that consist of vast arrays of pixels. Each pixel is a tiny square that has a single color. Raster maps have an accompanying world file that provides data on how to display the image in projected coordinates. The world file includes the x- and y-coordinates of the upper-left corner of the image in map coordinates and the width of pixels in map distance.

GIS queries include attribute queries, as are commonly used in databases, as well as spatial queries based on graphic features and their map coordinates. Spatial queries are unique to GIS.

Attribute queries applied to a GIS select records from the data stored in feature attribute tables. In turn, the corresponding graphic features in the map layer are selected automatically. The GIS usually uses yellow to make these selections visible.

A simple query has the form (<attribute name> <logical operator> <value>). Any attribute name of a feature attribute table can be used. Logical operators are the familiar ones from algebra (=, <, >, <=, >=), not equals (<>), and *like*. The *like* operator allows flexible queries of text values, such as all pool names starting with letters *Br*.

In ArcExplorer, text values and dates must be placed in single quotes, as in
(NAME = 'Riverview'), but numeric values appear without special characters, as in
(MAXLOAD >= 200).

Compound queries combine two or more simple queries with AND or OR logical connectors. All simple conditions connected by AND must simultaneously be true for a record to be selected. By contrast, OR selects a record if any or all conditions are true.

Direct spatial queries depend on you being able to see what you want to select on a displayed map layer. You can use an ArcExplorer tool to select any visible graphic features, highlighting them with the selection color. Such a spatial collection automatically selects corresponding records in the map layer's feature attribute table. With records selected spatially, you can then export and analyze them in Excel or another software package.

An indirect but powerful means of making spatial queries is to build and use buffers. Point buffers are circular with a user-supplied radius. Line buffers look like a worm, and polygon buffers extend polygons outward and round off corners. You can use a buffer to select features from another map layer. For example, you can select the points representing pool tag holders' residences within a one-mile radius of a pool.

Lastly, you can "trick" ArcExplorer to retrieve features within a polygon. You build a buffer for a selected polygon that has a very tiny buffer width, near to zero, and then use the buffer to select features from another map layer within the polygon.

Key Terms

Bit   The smallest storage unit within a computer. A bit, short for *binary digit*, is capable of having one of two values: on or off.

Boolean   A data type which has two possible values: true or false.

Byte   A storage unit on a computer, usually made up of 8 bits. Characters on a keyboard (and other special or foreign characters) are encoded as unique bit patterns of 8 bits in a byte.

Color depth   Also known as *bit depth*; the number of colors a computer system can display or store.

Compound query criteria   Two or more simple query criteria connected with AND or OR logical connectives.

Coverage   An outdated GIS map file format designed by ESRI. A coverage has many files stored in a folder given the name of the coverage. Several of the files store intermediate results needed to speed up processing of advanced GIS procedures.

Data dictionary   Documentation for a database that includes (at a minimum) the names of data tables and their attributes' names, definitions, and data types.

Date   A data type for attribute storage of calendar dates.

Decimal   A data type for storing numbers that have fractional parts.

Digitize   The process of tracing an image or other graphic manuscript for the purpose of producing a vector-based drawing or map layer.

E00 export format   A map file format from ESRI used to store and transmit a map coverage as a single file.

Event theme   A data table that includes x- and y-map coordinates of point features.

False colors   Colors in the visible spectrum used to represent satellite images of reflected electromagnetic energy from earth that is out of the color spectrum.

File compression   A technology for reducing the size of large files to facilitate storage or network transmission.

GIF (Graphic Interchange Format)   A digital image file format best suited for schematic drawings and other images without many color variations.

Integer   An attribute data type for storing numbers that do not have decimal parts.

JPEG (Joint Photographic Experts Group)   A digital image file format widely used for photographs. This format uses an adjustable amount of file compression to reduce file sizes, trading off image quality.

Logical connectives   The words AND or OR which are used to connect simple query criteria to produce a compound query criterion.

Proximity analysis   A study that identifies and analyzes entities of a selected type that are within a specified distance of other selected objects. An example is tabulating the number of 5- to 17-year-old youths within a one-mile radius of open swimming pools.

Query   A process of selecting data records or graphic features that meet selection criteria.

Shapefile   A simple map format developed by ESRI. It is much simpler than the older coverage format but depends more on computing power to carry out advanced GIS processing.

Simple query criterion   A logical condition for selecting records from a data table of the form (<attribute name><logical operator><value>).

Spatial query   A means of selecting graphic features based on location in map coordinates or distance.

Text   An attribute data format for text strings.

TIFF (Tagged Image File Format)   A digital image file format widely used in publishing and other applications that require high quality images.

Wild card   A special character used to represent 0, 1, or more characters in queries using the *like* logical operator.

Short-Answer Questions

1. What is file compression and why is it valuable for raster format maps?

2. Suppose that the following four values have text data types: 3.141592, 300, argyle, argument. Place these values in ascending order.

3. Sometimes a city is represented on a map as a point, and at other times as a polygon. What purposes and scales dictate such choices?

4. In advanced GISs, a street centerline map can be used to route vehicles across a street network. The routes attempt to minimize travel time. What do you think are some of the properties street maps need for such an application?

5. What are the important uses of raster maps? What are their limitations?

6. Would you ever expect to see a raster map, made from an aerial photograph, that is in geographic coordinates? Why or why not?

7. Give examples of state names that the following simple queries would select: (STATE like 'N%'), (STATE like '%a'), and (STATE like '%e%').

8. Suppose that there are 52 records describing the 52 playing cards in a deck. Attributes include Suit, Color, and Name (such as *7, ace, king*). All attributes are text data type. What cards are retrieved with the following query criteria? (Suit = 'diamonds') AND (Name >= '3') AND (Name <= '7'). (Name >= 'queen') And ((Suit <= 'diamonds') or (Color = 'red')).

9. Suppose that you have a boundary map that has the 89 neighborhoods of Pittsburgh. The Pool Tag Holders' Residences map layer does not include an attribute for neighborhood. Give two ways that you could select all the pool tag holders that live in the neighborhood of Shadyside.

10. Suppose that you have selected all of the block centroids in the Shadyside neighborhood of Pittsburgh. Explain how to get the population of 5 to 17 year olds in Shadyside.

Exercises

1. **Patterns in Use of Swimming Pools.** In this chapter you saw some interesting patterns in intended uses of Phillips pool. Moore is a nearby pool that has similar patterns. Your task here is to describe these two pools' intended use and see whether you can find some possible explanations for the differences between the two.

   a. In ArcExplorer, open **Queries.axl** (Win) or **Querymac.axl** (Mac) from **c:\LearningAndUsingGIS** (Win) or **/LearningAndUsingGIS/** (Mac).

   b. Add the two raster maps, **pittsburgh_east_pa.tif** and **pittsburgh_west_pa.tif**. ArcExplorer will add them to the bottom of your layer panel so they will not cover up other layers.

   c. Zoom into an area extending out about 2 miles from the Phillips and Moore pools. Select those pools and build buffers of radiuses 1.0 and 2.0 miles around them for visualization.

   d. Select the residences of pool tag holders intending to use Moore pool.

   e. Try out various layers, zooming in, and so on, to see if you can find explanations for the patterns.

   f. When you have a useful map, press the **PrtSc** key on your keyboard (Win) or press **[shift]+[command]+3** (Mac). This places a copy of the map on the Clipboard.

   g. Create a Word document, and then press and hold down the **Enter** key to create a page of blank lines. Right-click (Win) or control-click (Mac) the Word page and click **Paste**. This pastes a copy of your map into the document. Save your document in **c:\LearningAndUsingGIS\Outputs** (Win) or **/LearningAndUsingGIS/Outputs** (Mac) with the name **Exercise1<YourName>.doc** where you substitute your name for <YourName>.

   h. Repeat the selection of pool tag holders, but this time for Phillips pool and make another screen print to add to your document.

   i. Write a description of the patterns in your document and your possible explanations for them.

2. **Intended Use Rate Estimates for Selected Pools.** We define the intended use rate for a swimming pool to be the number of pool tag holders within one mile of a pool divided by the population of 5- to 17-year-old youths living within a mile of the pool. To estimate the total number of pool tag holders from the random sample, you have to multiply any count of pool tags within a mile by 20, as discussed in this chapter. *Note:* Estimated use rates are a bit high because roughly 1 out of 3 pool users is an adult. We will not have you make any adjustment here to your estimated use rates, but you will do so in Exercise 4.

   a. Estimate the use rate for Homewood, Jack Stack, and Magee pools. Make a table including all of your estimates and use rates. Use three rows (one for each pool). Include three columns (one for each of the two quantities tabulated from buffers and the third for the use-rate ratio).

b. If Ream pool were to be opened, predict the number of 5 to 17 year olds who would sign up to get pool tags within 1 mile of the pool. Apply the average use rate from your three estimates in the previous step to make this prediction. Write down your steps and estimates for each step.

c. Save the results of this problem in an Excel document called **Exercise 2<YourName>.xls** where you substitute your name for <YourName>. Save your document in **c:\LearningAndUsingGIS\Outputs** (Win) or **/LearningAndUsingGIS/Outputs/** (Mac).

3. **Estimate of McBride Pool Use by Residents of Munhall and West Mifflin.** The director of Pittsburgh's Citiparks Department asked us to estimate how many residents of West Mifflin and Munhall signed up to use McBride pool. He was going to a meeting to persuade officials in those communities to contribute financially to McBride's operating costs. He reasoned that if many West Mifflin and Munhall residents used the pool, his case would be strengthened.

a. Use the buffer "trick" to select features by polygon to determine the number of residents of each municipality that used Pittsburgh pools.

b. Determine how many residents intended to use McBride pool. For those residents who did not record a pool that they intended to use, include an estimate of how many likely used McBride. For example, if 90% of the persons who recorded a pool for intended use chose McBride, assume that 90% of those who did not record an intended pool also intended to use McBride.

c. Scale sample results for each municipality up to the total population level by using the factor 20, as explained in this chapter.

d. Save your results in a Word document called **Exercise3<YourName>.doc** where you substitute your name for <YourName>. Save your document in **c:\LearningAndUsingGIS\Outputs** (Win) or **/LearningAndUsingGIS/Outputs/** (Mac).

e. Use the **PrtSc** key (Win) or press **[shift]+[command]+3** (Mac) to get a good map showing locations of sampled pool tag holders' residences in these two municipalities and make it part of your document.

4. **Reduction of Use Rate with Distance from a Pool.** You would expect a high proportion of youths to use the pool nearest their home. Conversely, use rate should decline with distance from a pool. See Exercise 2 for the definition of use rate.

a. Estimate use rate for a 1-mile buffer and the ring between 1 and 2 miles for Phillips pool.

b. You have to make two adjustments to the count of the tag holders per buffer. First, we have only a random sample, so multiply by 20 to scale the sample estimate up to the full population of tag holders. The results will be subject to sampling error, but it will be in the right ballpark. Second, many tag holders are adults who accompany children to the pool. Use the approximation that 1 out of 3 tag holders is an adult, so multiply the scaled-up estimate of tag holders per buffer by 0.67. *Hint:* You have to get the numerators and denominators of the use rate ratios for each buffer and then subtract to get the ring's numerator and denominator.

c. Save all of your estimates and results in an Excel document called **Exercise4<YourName>.xls** where you substitute your name for <YourName>. Save your document in **c:\LearningAndUsingGIS\Outputs** (Win) or **/LearningAndUsingGIS/Outputs/** (Mac).

References

ESRI Support Center, "FAQ: What is the format of the world file used for georeferencing images?," Internet URL: http://support.esri.com/index.cfm?fa=knowledgebase.techArticles. articleShow&d=17489 (accessed February 25, 2005).

Koren, N., "Making fine prints in your digital darkroom: pixels, images, and files." Internet URL: http://www.normankoren.com/pixels_images.html (accessed February 25, 2005).

Wall, Roland, "Remote Sensing: The View From Above," The Academy of Natural Sciences. Internet URL: http://www.acnatsci.org/education/kye/te/kye52001.html (accessed February 27, 2005).

U.S. Census Bureau (2005), Tiger Line/Files Technical Documentation. Internet URL: http://www. census.gov/geo/www/tiger/tigerua/ua2ktgr.pdf (accessed March 3, 2005).

CHAPTER **4**

DESIGNING MAPS

LEARNING OBJECTIVES

In this chapter, you will:

- Learn the principle of graphic hierarchy
- Determine how to use color
- Understand map symbolization
- Learn to design maps for different audiences
- Preview map layers in ArcExplorer's Catalog
- Symbolize maps using ArcExplorer
- Set map layer properties in ArcExplorer

Maybe orange with yellow polka dots . . .

INTRODUCTION

Thus far, you have been using ArcExplorer map project files that we built for you, namely *Pools.axl* (Win)

or *PoolsMac.axl* (Mac) and *Queries.axl* (Win) or *QueriesMac.axl* (Mac). Now it is time for you to learn how

to design and build your own map projects.

When you design maps, you have a number of elements at your disposal. **Graphic elements** include

the shapes, sizes, and colors of point markers; colors of areas and lines; fill patterns of areas; and widths and styles of lines. Anybody can use a software package such as ArcExplorer and easily choose colors and other graphic elements for maps and other graphics. Setting you apart from the crowd, however, will be the graphic-design principles that you learn in this chapter, so your maps will be professional in appearance and effective for their purposes.

Graphic hierarchy is one of the most valuable principles for using graphic elements, one that compels the viewer to see important aspects of a composition. Color plays a central role in graphic hierarchy as well as in other aspects of graphic design, so we provide guidelines for using color. Another principle is to minimize ink: Make every pixel add value to the purpose of the graphic design, or leave pixels the equivalent of blanks—white, like paper, in most cases.

There are two major audiences for maps: analysts and the general public. An analyst needs many graphic details to aid in the discovery of spatial patterns. Analysts are willing to work hard, sorting through details, to find clues to the underlying behaviors of spatial phenomena. The general public is just the opposite: They need to get your message clearly and without working to obtain it. Obviously, these two groups need different kinds of maps.

ArcExplorer allows you to put graphic design principles to work. You can choose the color, size, widths, and shapes of graphic features based on the values of their attributes, using either unique values of codes or ranges of numeric variables. You also can label graphic features using attributes, such as names—and choose placement, fonts, and special effects. All your selections are saved in the ArcExplorer map project file.

MAP DESIGN

Cartography, the art of designing maps, is one of the oldest forms of graphic design. By **graphic design** we mean the choice of symbols, colors, text, patterns, and arrangements of graphic elements in visual displays with an aim to achieving communication and beauty. Mapmakers must represent much data on relatively small sheets of paper, and over time that has required the invention of many principles, concepts, standards, and skills. Even if you do not consider yourself an artistic person, the knowledge that you will gain in this chapter will make you a successful map designer. The same principles easily apply to other graphic applications, such as designing Web pages.

Graphic Hierarchy

As previously stated, one of the most useful and informative graphic design principles is graphic hierarchy, the use of color and edge effects to draw attention to parts of a graphic display (MacEachren, 1994). For an example, see Figure 4-1. In the left panel, it is not clear what you should be studying—the lines, squares, or circles. In the right panel, there is no doubt: The red circles almost jump off the page at you, while all else fades to context and background. The right panel uses graphic hierarchy.

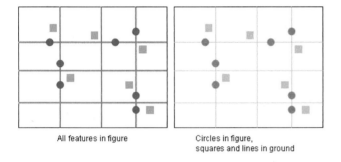

All features in figure

Circles in figure,
squares and lines in ground

FIGURE 4-1   Demonstration of graphic hierarchy

Here are guidelines for using graphical hierarchy:

- Put graphic elements that should get the most attention in bright colors, such as red, orange, yellow, green, or blue. Such graphic elements are called **figure**. These are the red circles in the right panel of Figure 4-1, which could mark the locations of some sort of incident type of interest in a neighborhood, such as vandalism of parked cars.
- Put graphic elements that orient you or provide a context for interpretation in drab colors, especially shades of gray. The lesser the importance, the lighter the shade of gray you should use. Such graphic elements are called **ground**. These are the gray elements in the right panel of Figure 4-1, and they represent streets and houses.

- Place a strong boundary, such as a heavy black line, around polygons that are important to increase figure. (You will see examples of this treatment in other chapter figures.)
- Use a coarse, heavy cross-hatch or pattern to make some polygons important, placing them in figure.

Principle of Minimizing Ink

A second important graphic principle, credited to Edward Tufte (2001), is simply this: *Minimize ink!* Make every pixel of a graphic design have a purpose. For example, as a guideline for map layouts in Chapter 6, we suggest not including a north-pointing arrow. Everyone already knows that the top of a map points north, so why waste ink on a *north* arrow? A *north* arrow is what Tufte calls **chart junk**, graphics with no payoff that clutter up a graphic design and may even be a distraction.

Part of the minimize-ink principle is to minimize use of color. Use color only for truly important elements, such as the graphic hierarchy principle suggests. Really good graphic designs, whether they are maps, Web pages, or PowerPoint slides, need a lot of white area and ground materials, and just a few valuable graphics and text in figure. For example, do not use color for areas such as states, counties, or zip codes unless you are color-coding them to represent a variable, such as population. Otherwise, leave them transparent with no fill.

Color

Color is one of the most effective graphic elements for communication of spatial information, but it is easy to overuse. There is quite a bit to learn about color. First you should learn these terms (Graphics Communication Program, 2005):

- **Hue** is the basic color. For example, green is the hue in both light green and dark green.
- **Color value** is the amount of black in the color. In relation to white paper or a white computer screen, white has low value and black has high value.
- **Monochromatic color scale** is a series of colors of the same hue with color value varied from low to high; for example, the value ranges from white to black on a monochromatic gray scale, from light to dark green on a green monochromatic scale, and so on.
- **Saturation** refers to a color scale that ranges from a pure hue to gray or black; for example, the closer to black, the more saturated the color.

Map designers use monochromatic scales or saturated colors to represent the magnitude of numeric attributes, such as youth population or number of swimming-pool users, in color-coded polygon layers, known as **choropleth maps**. Color value represents order in categories, ranging from low to high, and a key in a legend interprets the colors and magnitude ranges of ordered categories. For an example, see Figure 4-2. You can see that the increasing value in gray scale corresponds to increasing intervals for number of swimming-pool tag holders per zip code area. (We used a red line for Pittsburgh's boundary in Figure 4-2 to emphasize that zip codes are not coterminous with municipal boundaries, but they cross over them.) Note that shape and size are better graphic elements for differentiating point markers than color values of the same hue.

FIGURE 4-2   Choropleth map

Some guidelines for using color scale on maps are as follows:

- Use monochromatic color scales to color-code most choropleth maps. An exception is where there is a natural middle-point of a scale, such as 0 for some quantities (profits and losses, increases and decreases). In such a case, use a **dichromatic color scale**—two monochromatic scales jointed together with a low color value in the center, with color value increasing toward both ends. For example, a dichromatic color scale might have blues on one end, reds on the other end, and white in the center. White in the center assumes that such areas should be denoted as ground—often the centers of scales are the least important for purposes at hand. It is helpful to the reader if you can keep the negative and positive numeric scales symmetric (i.e., the same increments except for a sign (+ or -) or other designation as the number decreases or increases). See Figure 4-3.
- The darker the color in a monochromatic scale, the more important the graphic feature. In Figure 4-2, the darker shades of gray are assigned to high intervals for numbers of pool tag holders, because high values are important for meeting demand for swimming pools.
- Use more light shades of a hue than dark shades in monochromatic scales. The human eye can better differentiate among light shades than dark shades.

- Do not use all of the colors of the **color spectrum**, as seen from a prism or in a rainbow, for color coding. Yellow, in the center of the scale, has the lowest color value, which is confusing because color value starts at a high value for red, and then moving to the right of the spectrum, it decreases until attaining a minimum at yellow. Then, moving to the right again, color value increases through the end of the spectrum, ending at violet. Thus the sequence of colors and color values in the spectrum cannot signify steadily increasing or decreasing quantities. See Figure 4-4. Instead of the entire color spectrum, use either half of the spectrum, the hot-color (red) or cool-color (blue) side, for color-coding.

- If you have relatively few points in a point layer, or if a user will normally be zoomed in to view parts of your map, use size instead of color value to symbolize a numeric attribute. The relatively small area of a point marker does not give color much room to send its message.

- If you have a massive number of polygons to symbolize, then it is much better to symbolize polygon centroid points with color than to use choropleth maps. For example, we use block centroids for the youths and female-headed households attributes.

- Choropleth maps work well for attributes that are rates or densities, such as people per square mile. A polygon's color and size convey a consistent message—darker or larger polygons indicate more people live in an area. Although it is a common practice, you should not use choropleth maps for attributes that are actual counts, such as population numbers. In this case, size may provide spurious information: A dark polygon that is small is just as important as a dark polygon that is large, but the large polygon may dominate your attention. For count attributes, it is better to use centroid points and point markers to symbolize attributes of polygons.

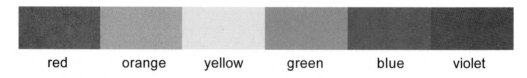

| red | orange | yellow | green | blue | violet |

FIGURE 4-3   Color spectrum

With the exception of choropleth maps, maps mostly use color to distinguish different kinds of graphic features from one another and to build graphic hierarchy. You already know to use bright colors for figure and dull, drab colors for ground. The **color wheel** is a device that provides further guidance in choosing colors, especially for differentiating features. It arranges colors in their order along the electromagnetic spectrum, but joins the two extremes, red and violet, on a circle. See Figure 4-5.

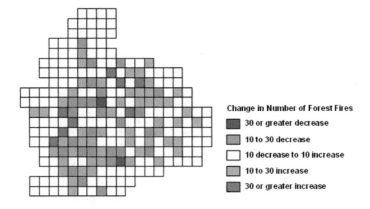

Change in Number of Forest Fires

- 30 or greater decrease
- 10 to 30 decrease
- 10 decrease to 10 increase
- 10 to 30 increase
- 30 or greater increase

FIGURE 4-4   Dichromatic color scale

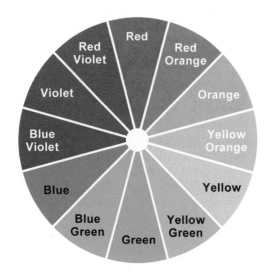

FIGURE 4-5   Color wheel

Guidelines for using the color wheel include the following:

- Use opposite colors—those directly across from one another—on the color wheel to differentiate graphic features. Opposites are known as **complementary colors**, such as yellow and violet or red and green. When placed next to each other, complementary colors make each other look brighter and produce a dramatic contrast.

Designing Maps

- Another good choice for differentiating graphic features are three or four colors equally spaced around the wheel, such as red, blue, and yellow or red, blue-violet, green, and yellow-orange. Use such choices for vector-based features (points, lines, and polygons) that have unique code values for classification and display. An example is point markers representing different types of recreation facilities with code values for swimming pool, tennis court, basketball court, and so on.
- Use adjacent colors for harmony, such as blue, blue green, and green or red, red-orange, and orange. These are known as **analogous colors**. They are less important in analytical mapping than complementary colors, because we usually need to strongly differentiate features. Reference mapping makes more use of analogous colors.

Keep in mind that colors can have meaning through common experience, conventions, or cultural uses. Sometimes, you can put such knowledge to work on a map, tying symbols to well-known meanings. For example, we used blue for open swimming pools because water is blue. We used red for closed swimming pools because red is the stop or danger signal. Color Wheel Pro (2005) has a fascinating list of colors and common uses and meanings.

Numeric Intervals

Oftentimes, in designing an analytical map, you will need to show variation in a numeric quantity, such as population. To do so, you must break the numeric scale up into **numeric intervals**, which are non-overlapping, and exhaustive intervals covering the range of values for an attribute. Maps have many details, so keep the number of intervals as small as possible to help simplify the user's ability to absorb information. Research has shown that most people can hold seven items (plus or minus two) simultaneously in short-term memory. With maps, we reduce that a bit, to five sets of intervals (plus or minus two).

The number of pool-tag-holder residences per zip code area in Pittsburgh ranges from 0 to 6,206. In this chapter's tutorial, you will use ArcExplorer to symbolize this attribute using equal intervals: 0 to 1000, 1000 to 2000, 2000 to 3000, 3000 to 4000, and 4000 and greater (up to 6,206). **Cut points**, also known as break points, are points at which we choose to break the total attribute range up into these intervals; namely, 1000, 2000, 3000, and 4000. The extremes, or range limits, of 0 and 6,206 already existed and so they are not designated as cut points. The numeric scale for the pool tag holders' attribute is thus defined by the four chosen cut points and the two occurring extremes.

Most analytical software packages include left ends of numeric intervals but not the right ends. For example, if you state an interval for an attribute as 10 to 20, it will include features with attribute values 10 and up to but not 20. The next interval, 20 to 30, picks up features with the attribute value 20. One map design issue on intervals is this: What labels should you use for intervals? ArcExplorer lets you input in your own labels, independent of cut point values, and this lets you decide how to handle the issue. Here are some initial guidelines:

- For a **continuous variable**, such as average percentage of pool capacity used or a discrete attribute with relatively large values, you can label intervals with overlapping end points, such as 0 to 10, 10 to 20, and so on.

- For a **discrete variable**, such as pools, that have relatively low values, use non-overlapping ends for intervals, for example, 1 to 5, 6 to 10, and so on. Implementing such a scheme takes a bit of thought. The cut point used to separate these two intervals is 6, not 5. This is because we want the 5 to be included in the first interval.
- Make interval labels easily understood by including measurement units and optional, additional words if you think they help, such as *to* instead of dashes. For example, use 10% to 15% or 10%–15% instead of 10–15.

Finally, there are several ways to select cut points. Always use a mathematical progression or formula instead of picking arbitrary cut points. You are less likely to be accused of manipulating a display to influence viewers' interpretation if cut points have a logical progression. Some options follow.

- **Equal intervals**: As you can guess, equal intervals have constant widths. An example with width 100 is 0–100, 100–200, 200–300, 300 and greater. Use equal width intervals in multiples of 2, 5, or 10. Equal intervals are easy to interpret.
- **Increasing interval widths**: Many populations in nature have **long-tailed distributions**, meaning that when data distribution is skewed and deviates from a bell-shaped curve by having one end elongated due to scant data, the widths between intervals are increased to accommodate the scant data. For example, many gymnasts have low-level skills, but a few have truly incredible skills, far higher than the rest of the crowd. In such cases, it is necessary to stretch out the intervals for high numbers. One approach is to keep doubling the interval of each category; for example, intervals 0–5, 5–15, 15–35, and 35–75 have interval widths of 5, 10, 20, and 40. ArcExplorer has a manual option for setting cut points that allows any progression, including this one.
- **Exponential scale**: This is a popular method of increasing intervals. For example, use cut points that are powers such as 2^n or 3^n, but generally you should start out with zero as an additional class if that value appears in your data. For example, 2^n for n=0, 1, 2, 3, 4, ... yields the sequence 1, 2, 4, 8, 16, ... to which it is often relevant to add a separate class for 0. Hence, corresponding classes or intervals are: 0, 1–2, 3–4, 5–8, 9–16, and so forth for integer-value quantities.
- **Quantiles**: This refers to separating a distribution into equal sizes of feature records per interval. For example **quartiles**—a special case of the more general quantile with four categories—use cut points that identify the 25% lowest values, the next 25% of values up to the **median** or middle point, the next 25% up from the median, and the top 25%. If there are five intervals, each has 20% of the distribution, and so forth with other numbers of cut points. Analysts use quantiles because they provide information about the shape of the distribution. For example, if the top quartile has a relatively long interval width, then the distribution is long-tailed. If the interval widths are all about the same size, the distribution is fairly uniform.

Point and Line Symbols

Points and lines are mathematical objects with no area or width. However, on a map or a graph, we use point markers with area and lines with width to make graphic elements visible. Location is the one aspect of point markers that we cannot vary as map designers. The other aspects are shape, size, color, and boundary. Here are some guidelines for varying these graphic elements for point markers:

- Use simple shapes. The simpler the shape, the easier it is to see spatial patterns. ArcExplorer has a good selection of shapes. We suggest that the order of preference be circles, squares, triangles, stars, and lastly crosses.
- If your GIS has point markers that have black boundaries and solid-color fill (ArcExplorer does not), use them for important points. A boundary makes point markers more prominent and also allows use of some color fills that otherwise do not display well, such as yellow and light cyan.
- If you are using the size of point markers to symbolize a quantity, you have to exaggerate the differences in areas. Make the differences in sizes as large as possible. The human eye does not discriminate proportional changes in areas very well. Also, include a key in the map legend to convey magnitude.

Lines are easier to symbolize than points. Besides line features themselves, the boundaries of polygons are lines. Here are a few guidelines:

- For analytical maps, most lines are ground and should be black or shades of gray.
- Consider using dark gray instead of black for boundaries of most polygons. Dark gray makes the polygons prominent enough, but also takes out some of the figure so as not to compete for attention with more-important graphic elements in figure.
- One option is to use dashed lines to signify less-important line features and solid lines for the important ones.

Map Audiences

Analytical maps have two primary audiences: analysts and the general public. The purposes of maps for these two audiences are different enough that mapmakers need to determine their audience before designing their maps. Analysts need maps with lots of details and layers so they can discover and analyze patterns. Once an important pattern is discovered, the general public, or some part of it, needs a simple but dramatic map that strongly portrays the pattern.

Consider the difference between maps of crimes used by uniformed officers versus maps of crimes provided on Web sites for the public. One of the authors built a crime mapping system for the Pittsburgh Bureau of Police. At roll call and before going out on patrol, uniformed officers study maps of their patrol areas with crimes plotted over the last four weeks. Originally, there were seven crime types displayed simultaneously on the same map—each with its own distinctive point marker—which made the maps quite cluttered from our perspective. Nevertheless, police officers wanted *more* crime types displayed. They wanted to study the entire crime picture—every crime point and type had meaning for them. By contrast, maps of crimes intended for the public, such as can be seen at the New Orleans Police Department's Web site *(www.cityofno.com/portal.aspx? portal=50)*, display only one crime type at a time unless zoomed in to small areas.

Guidelines for analyst and general public audiences include the following:

- Use mostly simple shapes for point markers, but consider using mimetic point markers for "general public" maps. **Mimetic symbols** bear a resemblance to what they represent; for example, a mimetic railroad line on a map has cross lines for railroad ties and the point marker for a state capital may look like a building with a flag on top. ArcExplorer has only simple shapes for point markers.
- Use many cut points for analytical choropleth maps, but use relatively few for general public maps.
- Use quantile numeric scales for analytical maps, but use equal interval scales for general public maps. Sometimes, you have to use an increasing interval scale for general public maps because of long-tailed distributions.
- Use a bright color for the monochromatic scale on a general public map.
- Build a stand-alone map layout for a general public map that includes map title, graphic scale, legend, and map (see Chapter 6).

ARCEXPLORER FOR MAP DESIGN

In this tutorial, you will build a map project from scratch similar to *Pools.axl*. In the process, you will use almost every kind of functionality that ArcExplorer has to offer for map design.

ArcExplorer's Catalog

One of your first tasks, after obtaining needed map layers, is to gain an understanding of them. ArcExplorer's Catalog tool is intended for this purpose, so let's start off using it.

1. Start **ArcExplorer**, click **Tools**, click **Catalog**, and then maximize the **Catalog window**. *(The Catalog window opens.)*
2. Click the **expander box with the plus sign** to the left of C: (Win) or / and then **ESRI** (Mac), then click the same to the left of **ArcExplorer Files** (Mac), then click the same to the left of **LearningAndUsingGIS**, and finally click the same to the left of **Maps**. *(These actions expand the folder and file tree of your computer to reveal map layers for the Pools project.)*
3. Click the **minorcivildivisions.shp** icon in the left panel. See Figure 4-6. *(With the Contents tab clicked in the right panel, you get a summary of the minorcivildivisions layer; for example, that it has polygon features and 130 records.)*
4. Click the **Preview** tab in the right panel. See Figure 4-7. *(Now you get a quick preview of the map layer in a random single color fill.)*
5. In the lower center of the Preview panel, click the **list arrow** in the field there and click **Table**. See Figure 4-8. *(This time you get to see the entire feature attribute.)*

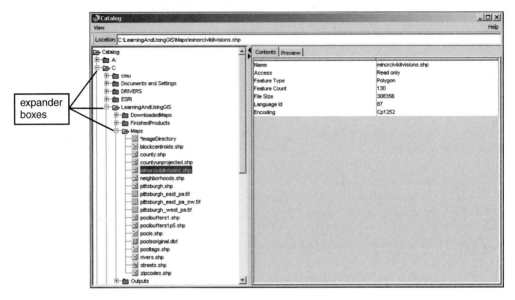

FIGURE 4-6   Catalog showing a summary of minor civil divisions map layer

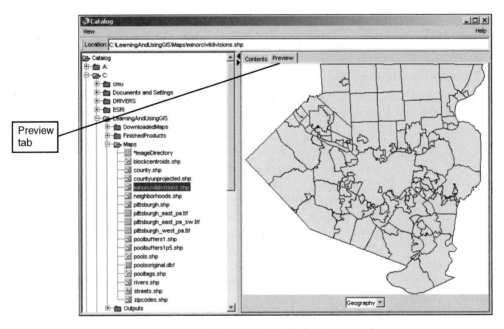

FIGURE 4-7   Catalog showing map preview of minor civil divisions map layer

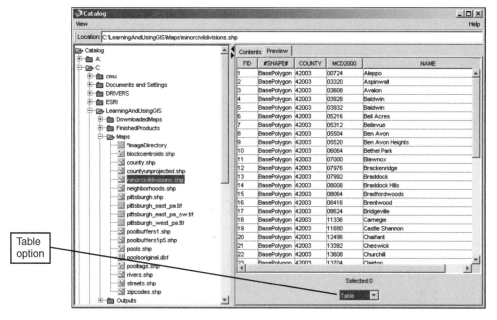

Table
option

FIGURE 4-8 Catalog showing attribute table preview of minor civil divisions map layer

PRACTICE 4-1

- Preview some other vector-based layers in the Pools GIS.
- Preview one of the raster-based map layers. Notice the Contents tab and that there is no feature attribute table to display.
- Close the Catalog window when you are finished.

New Map Project

1. Maximize the **ArcExplorer** window, which should still be open.
2. Click the **Add Data...** button, browse to **c:\LearningAndUsingGIS\Maps** (Win) or **LearningAndUsingGIS\Maps** (Mac). Hold down your **Ctrl** (Win) or **Command** (Mac) key in the resulting Content Chooser window and click the **blockcentroids.shp, county.shp, minorcivildivisions.shp, pittsburgh.shp, pools.shp, pooltags.shp, rivers.shp, streets.shp,** and **zipcodes.shp** layers, and then click **OK**. See Figure 4-9. *(This results in an incredible jumble of layers all turned on, but it is a start.)*
3. Click off **all layers** except **county**. Rearrange the **order of layers**, either by clicking, dragging, and dropping *(which sometimes does not work!)* or by right-clicking (Win) or control-clicking (Mac) and using the **Move Layer** action to achieve the following order of layers from top to bottom: county, pittsburgh, minorcivildivisions, rivers, pools, pooltags, blockcentroids, streets, and zipcodes. See Figure 4-10.

Designing Maps

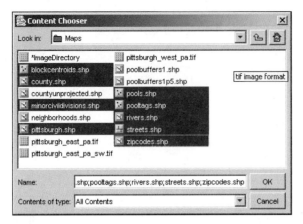

FIGURE 4-9   Adding map layers to ArcExplorer

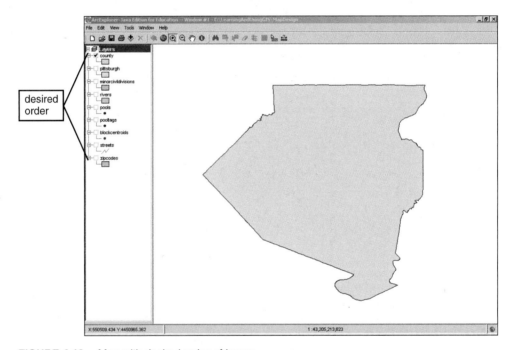

FIGURE 4-10   Map with desired order of layers

4. Click **File** and then click **Save**.
5. In the resulting Save window, browse to **LearningAndUsingGIS**, enter **MapDesign** (Win) or **MapDesignMac** (Mac) in the name field, and click **Save**.

- Turn off the county layer for now.
- Add the three raster-based maps in the Maps folder (*pittsburgh_east_pa.tif*, *pittsburgh_west_pa.tif*, and *pittsburgh_west_pa_sw.tif*) to your project.
- Keep them at the bottom of the Layers panel, but put the aerial photo on top of the two other raster layers.
- Turn the raster layers off, and then turn on the layer for county.

Transparent Color Fill

The county, pittsburgh, and minorcivildivisions layers have the purpose of displaying only boundaries. They will not be used as choropleth maps. Turn off the **county** layer and turn on the **minorcivildivisions** layer.

1. Right-click (Win) or control-click (Mac) **minorcivildivisions**, and in the resulting context menu, click **Properties**....
2. In the resulting minorcivildivisions Properties window, with the Symbols tab selected, click the **list arrow** in the **Style** field, and then click **Transparent fill**. *(This will eliminate the fill color.)*
3. In the Outline panel, click the **list arrow** in the **Color** field, and then click **Dark Gray**. See Figure 4-11.

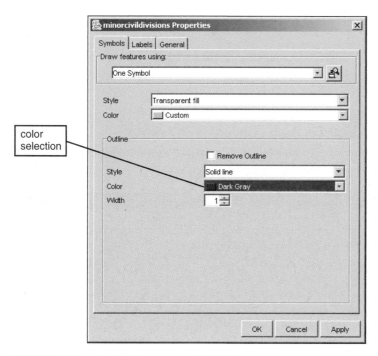

FIGURE 4-11 Symbolizing minor civil divisions

4. Click the **Labels** tab, click the **list arrow** in the **Label features using** field, and click **NAME**.
5. Click the **list arrow** in the **Color** field and click **Dark Gray**.
6. Click the **Bold** check box. See Figure 4-12.

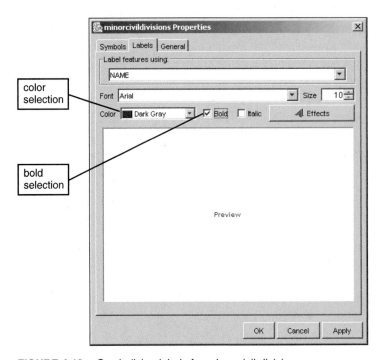

color selection

bold selection

FIGURE 4-12   Symbolizing labels for minor civil divisions

7. Click the **General** tab, change **minorcivildivisions** to **Cities**, and then click **OK**. See Figure 4-13. *(That finishes up minorcivildivisions.)*

(Note: *The next Practice exercise is needed to complete the remainder of the tutorial, so be sure to do it.*)

PRACTICE 4-3

-   Symbolize the layer for county in a similar way to the layer for minorcivildivisions, except do not label it, make its boundary width 2 instead of 1, and capitalize *county* to make it *County.* Turn this layer on.
-   Symbolize the layer for pittsburgh in a similar way: Do not label it, leave its boundary color black, make its boundary width 2 instead of 1, and capitalize *pittsburgh* to make it *Pittsburgh.* Turn this layer on.

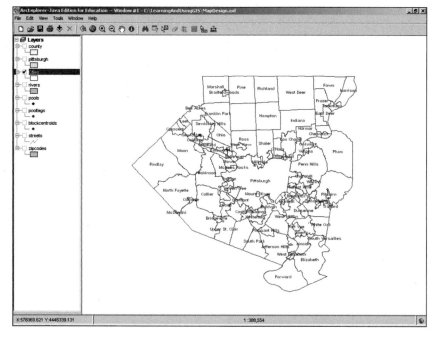

FIGURE 4-13   Finished map layer for minor civil divisions

Single Color

1. Turn rivers on, then right-click (Win) or control-click (Mac) **Rivers**, click **Properties...**.

2. In the Symbols tab of Rivers Properties, click the **list arrow** of **Color**, scroll down if necessary, and then click **Custom**.

3. In the resulting Color Chooser with the Swatches tab clicked, click on a **light blue** from the top row, and then click **OK**. See Figure 4-14.

4. Click the **Labels** tab, click the **list arrow** in the **Label features using** field, and then click **LANDNAME**.

5. Click the **Effects** button, and in the resulting Effects window, click the **check box** for **Glow**, and click **OK**. See Figure 4-15.

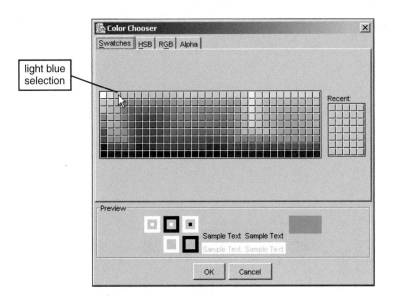

light blue
selection

FIGURE 4-14   Selecting a color for Rivers

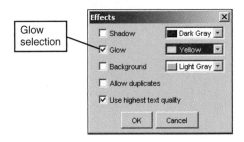

Glow
selection

FIGURE 4-15   Selecting a glow effect for the label of Rivers

6. Click the **General** tab, capitalize **rivers** to make it **Rivers**, and then click **OK**.
7. Right-click (Win) or control-click (Mac) **Rivers**, click **Move Layer**, and then
    click **Move Up**. *(The Rivers labels and Glow are not displayed unless they're
    moved above Cities. The Cities labels block the Rivers labels, but not visa
    versa.)*
8. Right-click (Win) or control-click (Mac) **streets**, click **Properties**, change its
    color to **Light Gray**, capitalize **streets**, and then click **OK**. See Figure 4-16.

PRACTICE 4-4

- Symbolize the layer for pooltags.
- Give it a color of your choice, not too much in figure though, and change its size to
  4. Do not label the points.
- Change its name to Pool Tag Holders' Residences.

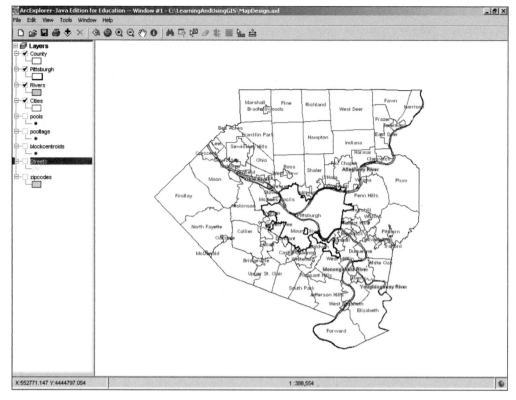

FIGURE 4-16   Finished map layer for Rivers

Unique Symbols

The option used here for symbolizing pools, unique symbols, depends on having an attribute that has a code for classification. The attribute OPEN has the value 1 for open pools and 0 for closed pools. You will give the 1s a blue square point marker and the 0s a red square point marker.

1. Click **Pittsburgh** in the Layers panel to make it the active layer, click the **Zoom to Active Layer** button, and then turn on the **pools** layer.
2. Right-click (Win) or control-click (Mac) **pools** and then click **Properties**.
3. Click the **list arrow** in the **Draw features using** field and then click **Unique Symbols**.
4. Click the **list arrow** in the **Field for values** field and then click **OPEN**.
5. Click the **list arrow** in the **Style** field and then click **Square**.
6. Click the **up arrow** in the **Size** field twice to change it from an **8** to a **10**.
7. Double-click the **color bar** under Symbol for the first row with value **1**. *(The value 1 signifies an open pool.)*
8. In the resulting color chooser, click a **bright medium blue color**, and then **OK**.
9. Repeat Steps 7 and 8, except for the second row, and select a **bright red**.

10. Double-click in the first row of the **Label** column and then enter **Open** to replace the **1**.
11. Do the same in the second row but enter **Closed** and press the **Enter** key. See Figure 4-17.

symbol settings

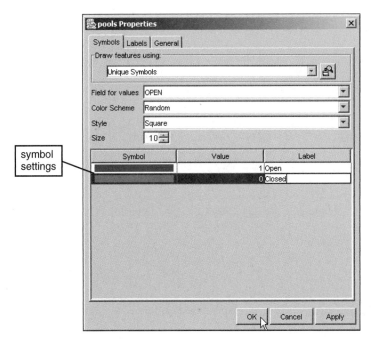

FIGURE 4-17   Selecting colors for pool point markers

12. Click the **Labels** tab, label the pools with the **NAME** attribute, change the font size to **12**, and then click the **Placement circle** at the top.
13. Click the **General** tab, capitalize **pools**, and then click **OK**. See Figure 4-18.

PRACTICE 4-5

- Symbolize the Streets layer with unique values based on the attribute named CFCC (Census Feature Class Code).
- Use the Identify tool to see what some of the major CFCC codes are for streets. Some code descriptions for this code are A15 = limited access w/ separated lanes, A31=secondary feeder road, and A41=city or neighborhood street. Remember to move the Streets layer to the top of the Layers panel before you use the Identify tool.
- When finished, re-symbolize the Streets layer to one symbol, light gray, size 1, and return it to second from the bottom in the Layers panel.

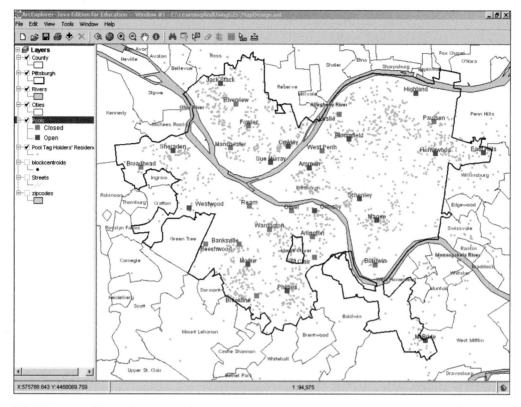

FIGURE 4-18   Finished map layer for residences

Choropleth Map

You will start by using the built-in equal interval option for specifying cut points, but you'll move on to using the manual option in order to get nicer values. The manual option is a bit tricky, so work carefully, especially in Steps 7 and 8.

1. Right-click (Win) or control-click (Mac) **zipcodes** and then click **Properties**.
2. Click the **list arrow** in the **Draw features using** field, and then click **Graduated Symbols**. *("Graduated" means symbols that change in size, color, or both. You will just use color for a choropleth map.)*
3. Click the **list arrow** in the **Field** field and then click **NUMTAGS**. See Figure 4-19. *(ArcExplorer responds immediately by providing a yellow-to-red color ramp and equal intervals, but with odd-width cut points.)*
4. Click **OK** and then click the **zipcodes** layer on. See Figure 4-20. *(The results have too much figure, dominating all other features. In addition, the automatic cut points are difficult to interpret.)*

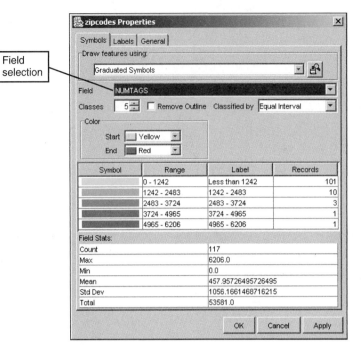

Field selection

FIGURE 4-19 Default color ramp for graduated symbols

5.   Right-click (Win) or control-click (Mac) **zipcodes** and then click **Properties**.
6.   Click the **list arrow** in the **Classified by** field and then click **Manual**. See Figure 4-21. (*Next, you need to enter 1000, 2000, 3000, and 4,000 as the cut points, one at a time, as described next.*)
7.   In the resulting Class Breaks and Histogram window, click in the **Current** field, select **1,242**, enter **1,000**, click the **list arrow** in the **Select Break** field, and then click **2483**. (*You just manually reset the first break point and selected the second in preparation of resetting it too.*)
8.   Repeat Step 7 two more times, first changing the **Current** value **2,483** to **2,000** and selecting the next **Select Break** value of **3724**. Then change the **Current** value to **3,000**, and select the next **Select Break** value of **4965**. Finally, change the **Current** value to **4,000**, and click **OK**. See Figure 4-22.
9.   In the **zipcodes** Properties window, click in the last row of the **Label** column with label **4000–6206**, double-click the same location, select **–6206**, and then enter **and greater**.
10.   Click the **list arrow** in the **Start** field and then click **White**; do the same in the **End** field and then click **Black**.

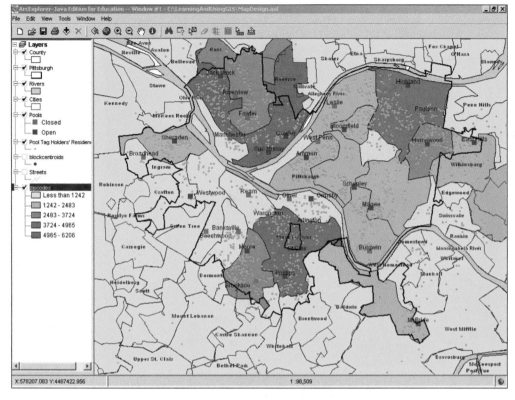

FIGURE 4-20   Choropleth map with default color ramp for zip codes

11. Click the **General** tab, change the layer name from **zipcodes** to **Number of Pool Tag Holders' Residences per Zip Code**, and then click **OK**. Change the order of layers in the Layers panel as seen in Figure 4-23. *(That is much better than the defaults. The choropleth map is distinctive but not overpowering, and it is easy to interpret.)*

12. Turn off the **Number of Pool Tag Holders' Residences per Zip Code** layer.

PRACTICE 4-6

- Click the Add Data button and add another copy of the layer for zip codes to your project.
- Re-symbolize the new copy of the layer for zip codes using the NUMTAGS attribute, 5 classes, and intervals starting at 250 that double in size: 0–250, 250–750, 750–1750, 1750–3750, 3750 and greater.
- Which set of cut points did you prefer? Equal interval or increasing interval? Delete the version that you do not like by using the Remove Layer button.

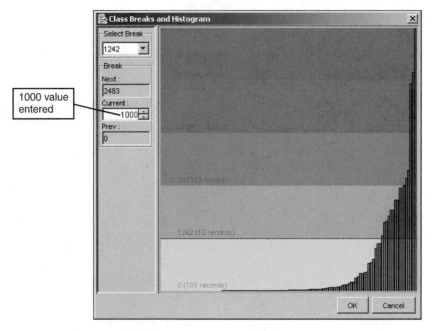

1000 value entered

FIGURE 4-21 Setting break points

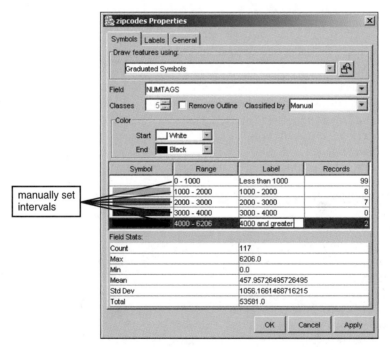

manually set intervals

FIGURE 4-22 Setting break points for intervals manually

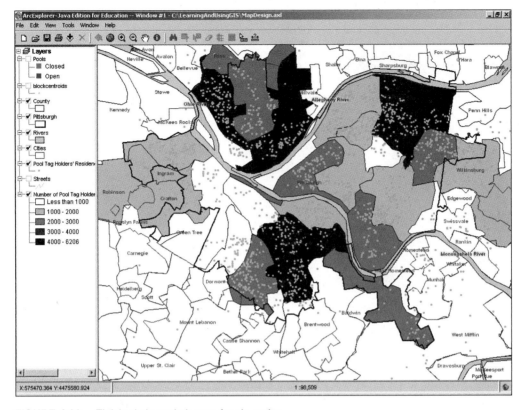

FIGURE 4-23   Finished choropleth map for zip codes

Size-Graduated Point Markers

1.   Turn off the **Pools** layer.
2.   Click the **Add Data** button, browse to the **LearningAndUsingGIS\Maps** folder, click **pools.shp**, and then click **OK**. *(This adds another copy of the Pools layer to the Layers panel. There is no limit to how many copies of a layer you can add to a map project.)*
3.   Right-click (Win) or control-click (Mac) the **new copy of pools** and then click **Properties....**
4.   Click the **list arrow** in the **Draw features using** field and then click **Graduated Symbols**.
5.   Click the **list arrow** in the **Field** field and then click **ATTEND04**. *(This is the average daily pool attendance in summer 2004.)*
6.   Change the **number of classes** from **5** to **4**, make both the **Start** and **End** colors **blue**, and make the **Start** size **1** and the **End** size **16**.
7.   Click the **list arrow** in the **Classified by** field and then click **Manual**.
8.   Set the cut points to **1, 50, 200**, and click **OK**.
9.   Change the **Less than 1** label to **None**, and change the **200–556** label to **200 and greater**.

10. Double-click the **blue color symbol** of the first row (0–1 Range), click the **white color swatch**, and then click **OK**. See Figure 4-24.

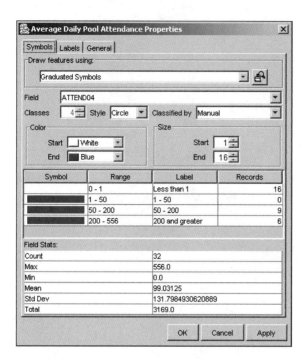

FIGURE 4-24   Selecting colors for attendance

11. Click the **General** tab, change **Pools** to **Average Daily Pool Attendance**, and then click **OK**. See Figure 4-25. *(That provides useful information. Now you can see the pools that had large and small numbers of swimmers in summer 2004.)*
12. Save and close MapDesign.axl.

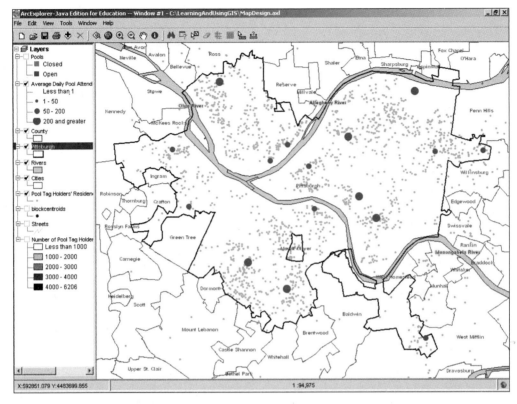

FIGURE 4-25 Finished size-graduated point markers for Average Daily Pool Attendance

PRACTICE 4-7

- Re-symbolize Average Daily Pool Attendance to have one more category. Use 1, 100, 200, and 300 as cut points.
- When you are finished, save your map project file and close ArcExplorer.

Chapter 4 Summary

Graphic design is an art, but it is informed by principles, concepts, and knowledge—thus making good graphic design possible by everyone, not just the artistically inclined.

Graphic hierarchy is a principle using the concepts of figure and ground to direct the viewer's attention to important parts of a map, chart, or other graphic design. Many of the graphic features on a map provide context or reference material. Such features should be put into ground by giving them dull colors (mostly grays), weak or no boundaries, and thin or dashed lines. The subjects of the map—the features that have important patterns—should be put into figure by giving them bright colors and wide, black edges, and other distinctive graphic elements.

As a graphic designer, be a minimalist: Make every pixel add meaning, or leave them white. Leave out chart junk, such as north arrows. Leave extra map layers out. Use color sparingly and for figure.

Hue, value, and saturation are terms associated with color. Blue is the hue in light blue and dark blue. Value signifies the amount of ink per square inch on an area, with a lot of white being low value, and a lot of black being high value. Saturation refers to a sequence of colors for a hue that runs from the pure hue to gray.

Mapmakers often use monochromatic scales to represent increasing magnitudes on choropleth maps, running from low to high color value, or low to high saturation. Avoid using multiple hues for the same choropleth map. An exception is a dichromatic scale that combines two monochromatic scales; for example, blue for negative quantities and red for positive quantities to represent numeric attributes with the natural center magnitude such as 0. Another exception is either half of the color spectrum (cool colors or hot colors) with yellow at one end, representing low value.

The color wheel is a device for picking good color combinations. Best for analytic maps are colors that provide the most differentiation: complementary colors (those that are opposite from each other or at equal intervals around the color wheel). Analogous colors are adjacent to each other on the color wheel and are used to show association (in contrast to differentiation).

Many map attributes have numeric scales, such as population counts and capacities of facilities. To represent such attributes on a map, the mapmaker must place these variables into intervals by choosing cut points along their range. Each interval is assigned a color from a monochromatic scale that portrays order through color value. A key in a legend must provide each interval's end point values and identify its color for interpretation. Good scales for general audiences are equal intervals in multiples of 2, 5, or 10—or exponential scales for long-tailed distributions, such as powers of 2 or 3. Quantile scales are for analysts so they can see the shape of distributions, for example, if they are long-tailed or uniform.

Points and lines are mathematical objects with no area or width; nevertheless, mapmakers must show points with shape and area and lines with width. It is best to use simple point marker shapes, such as circles and squares, because it is difficult to differentiate complex shapes and discover patterns among them. In analytic maps, most line features are ground and thus should have relatively narrow widths and gray color.

Analytical maps have two major audiences: the analysts who study them and the general public who need to get the message of a map. Analysts require maps with many layers and details. Use relatively few intervals (up to 7) for choropleth maps, many different kinds of point markers that have simple symbols, and so forth. Maps for analysts may be used only on a computer screen in a GIS package. Once analysts find an important pattern and want to make the public aware of it, then the map designer needs to create a simple map that dramatically portrays the pattern. Include the minimum layers to provide context and the subject, and make good use of graphic hierarchy. Consider several map outputs, including images for Web sites and paper maps using a map layout (described in Chapter 6).

ArcExplorer has powerful GIS functionality for symbolizing maps. The more complex layers get their symbols from the values of feature attributes; namely, from attributes that have code or numeric values. Use unique colors for point features that have codes, such as those for open and closed pools. Use a sequence of sizes for point features that have numeric values converted into intervals. It is easy to create monochromatic and dichromatic scales for choropleth maps. A key feature of ArcExplorer is that it allows the map designer to manually create cut points for numeric attributes, allowing the use of any set of cut points.

Key Terms

Analogous colors   Adjacent colors on the color wheel, used to depict association or harmony.

Cartography   The art of choosing map layers and graphic elements to yield a map composition that meets a specified purpose.

Chart junk   Graphic elements and symbolization that do not add value to charts, maps, graphs, or other graphic designs. Chart junk wastes ink and clutters up maps.

Choropleth maps   Polygon map layers that have fill using color value to signify magnitude of an attribute.

Color spectrum   The sequence of colors determined by the increasing frequency visible range electromagnetic waves as seen as light from prism or in a rainbow.

Color value   Amount of white or black in the color. In relation to white paper or a white computer screen, white has low value and black has high value.

Color wheel   A color-choosing guide, shaped like a wheel, that arrays colors in order of the color spectrum. Violet, the shortest-wavelength color is adjacent to red, the longest-wavelength color.

Complementary colors   Opposite colors on the color wheel. They combine a warm and cool color that look good together and provide large visual differentiation.

Continuous variable   A numeric variable with fractional parts, computed as a ratio or measured continuously, such as distances.

Cut points   Points chosen along the range of a quantitative attribute for creating non-overlapping, exhaustive intervals. The intervals make the attribute discrete so it can be represented as a bar chart or as a choropleth map.

Dichromatic color scale   Two monochromatic scales joined together with low color value in the center and color value increasing toward either end. Such a scale is used for attributes that have a natural center, such as the value 0 for measures of increases and decreases.

Discrete variable   A variable that may take values only from a small set, such as small, medium, and large. Generally such variables cover all possibilities, and all possible occurrences have values.

Equal intervals   Intervals with equal widths such as 0–5, 5–10, 10–15, and so on.

Designing Maps

Exponential scale   A numeric scale with cut points that follow an exponential sequence, such as 2n or 3n, where n takes on values 1, 2, 3, and so on. Often the value 0 is included if the corresponding attribute's data values include 0s.

Figure   A graphic feature given a bright color, distinctive boundaries, or other graphic designs to draw attention to it. Graphic features in figure are the subject being investigated or of other high importance.

Graphic design   Choice of graphic features and elements yielding a map or other graphic display that meets an intended purpose.

Graphic elements   The graphic variables used to impart meaning to graphic design including shape, size, width, and color.

Graphic hierarchy   A principle using color, strong edges, and other graphic elements to direct the viewer's attention to important parts of a map, chart, or other graphic.

Ground   A graphic feature given dull colors, dashed lines, or other graphic designs to place it in the background. Ground features provide context and supplemental information.

Hue   The essence or distinguishing feature of color that, for example, is the blue in light blue and dark blue.

Increasing interval widths   A sequence of intervals covering the range of a variable that accommodates long-tailed representations in bar charts and choropleth maps.

Long-tailed distributions   Samples or populations whose distribution deviates from the normal, bell-shaped curve by having one tail elongated. The performance of athletes and computer programmers are examples of such distributions, with long tails on the right side of the distribution, as are many entities in nature.

Median   The middle member of a distribution, with 50% of the sample being smaller and the other 50% being larger in magnitude.

Mimetic symbols   Graphic symbols that resemble what they represent, such as a cross-hatched line for a railroad on a map.

Monochromatic color scale   A series of colors of the same hue with color value varied from low to high; for example, the value ranges from white to black on a monochromatic gray scale, from light to dark green in a green monochromatic scale, etc.

Numeric intervals   Non-overlapping and exhaustive intervals covering the range of data values for an attribute, such as associated with bars on a bar chart.

Quantiles   Numeric intervals for the range of an attribute that have equal numbers of members in each interval. The intervals are constructed by sorting an attribute and choosing cut points along the sorted list of values that result in an equal number of data points in each interval.

Quartiles   Quantiles that have four intervals, each with 25% of an attribute's data values.

Saturation   A color scale that ranges from a pure hue to gray or black; for example, the closer to black, the more saturated the color.

Short-Answer Questions

1. Suppose that the following elements are individual map layers in ArcExplorer: streets, buildings, parks, motor vehicle accident points, stop signs, and stoplights. Write a description of symbols for use with each layer (shape, size, width, and color). Give a rationale for each choice that you make. Assume that you have only symbols that are available in ArcExplorer.

2. What is the best design for point markers classification using a numeric scale when there are relatively few points: a) monochromatic color scale, b) shapes ranging from circles through stars, c) sequence of sizes, or d) circles with increasingly thick black boundaries? Answer the same question for the case of a very large number of point markers (for example, 20,000). Provide rationales for your choices.

3. Suppose that you have a point layer for sources of particulate air pollution in a city and that particulate emission rates range from 0.1 to 135.0 tons of particulates per day. Describe a graphic design to portray this map layer for use in a brochure for the Group Against Smog and Pollution. Provide rationales for your choices.

4. Suppose that you have county-level data on the population of white-tailed deer in a state and a county polygon layer for the state. How would you portray these areas on a map, and why?

5. Suppose that you have crime data points for a neighborhood classified by crime type including larcenies, burglaries, motor vehicle thefts, and robberies. How would you symbolize these points?

6. Suppose that you have a polygon map layer for land use in an urban area that includes these non-overlapping categories: industrial, commercial, residential, and non-profit. How would you symbolize the polygons? Explain your choices.

7. Use the color wheel to produce four sets with three colors each for use in differentiating map features. Describe the four sets, indicate the one that you like the best, and tell why.

8. Suppose that you have used ArcExplorer's quantile option for an attribute that ranges from 0 to 72, and it produced cut points 22, 25, and 43. Describe the distribution of the attribute.

9. The map layers *Pools.axl* and *Queries.axl* used block centroids instead of block polygons to represent population of 5- to 17-year-old youths. What are the advantages of this choice?

10. Suppose that you have the following intervals for an attribute: (a) 0 to 50, (b) 50 to 100, (c) 100 to 200, and (d) 200 and greater. Which intervals include the following values: 75, 50, and 337?

Exercises

1. **Map with Two Point Markers Per Point.** You will display two copies of the Pool layer. One will display Average Daily Percent of Capacity and the other Average Daily Pool Attendance. This technique allows the viewer to compare two attributes of the same entities at the same time. It works very well here.

   a. Open **MapDesign.axl** (Win) or **MapDesignMac.axl** for (Mac) from **c:\LearningAndUsingGIS** (Win) or **/LearningAndUsingGIS/** (Mac). If you do not have the needed map project file, then follow steps in the tutorial of this chapter to create it in ArcExplorer.

   b. Add another copy of **pools.shp** to the *MapDesign.axl* (Win) or *MapDesignMac.axl* (Mac) project, and move it below **Average Daily Pool Attendance**. Leave **Average Daily Pool Attendance** turned on.

c. Use **PCTCAP** and construct a sequence of sizes for point markers with cut points of **0.001, 0.1, 0.2, 0.4,** and **0.8**. To handle the closed pools, the small value, 0.001, is a trick so the first interval represents *0*. There is no other way to put the closed pools in their own category.

d. Use large point markers ranging from size **8** to **26** and a complementary color, such as orange, to Average Daily Pool Attendance's blue color.

e. Save the project as **Exercise1<YourName>.axl**, substituting your name for <YourName>. Submit an electronic copy of this file if your instructor requires.

2. **Comparison of Different Ways to Symbolize an Attribute of City Blocks.** The number of vacant houses in a neighborhood is often a measure of poverty. In this exercise, you will compare four versions of maps showing the number of vacant houses per block in Allegheny County. One version is a choropleth map of block polygons. A second version uses color value for block centroid point markers, such as for the 5- to 17-year-old youth population and female-headed households with children that you have seen in the tutorials. A third version uses a sequence of sizes for block centroids. A fourth version combines versions 2 and 3. When you are done, you'll choose the best approach. Judge the competing symbolizations when zoomed in to Pittsburgh or closer and with your ArcExplorer window maximized. Note that you will have to wait after some of the steps in ArcExplorer for your computer to respond because the block map layers are huge.

a. Start **ArcExplorer** and start a new map project.

b. Add one copy of **c:\LearningAndUsingGIS\Maps\blocks.shp** (Win) or **/LearningAndUsingGIS/Maps/blocks.shp** (Mac) and three copies of **c:\LearningAndUsingGIS\Maps\blockcentroids.shp** (Win) or **/LearningAndUsingGIS/Maps/blockcentroids.shp** (Mac). While you are working, turn off all layers except the one on which you are working. As was previously mentioned, ArcExplorer is slow because these files are huge.

c. Add a copy of **minorcivildivisions.shp**. Give *minorcivildivisions.shp* a transparent color fill, add labels, and change the name to **Municipalities**.

d. Save your project as **c:\LearningAndUsingGIS\Outputs\Exercise2<YourName>.axl** (Win) or **/LearningAndUsingGIS/Outputs/Exercise2<YourName>.axl** (Mac) substituting your name for <YourName>.

e. Symbolize the **block polygon** layer for the field **VACANT** using cut points of 1, 5, 10, and 20. Use a gray monochromatic scale. Start with the equal interval scale before changing to manual scale. That approach assures that the starting cut points will be easy to change. Do the same for the other three layers in Steps f through h.

f. Symbolize one copy of the **block centroids** layer for **VACANT**, using square point markers size 3 and a gray monochromatic scale. Remember to use cut points of 1, 5, 10, and 20, and use them on the two remaining copies of the block centroids.

g. Symbolize another copy of the **block centroids** layer using medium gray circular point markers ranging in size from 1 to 7.

128

Chapter 4

h. Symbolize the last copy of **block centroids** the same as the previous one (with circular point markers), except include a monochromatic gray color scale.

i. Save the project as **Exercise2<YourName>.axl**, substituting your name for <YourName>. Submit an electronic copy of this file if your instructor requires you to do so.

3. **Map of the World.** In this exercise, you get to try out *all* your map design skills, including skills from previous chapters. Design a good map of the world for analysts.

a. Start **ArcExplorer** and add all of the layers from **C:\ESRI\AEJEE\Data\world** (Win) or **/ESRI/AEJEE/Data/world/** (Mac).

b. Use the **Robinson** projection.

c. Save your map project file as **c:\LearningAndUsingGIS\Outputs\ Exercise3<YourName>.axl** (Win) or **/LearningAndUsingGIS/Outputs/ Exercise3<YourName>.axl** (Mac), substituting your name for <YourName>.

d. Use **Catalog** to explore the layers.

e. Add threshold scales to display **World30** only when zoomed out and **latlong**, **rivers**, and **cities** only when zoomed in. Choose a single map scale for all thresholds that correspond to the zoomed in continent of Africa. Turn map layers on and off at this single map scale.

f. Symbolize **country** for an interesting attribute. Use **manual cut points** of your design. Label **countries** using the Name attribute.

g. Symbolize **cities** for an interesting attribute. Use **manual cut points** of your design. Label cities using the Name attribute.

h. Save the project as **Exercise3<YourName>.axl**, substituting your name for <YourName>. Submit an electronic copy of this file if your instructor requires.

4. **Map of the United States.** In this exercise, you will again have the opportunity to exercise your map design skills, including skills learned from previous chapters. Design a good map of the United States. This map project has the nice aspect of allowing the user to study an attribute at three geographic scales, states, counties, and cities, and to zoom in for detailed breakdowns.

a. Start **ArcExplorer** and add all of the layers from **C:\ESRI\AEJEE\Data\USA** (Win) or **/ESRI/AEJEE/Data/USA** (Mac). Add a second copy of states that you symbolize to have a transparent color fill and leave on at all scales.

b. Use a **Regional** projection of North America of your choice.

c. Use **Catalog** to explore the layers.

d. Add **threshold scales** to display counties and cities only when zoomed in at about the scale of a state. Turn off your color-coded version of the states layer (described as follows) at the same scale.

e. Choose an interesting attribute that is present in all three layers: states, counties, and cities; for example, you might choose **Hispanic population**.

f. Symbolize the **chosen attribute** using **manual scales** of your own design for each of the three layers. All three scales will be different because states are larger than counties, and counties are larger than cities, so each layer will have different ranges. (An exception may be any attributes that are averages, where variation between ranges may be smaller.) Use the same number of classes and the same color ramp for all three layers.

g. Save your map project file as **Exercise4<YourName>.axl**, substituting your name for <YourName>. Submit an electronic copy of this file if your instructor requires.

References

Tufte, E.R., *The Visual Display of Quantitative Information*, 2nd ed. Cheshire: Graphics Press, 2001.

MacEachren, A.M., *Some Truth with Maps: A Primer on Symbolization and Design*. Washington D.C.: Association of American Geographers, 1994.

Graphic Communications Program, NC State University College of Education "Color Principles—Hue, Saturation, and Value." Internet URL: http://www.ncsu.edu/scivis/lessons/colormodels/color_models2.html#saturation (accessed March 2, 2005).

Color Wheel Pro, "Color Meaning." Internet URL: http://www.color-wheel-pro.com/color-meaning.html (accessed March 2, 2005).

CHAPTER **5**

FINDING GIS RESOURCES

LEARNING OBJECTIVES

In this chapter, you will:

- Learn about free maps and data available from the U.S. Census Bureau and ESRI
- Discover other sources of map layers and data
- Download U.S. Census maps and data tables
- Download TIGER/Line maps and data tables
- Process downloaded layers in ArcExplorer

Arthur and his crew looking for more pieces to build the world's first floating map...

INTRODUCTION

In previous chapters, you learned how to navigate, query, design, and build GIS map compositions by using map layers we provided for the Swimming Pool Case Study. In this chapter, you will learn about two major sources of free map layers and spatial data: the U.S. Census Bureau and ESRI Web sites. Both Web sites provide TIGER/Line maps for the entire U.S. by county. We used these Web sites to obtain the blocks, municipalities, zip codes, streets, and river maps for the Swimming Pool Case Study (maps you will continue to use in Chapters 6 and 7). In Chapter 7, you will finish this case study in a project assignment, but you will also move away from Pittsburgh maps and start working on projects in your own community using maps from these Web sites.

In addition to map layers, both the Census and ESRI Web sites provide data tables of **spatially-referenced data**—data that is categorized by unique spatial identifiers. The identifiers—state names, county FIPS codes, 5-digit zip codes, census tract numbers, and so forth—enable you to join the data to corresponding map layers.

There are many more resources for map layers. In this chapter, we provide some ideas about where to search for specialized maps and data. Many states, counties, and cities have their own GIS departments that create map layers and make them available on the Internet. You will find that many map layers and data are free; others have a small fee (typically to cover just duplication and handling costs), but some are quite expensive. Your work in this chapter continues in Chapters 6 and 7. In those chapters, we provide additional Web sites for map resources.

FREE RESOURCES ON THE INTERNET

There are more than 10 million GIS Web sites on the Internet! Fortunately, to meet most analytical mapping needs in the U.S., you need to know about just *two* Web sites. One of the Web sites also has good map layers for other parts of the world.

Before learning about these two Web sites, you need to know that in ArcExplorer, you can use just shapefile-format maps and event themes. If you find map layers in any other format, such as ArcInfo coverages or ArcInfo E00 export format, you will need to find someone with a full-featured GIS (such as ArcView) who can convert such map layers to shapefile format for you.

Next, let's look at some background on U.S. Census Bureau map layers and data.

U.S. Census Bureau Map Layers and Data

The U.S. Census Bureau started building a map infrastructure in the late 1970s and early 1980s. Its mapping needs were twofold: first, to assign census employees to areas of responsibility, covering the entire country and its possessions, and second, to report and display census tabulations by area. Officials determined that the smallest area needed for these purposes is a city block or its equivalent. Consequently, Census Bureau officials decided to compile all line features that could be used to create a block layer for the entire country. The officials had a preference for visible features—streets, streams, shorelines, and so forth—but they also intended to use invisible features when necessary—county lines, city limits, and so forth—to build block layers. In the end, the Census Bureau met its needs, and as a by-product provided the major vector-based map infrastructure for the U.S.

Any map features smaller than blocks—such as deeded land parcels, building outlines, street curbs, and parking lots—are the responsibility of local governments. There is no central repository for local-government map layers, so obtaining local-government maps is a hit-or-miss proposition: You must search individual city and county Web sites. A small but increasing number of them provide GIS map layers.

TIGER/Line® Files

As discussed in Chapter 1, TIGER/Line (Topologically Integrated Geographic Encoding and Referencing) files are the Census Bureau's product for digital mapping of the U.S. The TIGER maps are available for the entire U.S. and its possessions, and the maps include geographic features such as roads and streets, railroads, rivers, lakes, political boundaries, and census statistical boundaries. Census statistical boundaries include the following:

- **Census tracts**: These are areas averaging 4,000 population. Census tracts are neighborhoods: Generally, they are homogeneous in population, social-economic status, and living conditions. There were more than 60,000 census tracts in the 2000 Census.
- **Census block groups**: These are subdivisions of census tracts averaging 1,000 population.
- **Census blocks**: These are subdivisions of block groups, the smallest geographic areas for which the Census Bureau collects and tabulates census data.

TIGER/Line files can be downloaded for free in shapefile format from the U.S. Census Bureau Web site, from ESRI's site, and many other sites. You can find definitions of all Census Bureau and TIGER/Line files at *www.census.gov/geo/www/tiger* and *www.census.gov/geo/www/garm.html*.

U.S. Census Bureau Data Files

The Census Bureau's boundary map layers do not contain demographic data. There are far too many census variables to be included with map layers—the maps files would become enormously large and slow to process on a computer. Thus, it is the user's responsibility to choose one or more of the large number of census data tables available and then join them to a map's feature attribute table. You'll learn how to join data tables in Chapter 6. Two major collections of data tables are the following:

- **Census Summary File 1 (SF 1)**: This collection has data tables on population, age, sex, race, Hispanic/Latino origin, household relationship, ownership of residences, and so forth for the entire population of people and housing units. This data is available for states, municipalities, zip codes, census tracts, census block groups, census blocks, and other types of areas.

- **Census Summary File 3 (SF 3)**: This collection has data tables for detailed population and housing characteristics—such as place of birth, educational attainment, employment status, income, value of housing unit, and the year in which a structure was built—collected from a 1-in-6 random sample and then weighted to represent the total population. This data is not available at the census-block level, but it is available for census block groups and larger areas.

U.S. Census Bureau Web Site

The American Fact Finder Web site of the U.S. Census Bureau, *factfinder.census.gov*, has documentation for all census data sets and map layers. Downloadable map layers are in shapefile format; data is available in tabular format. This chapter's tutorial and the solved projects in Chapter 7 provide sufficient instruction so you will be able to obtain maps and data that you need from the Census Bureau.

ESRI Web Sites

As mentioned in previous chapters, ESRI is the world leader in GIS software and produces ArcExplorer. ESRI's data Web site, *www.esri.com/data*, is one of the first places that many people visit when looking for map layers. It provides links to download data, to order data on CDs, or to locate GIS data providers for a variety of industries. Examples of data you can download for free, or for a small fee, include the following:

- *ESRI World Basemap Data (free):* These maps provide GIS layers from countries around the world in shapefile format.
- *Census 2000 TIGER/Line Data (free):* These maps provide Census 2000 TIGER/Line maps in shapefile format by county.
- *United States Geological Survey (USGS) National Elevation Dataset (NED) Shaded Relief Imagery Data (free):* These maps provide the highest-resolution elevation data available for the United States, in raster format.
- *GDT Dynamap/2000 U.S. Street Data (small fee for individual zip code layers):* These map layers are the highest quality street-map layers in terms of appearance, completeness, and accuracy. These maps include more than 14 million U.S. street segments and include postal boundaries, landmarks, water features, and other features.
- *Titan Sure!MAPS RASTER Data (small fee for single map):* These color raster maps are for selected areas. They include the U.S. Geological Survey topographic maps at 1:24,000; 1:100,000; and 1:250,000 scales. Each map contains topographic contours, land-use features, political boundaries, streets, buildings, landmarks, and other cultural information.

ESRI's Geography Network site, *www.geographynetwork.com*, offers links to on-line dynamic maps and downloadable data. It provides a mechanism for GIS users to access GIS data and services worldwide. It is possible to search not only by location but also by industry-specific categories such as agriculture and farming, biology and ecology, business and economy, and human health and disease. For example, you could search for all the map layers for agriculture and farming near Cape Town, South Africa.

In addition to ESRI Web sites, several states have GIS clearinghouses that provide map data. You can find links to many state GIS clearinghouses on *www.gis.com*. The GIS Data tab on this site lists all states and the number of GIS links that are available for that state. For example, the Pennsylvania Spatial Data Access site (PASDA) is hosted and maintained by The Pennsylvania State University and is Pennsylvania's official geospatial data clearinghouse. The data on PASDA is provided by federal, state, local and regional government agencies, non-profit organizations, and academic institutions throughout the region. We obtained the Swimming Pool Case Study's raster maps from PASDA.

U.S. CENSUS BUREAU WEB SITE DOWNLOADS

Next, you will follow steps for downloading Census map files and spatially-referenced data tables. After downloading map files, you will use them in ArcExplorer. You will join spatially-referenced data tables to map files in Chapter 6.

Map Boundary Files

The following steps show you how to log onto the U.S. Census Bureau site and download a shapefile of county outlines for Florida. The following steps require that you use a file compression program to decompress downloaded files. Windows users can get a free, trial copy of such a program at WinZip at *www.winzip.com* or PKZIP at *www.pkware.com*. There are several other such programs, and you can use any of them for this tutorial.

1. Start a Web browser such as **Internet Explorer** or **Netscape**.
2. Enter **http://www.census.gov** as the Internet address.
3. In the Geography section of the Census home page, click **TIGER**. *(This is about halfway down and in the middle of the page.)*
4. From the left side of the TIGER page, click **Cartographic Boundary Files**.
5. From the Cartographic Boundary Files page, click **Download Boundary Files**.
6. Click **County and County Equivalent Areas: 2000**.
7. Scroll about halfway down the next page to the section entitled **Census 2000 County and County Equivalent Areas in ArcView Shapefile (.shp) format** and then click **Florida - co12_d00_shp.zip (174,373 bytes)**. *(Be sure that you scroll to the ArcView Shapefile section of this page.)*
8. Click **Save** from the File Download dialog box. Windows users: Browse to the folder **c:\LearningAndUsingGIS\DownloadedMaps**, and then click **Save**. Mac users: The **co12_d00_shp.zip** file will be downloaded to your default download folder, usually your desktop. Then it will be automatically decompressed. Move the decompressed files to the **LearningAndUsingGIS/DownloadedMaps** folder on your hard drive. The procedure for downloading and saving the file will be different on Windows XP depending on if Service Pack 2 is installed or not.
9. Windows users: Use PKZIP or WinZip to extract the files in **co12_d00_shp.zip** to the **c:\LearningAndUsingGIS\DownloadedMaps** folder.

- From the Census Web site's Cartographic Boundary section, download Florida's census tract file, *tr12_d00shp.zip. Hint:* When you get to the Web page with tract files for downloading, you have to scroll down to the section entitled Census 2000: Census Tracts in ArcView Shapefile (.shp) format.
- Choose another state (perhaps the state where you live), and download its county and census tract boundaries.

Summary File Tables

Next, you will download county-level census data for Florida that includes income and poverty variables.

1. Start a Web browser such as **Internet Explorer** or **Netscape**.
2. Enter **http://factfinder.census.gov** as the Internet address.
3. Click **DATA SETS**.
4. Click the option button for **Census 2000 Summary File 1 (SF 1) 100-Percent Data**.
5. In the box to the right of the option button, click **Geographic Comparison Tables**.
6. From the Select a geographic type menu, click **State**.
7. From the Select a geographic area menu, click **Florida**.
8. Select **State -- County** as the table format and then click **Next**.
9. Click **table GCT-PH1. Population, Housing Units, Area, and Density: 2000**, and then click **Show Result**. See Figure 5-1.
10. From the Print/Download menu, click **Download**.
11. Click the **Microsoft Excel (.xls)** option button and then click **OK**. *(The saved file will be a compressed file called* output.zip *that includes the Excel Spreadsheet and* readme.txt *text documents describing geographic comparison tables.)*
12. Windows users: Save the file to **c:\LearningAndUsingGIS\DownloadedMaps\ Output.zip**. Mac users: The **Output.zip** file will be downloaded to your default download folder, usually your desktop. Then it will be automatically decompressed. Move the decompressed files to the **LearningAndUsingGIS/ DownloadedMaps** folder on your hard drive.
13. Windows users: Extract the files using WinZip or PKZIP, open the resulting spreadsheet file in Microsoft Excel, and scroll through the columns and rows to see the population, area, and housing data.

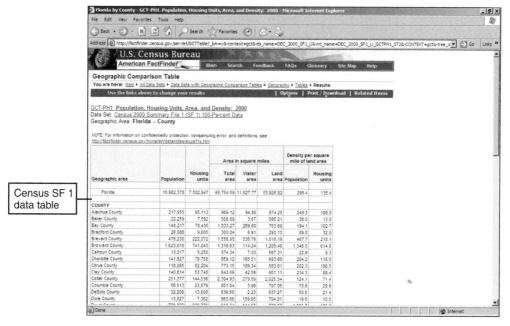

Census SF 1 data table

FIGURE 5-1 Census SF 1 data table for Florida counties

PRACTICE 5-2

- For Florida counties, download Geographic Comparison Tables from the Summary File SF3 table for Income and Poverty (GCT-P14).
- Choose another state, and download the same Geographic Comparison Tables for that state.

ArcExplorer Map of U.S. Census Bureau Files

After you download the county boundary outlines for Florida and extract them, you can add the shapefile to your ArcExplorer project.

1. On your computer's desktop, click **Start**, **All Programs**, **AEJEE**, **AEJEE**.
2. Click the **Add Data** button.
3. In the Content Chooser window, click the down arrow in the **Look in** field, browse to **c:\LearningAndUsingGIS\DownloadedMaps**, and double-click the **co12_d00_shp** folder, click **OK**, and then click **co12_d00.shp**. See Figure 5-2.

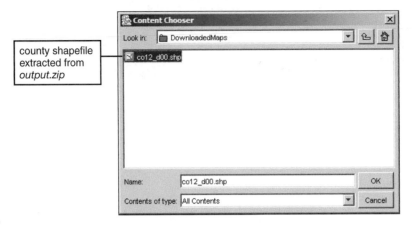

FIGURE 5-2 Adding extracted map layer for Florida counties

county shapefile extracted from *output.zip*

4. Click the **Zoom to Full Extent** button to see all of the Florida counties.
5. Click the **Identify tool** to see the attribute data about the counties. See Figure 5-3.

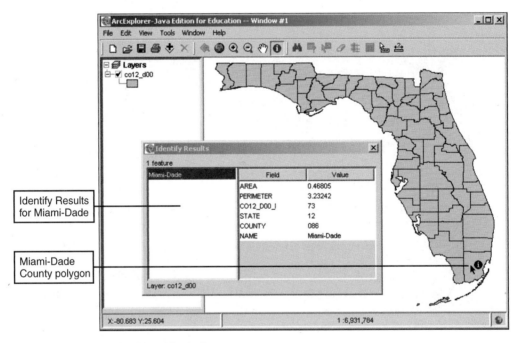

Identify Results for Miami-Dade

Miami-Dade County polygon

FIGURE 5-3 Identifying Miami-Dade County

ESRI WEBSITE DOWNLOADS

Next, you will visit ESRI's Web site to download additional Census Bureau TIGER/Line files. This Web site has some unique features; for example, it provides map layers for census blocks even though the Census Bureau does not make them available. It also has frequently used SF 1 Census variables already joined to census boundary maps.

TIGER/Line Files

You will start using the ESRI Web site by downloading shapefiles for Travis County, Texas.

1.   Start a Web browser such as **Internet Explorer** or **Netscape**.
2.   Enter **http://www.esri.com** as the Internet address.
3.   From ESRI's home page, click the **Products** tab and then click **Data**.
4.   From the Browse, Subscribe, and Download section, click **Downloadable Data**.
5.   Click **Census 2000 TIGER/Line Data Free!**
6.   From the Census 2000 TIGER/Line Data page, click **Download Data**.
7.   Click the state of **Texas** on the map (or click **Texas** from the drop-down menu).
8.   From the drop-down menu for Select by County, click **Travis** as the county name, and then click **Submit Selection**. *(Travis County is the home of Texas' state capital, Austin. The next screen will show all of the TIGER data layers that are available for Travis County, Texas.)*
9.   From the Available Layers, click the boxes next to **Census Blocks 2000** and **Line Features-Roads**.
10. Scroll to the bottom of the page and then click **Proceed to Download**.
11. Click **Download File**. *(The procedure for downloading and saving the file will be different on Windows XP, depending on whether Service Pack 2 is installed.)*
12. Windows users: Save the file to **c:\LearningAndUsingGIS\DownloadedMaps**. Mac users: Move the file from your desktop (or default download folder) to the **LearningAndUsingGIS\DownloadMaps** folder.
13. Windows users: Using PKZIP or WinZip, extract the shapefiles for Travis County Census Blocks and Roads, saving the files to **c:\LearningAndUsingGIS\ DownloadedMaps**.

PRACTICE 5-3

Download additional TIGER files for Travis County, Texas, including Census Tracts, Census Block Groups, Water Polygons, and Urban Areas.

Summary File (SF 1) Tables

Besides the TIGER map files, you can download spatially-referenced data tables from the ESRI Web site.

1.   Repeat Steps 1–8 from the previous set of 13 steps.
2.   Turn off any selected layers.

3. From the Available Layers, click the **Census Tract Demographics (SF 1)** check box.
4. Scroll to the bottom of the page and then click **Proceed to Download**.
5. Click **Download File**. Mac users: You may get a message noting that the file is not a recognizable type. You may be asked to choose a default application to open the file; Stuffit Expander is a good choice.
6. Windows users: Save the file to **c:\LearningAndUsingGIS\DownloadedMaps**. Mac users: The compressed folder will be downloaded to your default download folder, usually your desktop. Then it will be automatically decompressed. There will be another compressed file inside the folder, which you will also need to decompress. Move the decompressed file, which will have a *.dbf* file extension, to the **LearningAndUsingGIS/DownloadedMaps** folder on your hard drive. Mac does not recognize files with *.dbf* extensions, so to open this file in Excel, begin by starting Excel. Next, select **File** on the menu bar and then click **Open**. Click the **list arrow** in the Enable list, scroll to the bottom of the list, and select **All Documents**. (Note that All Documents is not the default, and you must select it to open the file.) Navigate to the *.dbf* file, select it, and click **Open**. The file will open in Excel.
7. Windows users: Use PKZIP or WinZip to extract the database **tgr48000sf1trt.dbf** to **c:\LearningAndUsingGIS\DownloadedMaps**. *(When you unzip the downloaded file, the result is another zipped file that you must unzip.)*
8. Open the file in Microsoft Excel to see the SF 1 data for census tracts.

PRACTICE 5-4

Download the Census Block Group Demographics (SF 1) file for Travis County, Texas.

ArcExplorer Map of ESRI Files

Next, you will use ArcExplorer to view a map of Austin, Texas, which is in the Travis County map layers you just downloaded.

1. Click **Start**, click **All Programs**, and then click **AEJEE, AEJEE**.
2. Click the **Add Data** button.
3. In the Content Chooser window, click the **list arrow** in the **Look in** field, browse to c:\LearningAndUsingGIS\DownloadedMaps, and click **tgr48453lkA** and click **OK**. Repeat this step to add **tgr48453blk00**.
4. Change the fill for the census blocks to a **transparent fill** and the roads to a **medium gray color**.
5. Zoom in to a closer view of Austin, Texas, to see the census blocks and roads. See Figure 5-4.

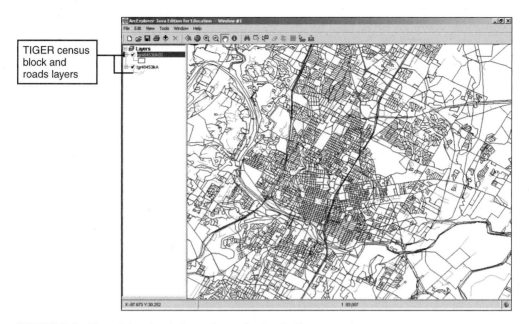

TIGER census block and roads layers

FIGURE 5-4 Map of downloaded map layers for Austin, Texas

PRACTICE 5-5

- Add the other TIGER files for Travis County, Texas, including Census Tracts, Water Polygons, and Urban Areas to your map project. Symbolize the additional layers to your liking.

Chapter 5 Summary

We obtained most of the base-map layers for the Swimming Pool Case Study—the blocks, municipalities, zip codes, streets, and rivers—for free on the Internet. You can get these and additional map layers and data for GIS projects for your own or other communities.

The U.S. Census Bureau is a good source of map layers and data that you can add to a GIS project. These resources are free for all states and counties. GIS resources provided include TIGER/Line map layers—which show streets, rivers, states, counties, municipalities, census tracts, and so forth—and summary file tables, which contain census data tabulations that can be joined to corresponding map boundary layers. Two important summary files are Summary File 1, which has census data on basic population and housing characteristics from the complete census, and Summary File 3, which has tabulations from a random sample of the population and housing with detailed characteristics including place of birth, educational attainment, employment status, income, value of housing unit, and so forth. You can download these map layers and data tables from *www.census.gov* or *www.esri.com/data*.

The ESRI Web site has several additional map resources, from maps for countries around the world including maps at the province/state level, to shaded relief maps for elevation and topographic raster maps. In addition, ESRI sponsors the *www.geographynetwork.com* Web site that has unique search capabilities by industry type and location for many map-layer vendors' products. Another Web site sponsored in part by ESRI is *www.gis.com*, which also has links to map sources.

Many states have GIS clearing houses on the Internet, such as the Pennsylvania site, PASDA, to provide map layers and data (see *www.pasda.psu.edu/*). Local governments are sources for map layers for features smaller than city blocks, such as building outlines, curbs, parking lots, and deeded properties. An increasing number of local governments are making their specialized GIS layers available for public use.

Key Terms

Census blocks   The smallest statistical tabulation area used by the U.S. Census Bureau for reporting census variables. In urban areas, census blocks are also city blocks. Their boundaries are made up mostly of streets, but they also include rivers, lakes, county lines, and many other line features.

Census block groups   Collections of census blocks yielding approximately 1,000 population. This is the smallest tabulation available for SF3 data.

Census Summary File 1 (SF 1)   A collection of data tables from the complete census of persons and households. Included are population, age, sex, race, Hispanic/Latino origin, household relationship, and ownership of residences, and so forth.

Census Summary File 3 (SF 3)   A collection of data tables from the 1-in-6 random sample of the population. Included are variables such as place of birth, educational attainment, employment status, income, value of a housing unit, and construction year for structures.

Census tracts   Collections of census block groups yielding approximately 4,000 population each. Census tracts are the primary statistical tabulation area for the census.

Spatially-referenced data   Data tables that include unique identifiers for geographic area such as state names, county FIPS codes, 5-digit zip codes, or census tract numbers. Such tables can be joined to feature attribute tables of corresponding map layers.

Short-Answer Questions

1. Suppose that you have a map layer of U.S. Census Bureau tract boundaries for a county that has urban, suburban, and rural areas. How would you expect the size of census tracts, in acres, to vary across those three kinds of areas? Why?

2. Describe the relationship between Census Bureau tracts, block groups, and blocks. What are advantages of such a design for reporting the census?

3. Explain the differences between the Census Summary File 1 and Census Summary File 3 data collections. What do you think the Census Bureau's motivation was for designing these two data collections?

4. Why are Census Bureau boundary files supplied without census data already attached to them? Describe the computer skills that you need to use SF1 and SF3 data in a GIS.

5. Why doesn't the Census Bureau build map layers of deeded land parcels?

6. What Web sites would you visit to download free maps of Asia?

7. What Web site would you visit to learn about map layers depicting human health in Africa?

8. What data would you download to identify the poverty-stricken areas of a state?

9. If you were the city official in charge of GIS and needed a street layer for use in dispatching emergency vehicles (police, fire, and ambulances), which map layer would you obtain? Why?

10. Why did the Census Bureau base its map layers on line features?

Exercises

1. **Download Map Layers for Oregon's Urban Growth Areas.** Oregon's 241 cities are surrounded by urban growth areas delimited by urban growth boundaries (UGBs). A UGB shows where a city expects growth; land outside the UGB will remain rural.

   In this exercise, you will download Census Bureau boundary maps necessary to build a map composition showing where Oregon's urban growth boundaries are compared with existing urban and rural areas. Growth can be determined by comparing 1990 and 2000 Census maps and data with the UGB boundaries.

   a. Create a subfolder in the Outputs folder called OregonExercise1.

   b. Start your Web browser and go to the *www.census.gov* Web site. Download the following boundary map layers for Oregon into the OregonExercise1 folder: 2000 Oregon Urban Growth Areas (*ou99_d00_shp.zip*), 2000 County and County Equivalents (*co41_d00_shp.zip*), 2000 Census Tracts (*tr41_d00_shp.zip*), and 1990 Census Tracts (*tr41_d90_shp.zip*).

   c. Use WinZip or PKZIP to extract the shapefiles from the downloaded files and explore the map layers and attribute tables using ArcExplorer's Catalog.

   d. Create an ArcExplorer map with the downloaded map layers. Symbolize layers to your own liking. Save the project as *OregonInterestingMaps<YourName>.axl*, where you substitute your name for <YourName>. If required, turn in a screen print of your finished map in a Word document that includes your name and a title for your map.

2. **Download TIGER Maps for Multnomah County Oregon.** In this exercise, you will download TIGER/Line files from ESRI's site that could be used to build a detailed map for the Portland, Oregon, area of Multnomah County.

   a. Create a subfolder in the Outputs folder called OregonExercise2.

   b. Start your Web browser and open the ESRI's Web site data download section, *http://arcdata.esri.com/data/tiger2000/tiger_download.cfm*. Download into your OregonExercise2 folder the following files from Multnomah County, Oregon: Block Groups 2000, CMSA/MSA Polygons 2000, Landmark Points, Line Features—Rails, Line Features—Roads, and Census Block Group Demographics (SF1).

   c. Use WinZip or PKZIP to extract the shapefiles and explore the map layers and attribute tables using ArcExplorer's Catalog.

   d. Create an ArcExplorer map with the downloaded map layers. Symbolize layers to your own liking. Save the project as *OregonInterestingMaps<YourName>.axl*, where you substitute your name for <YourName>. If required, turn in your *.axl* file and a screen-print of your finished map in a Word document that includes your name and a title for your map.

3. **Find Your Own Oregon Data.** There are many GIS layers for the state of Oregon that might not be found on the ESRI or Census Web sites. In this exercise, you will find and download your own interesting GIS layers to build a map.

   a. Create a subfolder in the Outputs folder called OregonExercise3.

   b. Use an Internet search engine or visit the sites listed on *http://www.gis.state.or.us/links.html* to find interesting shapefiles to create a new map.

   c. Use WinZip or PKZIP to extract the shapefiles from any compressed files and explore the map layers and attribute tables using ArcExplorer's Catalog.

   d. Create an ArcExplorer map with the downloaded map layers. Symbolize layers to your own liking. Save the project as *OregonInterestingMaps<YourName>.axl*, where you substitute your name for <YourName>. If required, turn in your *.axl* file and a screen print of your finished map in a Word document that includes your name and a title for your map.

4. **Download GIS Layers from a local government site.** An example of a local government providing map layers on the Internet is Sarasota, Florida. Detailed layers that you can find at *http://gis.co.sarasota.fl.us/* include buildings, parcels, sidewalks, schools, and so forth. With a growing interest in solving the childhood obesity epidemic, many school districts are looking for alternative ways to integrate exercise into the school day, such as encouraging activities at nearby parks. In this exercise, you will download files suitable for building a map for the Sarasota public schools to determine how many parks are near elementary schools.

   a. Create a subfolder in the Outputs folder called FloridaExercise4.

   b. Start your Web browser and then open Sarasota County's Web site, *http://gis.co.sarasota.fl.us*. Scroll to the MAPS and DATA section.

   c. Click on GIS data and download the following layers: Parks Polygons, Sarasota County Outline, Sidewalks, School Points, and Streets.

d. Use WinZip or PKZIP to extract the shapefiles and to explore the map layers and attribute tables using ArcExplorer's Catalog.

e. Create an ArcExplorer map with the downloaded map layers. Query the Schools layer to show only elementary schools, and create a 1/2-mile buffer (which is about a 10-minute walking radius) around those schools.

f. Save the project as *SarasotaSchools<YourName>.axl*, where you substitute your name for <YourName>. If required, turn in your *.axl* file and a screen print of your finished map in a Word document that includes your name and a title for your map.

145

References

Department of Land Conservation and Development (DLCD), Oregon Urban Growth Boundary, Internet URL: darkwing.uoregon.edu/~pppm/landuse/UGB.html (accessed March 23, 2005).

ESRI Downloadable Data, Internet URL: www.esri.com/data/download/index.html (accessed March 5, 2005).

ESRI Geography Network, Internet URL: www.geographynetwork.com (accessed March 7, 2005).

U.S. Census Bureau Tiger Overview, Internet URL: www.census.gov/geo/www/tiger/overview.html (accessed March 11, 2005).

U.S. Census Bureau Cartographic Boundary Files, Internet URL: www.census.gov/geo/www/cob/index.html (accessed March 12, 2005).

USGS National Elevation Dataset, Internet URL: gisdata.usgs.net/ned (accessed March 23, 2005).

CHAPTER 6

EXTENDING ARCEXPLORER'S CAPABILITIES

LEARNING OBJECTIVES

In this chapter, you will:

- Learn about map layouts
- Learn about creating new attributes
- Understand address matching
- Understand table joins for adding data to feature attribute tables
- Build map layouts by using ArcExplorer, Microsoft Paint, and Microsoft PowerPoint
- Create new variables by using Microsoft Excel
- Address-match data by using ArcExplorer and event themes
- Join tables by using Microsoft Excel

Staying afloat on software...

INTRODUCTION

When you use a computer to work on a complex project, such as the Swimming Pool Case Study, you inevitably use several software packages. For example, you might need to make changes or additions to tabular data, such as the feature attribute table of the Pools map layer. We used Microsoft Excel to create the PCTMAX attribute in that table: We divided average daily attendance by maximum capacity for each pool. Then we were able to use PCTMAX to symbolize pools for display in a map.

Although ArcExplorer has impressive capabilities for a free software package, it cannot do everything that a commercial GIS package can do. However, you can extend ArcExplorer's capabilities by using other common software packages with it. For example, ArcExplorer does not have the built-in functionality to create a publication-quality map layout, but it does produce all of the critical components. Thus, you can use Microsoft Paint (Win) or AppleWorks (Mac) to clip out the legend from a screen print of ArcExplorer's program window and touch up the legend by erasing unwanted lines. Then you can import the legend and an exported ArcExplorer map into Microsoft PowerPoint to assemble those pieces and to add other components. The result is a professional-quality map layout, suitable for use in a project report or presentation. Later in this chapter, you will build such a layout for the Swimming Pool Case Study.

Another important GIS task not available in ArcExplorer is **address matching**. Often, you will have tabular data that includes street addresses, but you won't have a corresponding point map layer. In a commercial GIS, such as ArcView, address matching is an automated function that places points on street-centerline maps by matching street addresses in tabular data with street addresses recorded in the feature attribute table of a street-centerline base map. ArcExplorer cannot automatically address-match data, but you can use it in a series of manual processing steps to accomplish the same end.

A benefit of doing the manual steps is that you will learn a lot about the address-matching process and about TIGER street-centerline maps—certainly more than you would using automated address matching in ArcView.

Another way of extending ArcExplorer's capabilities is to use Excel to join a spatially-referenced data table to a polygon feature attribute table. As you saw in Chapter 5, you can download Census Bureau data, but generally such data is not part of a map. To connect the Census Bureau data to a map layer, you need to use a **table join**, a procedure that matches records from two tables by using a common attribute. For example, you could use a spatial identifier such as a census tract number to create joined records in a new table. With a commercial GIS, you can make a table join automatically, as you can with a database program such as Microsoft Access, but with ArcExplorer you need to do it manually. Because the table-join needs of GIS are simple ones, you can use the Excel spreadsheet program and manual processing. As with address matching, you will learn a lot about table joins by completing the extra manual steps needed in Excel.

EXTENSIONS TO ARCEXPLORER

As you work through this chapter, you will learn how to use several software programs, one after another, to accomplish a task: One program accomplishes the first step, another accomplishes the second step, and so forth, until the larger task is done. First, we describe the desired end product, and then we show you how to use several programs to obtain that end product. These software additions extend ArcExplorer's capabilities.

Map Layouts

A **map layout** includes all of the elements of a stand-alone map that you might use in a PowerPoint presentation, a Word document, or a bulletin-board paper map (see Heywood, Cornelius, and Carver 2002). Figure 6-1 is a sample map layout for the Swimming Pool Case Study; it has a title, map, legend, and graphic scale. You will build this map layout later in this chapter. Here are the guidelines behind its design:

- *Make the map the largest and most prominent element of the layout:* Put a line boundary around the map (called a **neat line** by cartographers) to help draw attention to it as the central element.
- *Include a map title:* The title needs to include information minimally answering the three questions *what, where,* and *when.* In Figure 6-1, the what is "Random Sample of Pool Tag Holders' Residences," the where is "Pittsburgh, Pennsylvania," and the when is "Summer 2004." Center the title on the top of the map layout, and give it the largest font size on the map layout.
- *Include a legend for symbols:* Place it in the lower-right of the layout. There is no need to label it "Legend." Everyone will know what it is (this eliminates "chart junk").
- *Include data sources:* Maps that will be used by individuals not familiar with the mapped data need a note on the map layout stating data sources. Map users can then better judge the quality or nature of the data. However, maps for a client, such as Citiparks, may not need data sources listed because the intended map users already know that information. Thus, we did not include data sources in Figure 6-1. If, however, we determined that the map will be circulated widely, we would move the legend up an inch or so and add a note such as "Data Source: Pittsburgh Citiparks Department provided data on pools and pool tag holders' residences."
- *Ensure legibility:* Make sure that the font sizes for labels on the map and legend are large enough to read.
- *Include a graphic map scale:* If your audience might not be familiar with the area shown, then a graphic map scale is a valuable addition. Otherwise, you can omit a scale.
- *Do not include a* north *arrow unless the top of your map is not north:* Everyone knows that north is in the direction from the bottom to the top of a map. (Even cartographers in the Southern Hemisphere use north as the direction from the bottoms to the tops of their maps.)
- *Occasionally include other components as needed:* Sometimes, your map layout will need additional information, such as a data table listing, a frequency bar chart for the attribute of a choropleth map, or a photograph.

Creating New Attributes

Frequently, you will need to create new attributes in a map layer's feature attribute table. You can do this by combining the existing attributes using arithmetic or text-processing operators. *Note:* We will start using the terms "attribute" and "column" interchangeably because table operations involve columns and rows, and attributes are table columns.

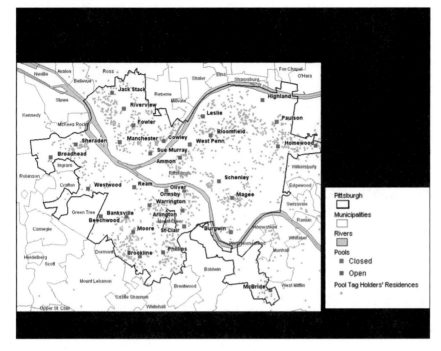

FIGURE 6-1 Map layout

To create a new attribute from one or more existing columns, you will need to insert new columns into your Excel spreadsheet. Here is an important guideline for this task:

Always insert a new blank column inside the existing feature attribute table, instead of adding a new column at the right end of the table. If you add a new column to the right, it will be outside the defined table and will not be saved. If you insert a new column within the existing columns, Excel will automatically expand the table definition area.

Usually, new attributes will be either the numeric or text data type. Let's start with numeric data type attributes. The *blockcentroids.dbf* feature attribute table has population counts for several age categories. Suppose that the Citiparks director were to tell us that he wants information on a slightly broader range of ages for pool users; namely, infants through 21-year-old people. You could meet this requirement by creating a new attribute: AGE_0_21 (AGE_0_21 = AGE_UNDER5 + AGE_5 _17 + AGE_18_21) and then use it in maps to indicate demand for pools. In Excel, you simply need to add three columns of data together, row by row, to create the new column. Figure 6-2 illustrates this calculation. The cursor is in cell Q2, so you can see its cell formula in the formula bar, =R2+S2+T2, yielding the value *1* for new attribute AGE_0_21.

Obviously, there are many other ways to combine existing attributes to create new ones. There are several additional arithmetic operators besides the plus (+) sign: The minus sign (-) for subtraction, the asterisk (*) for multiplication, the slash (/) for division, and the carat (^) for exponentiation. Most of the time, however, your needs will be simple—either adding up columns or dividing one column by another.

	Q	R	S	T
1	AGE_0_21	AGE_UNDER5	AGE_5_17	AGE_18_21
2	1	0	0	1
3	11	5	4	2
4	14	4	9	1
5	14	5	8	1
6	3	1	2	0
7	0	0	0	0
8	35	8	22	5

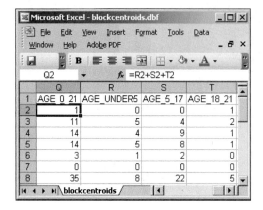

FIGURE 6-2 Summing three columns

One area for potential confusion involves operations that need to be done in a specific order. In any expression involving two or more arithmetic operators, the operations are carried out in this order: Exponentiation is first, followed by multiplication and division, and lastly by addition or subtraction—with ties broken by starting with the left-most operation and proceeding to the right. To override these rules, you must use parentheses: Any expression in parentheses is evaluated first. If there are nested parentheses, the innermost parentheses are evaluated first.

If the attributes for combination are text data type (also known as *string*), then the situation is different. For example, if you need to combine the STATE, COUNTY, TRACT, and BLOCK text attributes, then you would use the **concatenation** operator (&), which combines two or more existing text values into a single text value. See the cell formula in Figure 6-3. There you can see that concatenation "pastes" each component in order, from left to right, with no spaces between components.

	A	B	C	D	E	F
1	STATE	COUNTY	TRACT	BLOCK	BLOCKID	STFID
2	42	003	010300	1000	420030103001000	420030103001000
3	42	003	010300	1001	420030103001001	420030103001001
4	42	003	010300	1002	420030103001002	420030103001002
5	42	003	010300	1003	420030103001003	420030103001003
6	42	003	010300	1004	420030103001004	420030103001004
7	42	003	010300	1005	420030103001005	420030103001005

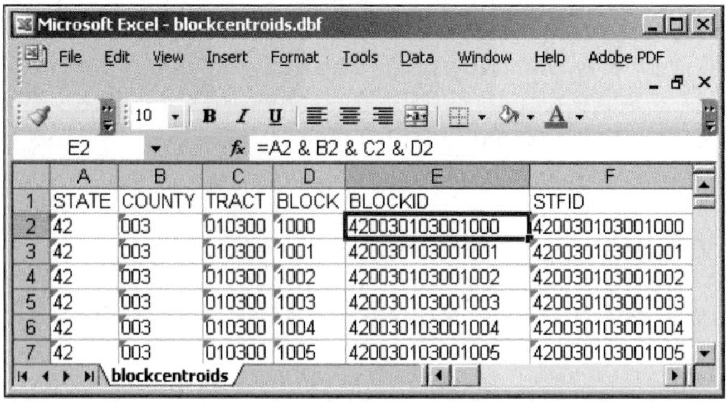

FIGURE 6-3 Concatenation of text hierarchical ID

Address Matching

Data often includes street addresses; for example, the original spreadsheet that we obtained for Pittsburgh's public swimming pools had street addresses. The question is this: How can you transform street address data into a point map layer?

The answer is to find the address on a TIGER/Line or other street-centerline map and to use coordinates found on the street segment for the location of the address's point. You can expect, however, that the exact text value for a street address in your data file and the value stored in a TIGER/Line map will be different for the same address. For example, your value might be *West Ridge Road* for the location of a retail store (exclusive of the street number, which requires special handling, as you will see later in this chapter), while the TIGER/Line map has *W Ridge Rd.* for the same location.

As a result, address-matching programs have built-in "intelligence" that provides some of the skills that your postal carrier has in interpreting addresses and delivering the mail. Mail carriers have no problem with abbreviations, but a simple matching program would not match the previous two addresses. So, when you match addresses manually in the tutorial that follows, you too may need to interpret the street addresses.

Next, let's consider a limitation of TIGER street maps. The U.S. Census Bureau designed the TIGER street-centerline maps to help take the census. The result is that street addresses are complete only to a level called **block face** (Clarke 2003, p 96). Each block-long street segment has a line graphic with coordinates and a record. Usually, there are houses or commercial buildings along both sides of a street, and each has an even or odd street address number. TIGER/Line records have only the beginning and ending address numbers for the even- and odd-numbered addresses in the block. Some example records are shown in Figure 6-4, where we show only the columns being discussed. (Attribute definitions for column headings are given in Table 3-1 in Chapter 3.) These are all of the records for *W Ridge Rd* in Allegheny County (a road near the home of one of the authors!). If you put on your address-matching hat, you can see that the first record matches *750 West Ridge Road*. The range of house numbers on the even-numbered side of the street is *700 to 856*, including our *750*. So, with this limited information available from TIGER, how can you locate the street address *750 West Ridge Road* as a point on the map?

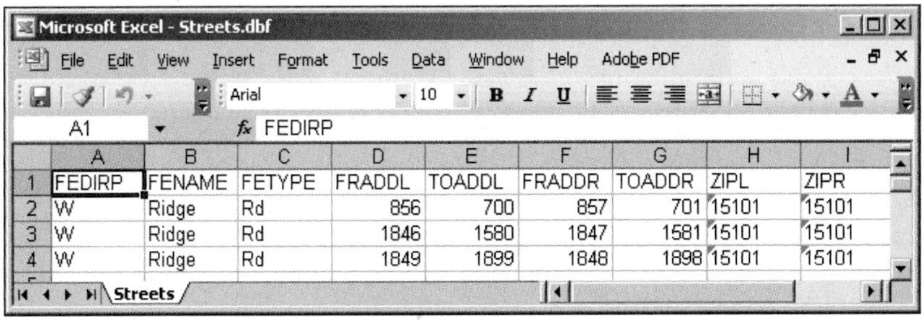

	A	B	C	D	E	F	G	H	I
1	FEDIRP	FENAME	FETYPE	FRADDL	TOADDL	FRADDR	TOADDR	ZIPL	ZIPR
2	W	Ridge	Rd	856	700	857	701	15101	15101
3	W	Ridge	Rd	1846	1580	1847	1581	15101	15101
4	W	Ridge	Rd	1849	1899	1848	1898	15101	15101

FIGURE 6-4 TIGER street centerline records

First, in ArcExplorer you can select the desired street-record data row in the feature attribute table which, in turn, automatically selects the corresponding street graphic line on the map. Next, you can zoom into the area of the selected street graphic and estimate the location of the street number. Mathematically, using linear interpolation (or the assumption that street numbers are equally distributed along the block-long street segment), 750 is 100*(750-700)/(856-700) = 32% up the street from the start of the block. For simplicity, we will have you just roughly interpolate with your eye and not do any calculations or measuring. That gets you a point on the map. If you hover your cursor over that point, you get x- and y-coordinates. We will have you save those coordinates in a database file, which ArcExplorer considers to be an *event theme* because the table has geographic coordinates. ArcExplorer can import an event theme and convert it to a permanent point shapefile.

That is how you will do address matching. On your own, you can easily address-match about 20 to 30 locations in an hour, so a team of four can comfortably do approximately 100 addresses in an hour. If you get stuck and cannot find a street, use an Internet-based map tool, such as *www.MapQuest.com* (2005), to find the address, and then you can find it on your TIGER/Line map.

Another address-matching issue is that some street names and numbers are not unique. Generally, street names and numbers are unique within any single municipality, but they may repeat across multiple municipalities. For example, *50 Main Street* probably exists in several municipalities in your county. In such a case, you need a "tie breaker" to locate a particular *50 Main Street*. The TIGER/Line street maps have zip codes for this purpose: Street addresses are usually unique within the same zip code. If you need a zip code to complete an address, you can use the U.S. Postal Service Zip Code Lookup (2005).

Table Joins

Frequently, you will obtain a map layer from one source and additional data for the mapped features from another source. If the additional data are already in a data table in some common format, it is a lot easier to add the data electronically by joining tables rather than to type all the data into the feature attribute table of the map.

Putting two tables together to make one table, a table join, is a common task. Our needs in GIS are simple: We need to join two tables, one-to-one, by row. This means that for every row of data in one table, we expect to find one—and only one—matching row in the other table. The major question at this point is this: How can you match records?

The answer is that each table must have the same **primary key**. This is an attribute, or column, that has two properties:

1. Each value in the column is unique. There are no duplicates of the same value in different rows.
2. There are no **null values**, which refers to cells that are missing values or that never were assigned values. Note that a null value is not the same as 0 or a blank space that was entered in the cell—both a 0 and a blank are values.

The BLOCKID attribute in Figure 6-3 is a primary key for any table of block data for the U.S.: The concatenated STATE, COUNTY, TRACT, and BLOCK values of BLOCKID make it unique, and there are no null values. Sometimes a table has two or more columns that have the properties needed to be a primary key. Then, one such column is designated to be the primary key and the other qualifying columns are called **candidate keys**. You can use matching candidate keys from two tables as well as the designated primary keys to join them.

Figure 6-5 shows an example of a table join. It shows the two input tables—the feature attribute table for the Allegheny County blocks with file name *tgr42003blk00.dbf*, and the Census Bureau data table with name *tgr42000sf1blk.dbf*. It also shows the resultant output table, *Blocks.dbf*. Notice that the *Blocks.dbf* table contains, in sequence, the columns of table *tgr42003blk00.dbf* and then those of table *tgr42000sf1blk.dbf*. The column STFID is the primary key, and it is repeated in columns A and E of table *Blocks.dbf*.

tgr42003blk00.dbf

	A	B	C
1	STFID	TRACT2000	BLOCK2000
2	420030103001000	010300	1000
3	420030103001001	010300	1001
4	420030103001002	010300	1002
5	420030103001003	010300	1003
6	420030103001004	010300	1004

tgr42003blk00

+

tgr42000sf1blk.dbf

	E	F	G	H
1	STFID	POP2000	WHITE	BLACK
2	420010301011000	2	2	0
3	420010301011001	41	40	0
4	420010301011002	55	55	0
5	420010301011003	85	82	0
6	420010301011004	36	36	0

tgr42000sf1blk

=

Blocks.dbf

	A	B	C	D	E	F	G
1	STFID	TRACT2000	BLOCK2000	STFID	POP2000	WHITE	BLACK
2	420030103001000	010300	1000	420010301011000	2	2	0
3	420030103001001	010300	1001	420010301011001	41	40	0
4	420030103001002	010300	1002	420010301011002	55	55	0
5	420030103001003	010300	1003	420010301011003	85	82	0
6	420030103001004	010300	1004	420010301011004	36	36	0

Blocks

FIGURE 6-5 Table join

For GIS, one of the input tables becomes the output joined table; namely, the feature attribute table. This does not cause any difficulties, but you will need to follow guidelines:

- *To finish the join, the result of which is seen in Figure 6-6, delete one of the duplicate primary key columns:* Data tables must have unique column names. Duplicate columns will lead to failure later, when data is processed. Delete the duplicate column on the right, column E, in Figure 6-5 to preserve the original primary key in the feature attribute table.
- *Never change the order of the rows in a shapefile's feature attribute table:* If you do, you will scramble the data and graphic features, and you will have a nonsense map layer as the result. Shapefile-format map layers depend on the physical order of rows in the feature attribute table for linking to graphic features. To preserve the original row order of a feature attribute table, add a new column to the table with a sequence number when first opening the table in Excel. Then, check before saving that the row order has not changed. If it has, sort the rows by the sequence number.

MICROSOFT SOFTWARE FOR EXTENSIONS

This chapter has fewer Practice exercises than in earlier chapters because when you're using several software packages, it's often difficult to interrupt your work to perform another task. Thus, we include Practice exercises that do not interrupt your work and also add value. Sometimes, you must complete a Practice exercise for use in following tutorial steps, and we will point out such instances.

Map Layouts Using ArcExplorer, Paint, and PowerPoint

Your work begins with opening ArcExplorer, arranging and exporting a map, and then getting a screen print of ArcExplorer's program window. Then, you will paste the screen print into Microsoft Paint (Win) or AppleWorks (Mac), clip out the map's legend, and clean it up by erasing some extra lines. With that done, you'll use PowerPoint to assemble the map and the legend, and then add features such as a title, a neat line for the map, and a graphic scale. See Figure 6-1 for the finished product.

1. Start ArcExplorer, open **c:\LearningAndUsingGIS\Queries.axl** (Win) or **/LearningAndUsingGIS/QueriesMac.axl** (Mac), and zoom into **Pittsburgh**.
2. Turn on only the following layers and arrange them in the order given, from the top down: **Pittsburgh**, **Municipalities**, **Rivers**, **Pools**, and **Pool Tag Holders' Residences**.
3. Drag the **sizing line** between the Layers and Map panels to the right so that you can see the entire Pool Tag Holders' Residences label in the Layers panel. See Figure 6-6.
4. Click **File**, click **Export to Image . . .**, and then click the **Export** button at the lower right of the resulting Export window.
5. In the Save in field in the resulting Export window, browse to **c:\LearningAndUsingGIS\Outputs** (Win) or browse to **LearningAndUsingGIS/Outputs** (Mac), click the **list arrow** in the Files of type (Win) or File Format (Mac) field, click **JPEG**, enter **PittsburghMap** in the File name field (Win) or Save As field (Mac), click **Save**, and then close the **original Export** window. *(That saves your map as an image file so it can be pasted into any document.)*
6. Click the word **Layers** at the top of the layers panel to take the reverse video off any layer that may be selected.
7. Press your **PrtSc** key (Win) or **Command + Shift + 3** keys (Mac). *(That action places a copy of the entire screen on the clipboard.)*
8. Click the **Start** button, **All Programs**, **Accessories**, **Paint** (Win) or click **Finder**, **Applications**, double-click the **AppleWorks 6** folder, click **AppleWorks**, and select **Painting** (Mac).
9. Click **Edit**, and then click **Paste** (Win) or click **File**, click **Insert**, change the File Format to **All Available**, select the file that is your screen shot, and then click the **Insert** button (Mac). *(This pastes the ArcExplorer screen capture into Paint (Win) or AppleWorks (Mac).)*
10. Close ArcExplorer without saving the map project.

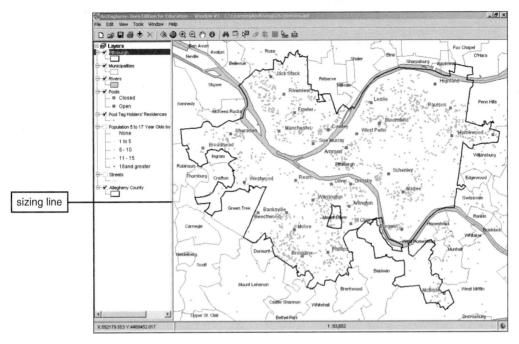

sizing line

FIGURE 6-6   Map composition for export

Next, you will need to do some image processing in Paint (Win) or AppleWorks (Mac).

1. Click the **Select** button in Paint (Win) or the **Selection Rectangle Tool** in Apple-Works (Mac). *(This releases the dotted "select" line around the entire image and allows you to make a new selection for cropping the image.)*

2. Drag a **rectangle** around the desired part of the legend from the Layers panel for all layers that are turned on, and then release your mouse button. See Figure 6-7.

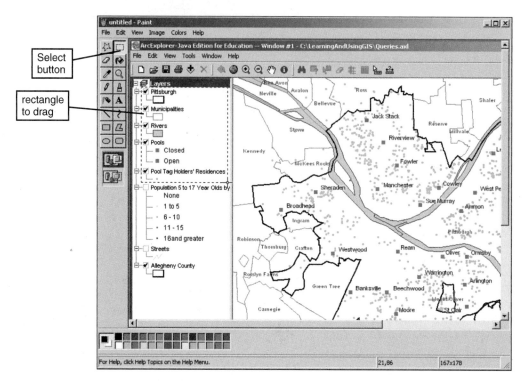

FIGURE 6-7 Clipping the legend

3. In the top horizontal menu in Paint (Win) or AppleWorks (Mac) *(and not the ArcExplorer screen print)*, click **Edit**, and then click **Cut**.

4. Click **File**, **New**, **No**, **Edit**, **Paste** (Win) or click **File**, **New**, **Painting**, then click **Edit** on the menu bar and click **Paste** (Mac). See Figure 6-8. *(That results in just the legend portion of the original screen print in Paint (Win) or Apple-Works (Mac). You can change the size of the image through experimentation, if you wish, using Image, Attributes... and changing the width. The image we created is 192 pixels wide.)*

5. Click **View**, **Zoom**, **Large Size** (Win), or click the **image size** button in the bottom-left corner of the AppleWorks window, type **300** in the View scale box, and click **OK** (Mac); then click the **Eraser/Color Eraser** button.

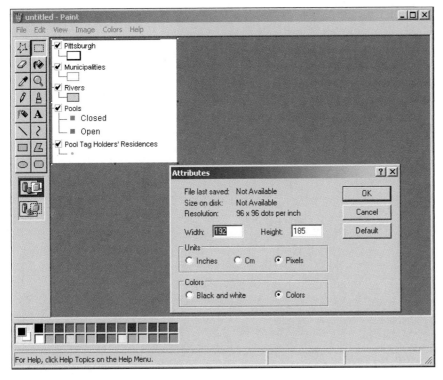

FIGURE 6-8 The clipped legend

6. Carefully position the eraser's **square cursor** over an area to erase and click your mouse button. See Figure 6-9. *(You can drag the cursor along to erase, but be careful. To start all over, click Edit, Undo.)*

7. Continue to erase all extra pixels, as seen in Figure 6-9 for the Pittsburgh map layer, and then click **View, Zoom, Normal Size** (Win), or click the **image size** button in the bottom-left corner of the AppleWorks window and click **100%** (Mac). See Figure 6-10.

8. Click **File, Save As...**, browse to **c:\LearningAndUsingGIS\Outputs** in the Save in field, enter **PittsburghMapLegend** in the File name field, (Win) or **Save As: field** (Mac), click the **list arrow** in the **Save as type** field (Win) or **File Format** (Mac) and click **JPEG**, click **Save** (Win) or **Save** and then **OK** (Mac), and then close **Paint** (Win) or **AppleWorks** (Mac). *(That completes the legend.)*

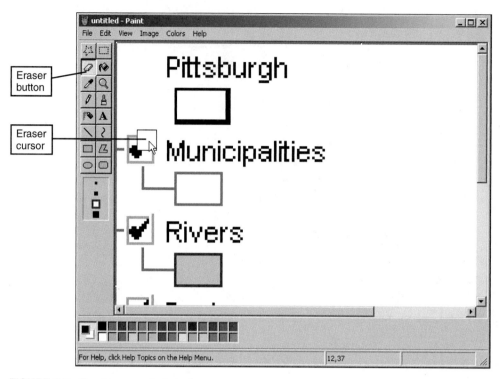

FIGURE 6-9   Erasing unwanted pixels

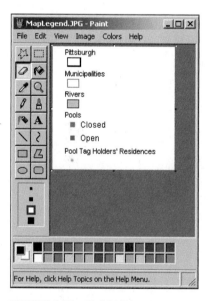

FIGURE 6-10   Finished legend

Finally, you get to use PowerPoint to put the map layout together.

1. Click **Start**, **All Programs**, **Microsoft Office**, **Microsoft Office PowerPoint 2003** (Win) or **Finder**, **Applications**, **Microsoft Office**, **PowerPoint** (Mac).
2. Click **Format**, **Slide Layout**, and then click the **blank template** in the right panel. See Figure 6-11.

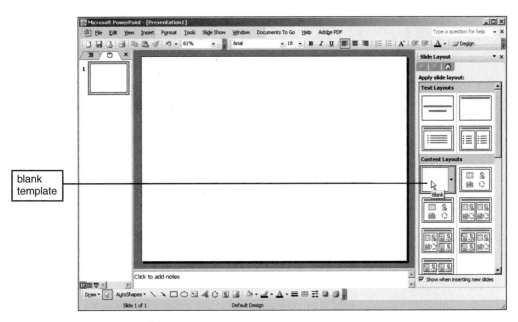

blank template

FIGURE 6-11 Formatting slide layout

3. Close the **Slide Layout** and **left** panels (Win) or click the **Slide View** button on the bottom left (Mac), leaving just the blank slide on the screen.
4. Click **Insert**, **Picture**, **From File...**, browse to **c:\LearningAndUsingGIS\ Outputs** (Win) or **/LearningAndUsingGIS/Outputs** (Mac), click **PittsburghMap.JPG**, and then click **Insert**.
5. Click and drag **a corner of the map image** to resize it to about 60% of the slide area.
6. Position your **cursor** over the map, click and drag to position the map down and left on the slide, but retain a good left margin. See Figure 6-12.
7. Click **File**, **Save**, browse to **c:\LearningAndUsingGIS\Outputs** (Win) or **/LearningAndUsingGIS/Outputs** (Mac), enter **PittsburghMapLayout.ppt** in the File name field (Win) or **Save As** field (Mac), and then click **Save**.

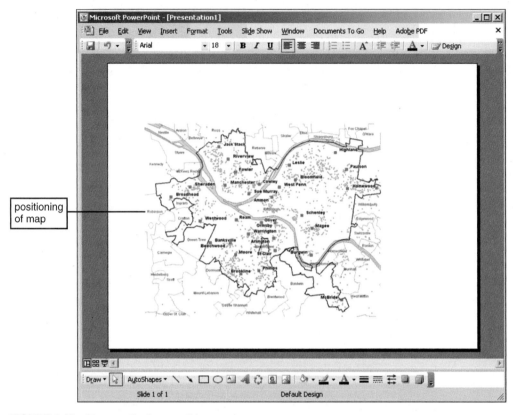

FIGURE 6-12 Map positioning on slide

PRACTICE 6-1

Repeat Steps 4 through 6, with appropriate modifications, to insert *PittsburghMapLegend.jpg* and place it to the right of the map. The bottom of the legend should align with the bottom of the map.

Next, you will add some finishing touches. First, you'll add the title, then the neat line, and finally the graphic scale. Your finished product should look like the map layer shown in Figure 6-13.

1. Click **View**, **Toolbars**, **Drawing** to turn on the drawing toolbar at the bottom (Win) or left side (Mac) of the PowerPoint window, if it is not already on.
2. Click the **Text Box** button, click at the top of the slide, and enter **Random Sample of Pool Tag Holders' Residences:** (press Enter for a new line) **Pittsburgh, Pennsylvania, Summer 2004**, select the text you just entered, and then click the **Bold** button.

3. Click the **Rectangle** button, drag a rectangle around **the map**, and then release the mouse button. *(The rectangle will cover up your map, but in the next step, you'll give the rectangle transparent fill to fix this. Also, the rectangle will need better alignment with your map, so you will fix that as well.)*
4. Click the **list arrow** on the **Fill Color** button, and then click **No Fill**.
5. Press and hold down your **Alt** (Win) or **Option** (Mac) key to override graphics snapping to the invisible grid in PowerPoint, click a **circular grab handle** on the rectangle's border, and then drag to align the rectangle with the map's edge.
6. Click the **Line** button on the drawing toolbar, and then drag **a line from left to right** across the widest part of the municipality of **Rankin**. *(We measured in ArcExplorer until we found a feature that was one mile wide for use in building a graphic scale.)*
7. Drag down the **line** you just drew below the right side of the map.
8. Click **View**, **Zoom...**, the **200%** option button, **OK**, and draw two short vertical lines on either end of the horizontal line of the graphic scale.
9. Click the **Text Box** button, click under your graphic scale, change the font size to **10**, enter **1 mile**, and then press **Enter**. See Figure 6-13.

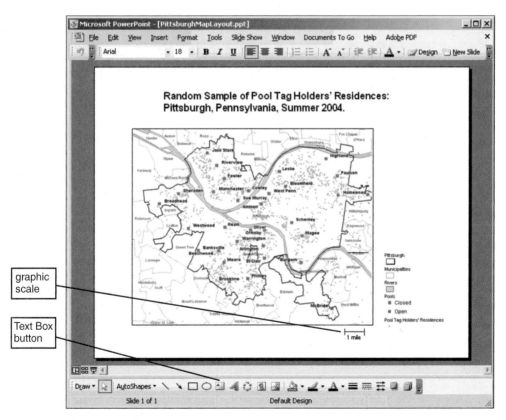

FIGURE 6-13 Creating the graphic scale

10. Click **View, Zoom...**, the **66%** option button, and then click **OK**.
11. Click **File, Save**, and then close **PowerPoint**.

New Feature Attributes Using Excel

In the next set of steps, you will create the new attribute, AGE_0_21, (AGE_0_21 = AGE_UNDER5 + AGE_5_17 + AGE_18_21). You will be working with a very large data table, so there may be delays while your computer processes the data.

1. Start **Excel** and then click **File, Open....**
2. In the Open window, browse to **c:\LearningAndUsingGIS\Maps** (Win) or **/LearningAndUsingGIS/Maps/** (Mac), click the **list arrow** in the **Files of type** field (Win) or **Enable** field (Mac), scroll down and click **dBase File (*.dbf)** (Win) or **All Documents** (Mac), click **blockcentroids**, and then click **Open**.
3. Click the **gray selector cell** in the upper-left corner of the sheet to select all cells, and then double-click **the line between the A and B header cells** to automatically size all the columns so you can read all the values. See Figure 6-14.

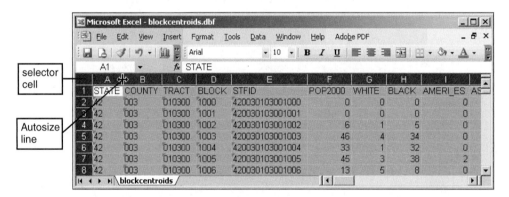

FIGURE 6-14 Autosizing columns

4. Scroll to the right in the spreadsheet until you can see at least **AGE_UNDER5** through **AGE_18_21**, click on the **gray cell Q** above AGE_UNDER5, and then click **Insert**, and click **Columns**.
5. Click in cell **Q1**, enter **AGE_0_21**, and then press **Enter**.
6. Click in cell **Q2**, enter **= R2+S2+T2**, and then press **Enter**. See Figure 6-15. *(That yields the correct sum of 0 in this case. Next, you will copy this cell formula to the remaining cells in the Q column.)*

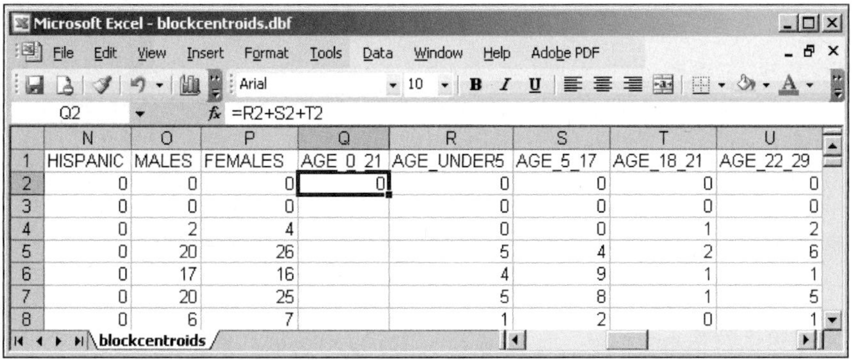

FIGURE 6-15 Entering a cell formula

7. Click in cell **Q2**, click **Edit**, and then **Copy**.
8. Click in cell **Q3**, hold your **Shift** key down, click and hold the **scroll slider** at the right of the spreadsheet, drag it down to the bottom of the spreadsheet to row 24284, click in cell **Q24284**, and then click **Edit**, **Paste**. See Figure 6-16. *(That finishes the task of creating the new attribute.)*

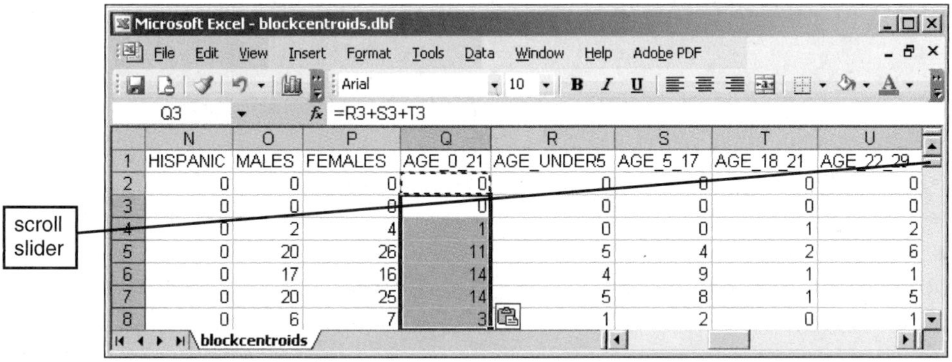

FIGURE 6-16 Pasting a formula

9. Click **File**, **Save**, **Replace** (Mac only), **Yes** (keep the DBF4 file format), and leave Excel open to this spreadsheet.

(Note that the next Practice exercise is needed to complete the remainder of the tutorial, so be sure to do it.)

Create another new attribute, P5_17YOUTH in *blockcentroids.dbf* —P5_17YOUTH = AGE_5_17/AGE_0_21 (or =T2/R2 in the first data row)—which is the fraction of youth aged 0 to 21 who are 5 to 17 years old. Save your results as a DBF4 file, and then close Excel. The following hints will help you to get the desired output.

1. Ignore the resulting #DIV/0! code for the first data row, and copy it as if it were a legitimate value throughout the rest of the new column. The formula will calculate legitimate values.

2. To replace the #DIV/0! code values with 0s, use the following steps:
   - After you create the column for P5_17YOUTH, create another new blank column to the right of it.
   - Select and copy the entire P5_17YOUTH column, click in the top cell of the new blank column, click Edit, Paste Special, click the Values option button, and then click OK.
   - Delete the original P5_17YOUTH column, and use the Replace function on the copy you just pasted. Click Edit, Replace..., enter #DIV/0! in the Find what field, enter 0 in the Replace with field, click Replace All, and then click Close. Excel should make 6116 replacements. The Replace function will work on the new column but not the old column, because the #DIV/0! codes for dividing by 0 were not stored values in the original version, but they are in the pasted version.

3. When you have a new column created and selected, click Format, Cells..., Number in the Category panel, enter 4 in the Decimal places field, and then click OK. This will let you see the results, which will be 0 or fractions.

4. Save your results and close Excel.

Address Matching Using Excel and ArcExplorer

The process of turning street address data, such as *5000 Forbes Ave, Pittsburgh, PA 15213* (our university's mailing address), into a point on the map requires several steps in ArcExplorer. They include sorting the feature attribute table for streets by street name, finding the right street segment, looking at it on the map, hovering over the right point to get coordinates, entering coordinates into an Excel spreadsheet, and finally, adding the spreadsheet to ArcExplorer as an event theme.

1. Start **ArcExplorer** and leave its window unmaximized for convenience.

2. Click the **Add Data...** button, and in the resultant Content Chooser window, browse to **c:\LearningAndUsingGIS\Maps** (Win) or **/LearningAndUsingGIS/ Maps** (Mac), click **streetspartial.shp**, and then click **OK**. *(The* streetspartial. shp *file is a portion of the* streets.shp *map layer that you have been using. We cut it down to speed up processing because ArcExplorer's Attribute Table is slow to load.)*

3. Right-click (Win) or control-click (Mac) **streetspartial** in the Layers panel, and then click **Attribute Table**.

4. Make the resultant table wide, and make some of the first three or four columns narrow so you can see **FENAME** through **TOADDR**.

5. Right-click (Win) or control-click (Mac) **FRADDL** (from address left side of street), and then click **Sort Ascending**; then do the same for **FENAME**. *(ArcExplorer first puts all the streets in order by their street numbers and then uses this as the starting point to sort by the name. The end result is a very nice sort by name and then street number. Note: This step does not change the order of rows in the stored streets shapefile; it merely changes their order in the computer screen display.)*

6. Start Excel, open **c:\UsingAndLearningGIS\Maps\Universities.dbf**, and rearrange your desktop similar to that shown in Figure 6-17. *(This is a database table with some Pittsburgh universities and their addresses. You will fill in the X and Y columns.)*

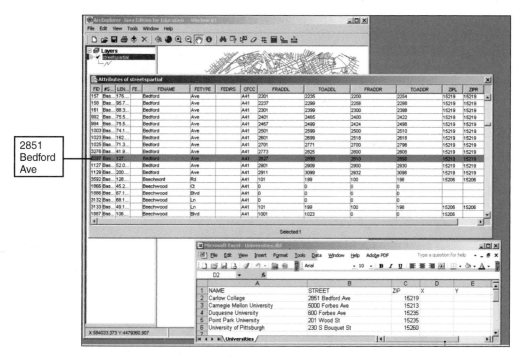

FIGURE 6-17 Reviewing a street record

7. Scroll down in the **Attributes of streetspartial** table until you find the record that contains **2851 Bedford Ave**, and then click it. See Figure 6-17. *(Note that the street segment is selected on the map, in the blue selection color.)*

(Note that the next Practice exercise is needed to complete the remainder of the tutorial, so be sure to do it.)

The next step is to get coordinates for each address from the map.

1. Close the Attributes of streetspartial table. *(Even with this table closed, your selections from Practice Exercise 6-3 persist in the table and map with the five selected street segments in the blue selection color.)*
2. Zoom into the **left-most selected street segment** (which is the 200-block of Wood St), click the **Identify** tool, and then click the **street segment on either side** to determine the direction in which street numbers increase. See Figures 6-18 and 6-19. *(From this you can roughly determine where 201 Wood St should be: On the lower end.)*

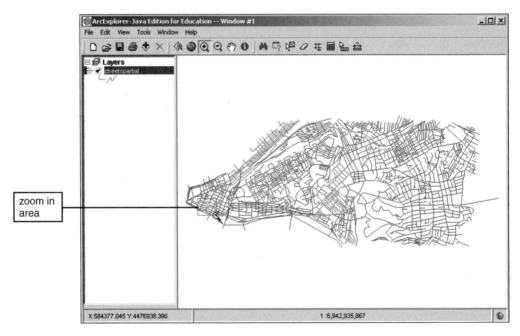

FIGURE 6-18 Rectangle to drag for zoom in

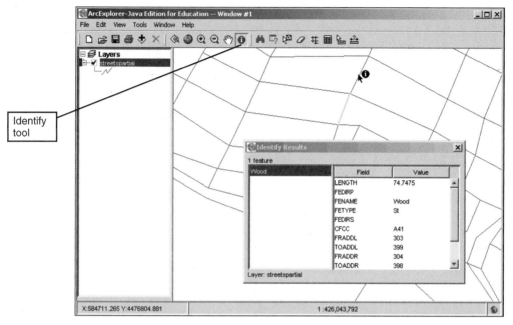

FIGURE 6-19 Identified street segment

3. Hover your cursor over roughly where you think the address should be, and make a note of the **x and y coordinates**. *(We get x=584676.797, y=4476720. 739, and yours should be similar.)*

4. Switch to the Excel spreadsheet, and then enter these x- and y-coordinates for Point Park University.

(Note that the next Practice exercise is needed to complete the remainder of the tutorial, so be sure to do it.)

PRACTICE 6-4

- Continue to zoom in and out of the map to get coordinates for each of the selected street segments you found in Practice 6-3, and enter them into the spreadsheet.
- When you are finished, save your file in a DBF4 format, and then close Excel.

There is just one more step: Add the finished event theme *(universities.dbf)* to the map. When you do this, ArcExplorer automatically converts the event theme to a permanent shapefile.

1. Zoom your **map out** so you can see all of the streets.
2. Click **View**, and then click **Add Event Theme**.

3. In the resulting Add Event Theme window, click the **Browse** button to the right of the **Table** field, and browse to **c:\LearningAndUsingGIS\Maps\ Universities.dbf** (Win) or **/LearningAndUsingGIS/Maps/Universities.dbf** (Mac), and then click **Open**. See Figure 6-20. *(ArcExplorer automatically figures out that your coordinates are the attributes X and Y.)*

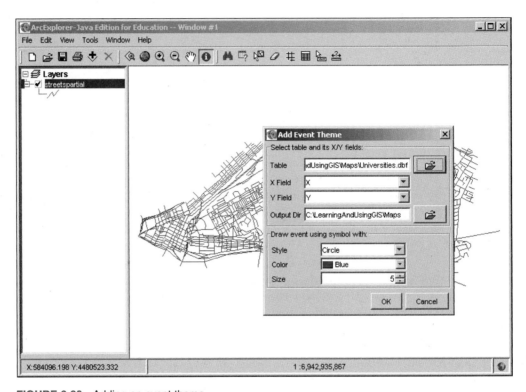

FIGURE 6-20 Adding an event theme

4. Leave the default value in the **Output Dir** field, change Size to **8**, and then click **OK**. *(ArcExplorer creates the Universities_ shapefile and adds it to your project.)*
5. Close ArcExplorer.

Table Joins Using Excel

We downloaded the Allegheny County zip code map from the U.S. Census Bureau for the Swimming Pool Case Study. We obtained counts of pool tags by zip code in a separate file from a consultant working for Pittsburgh's Citiparks Department. Then we joined the consultant's data to the zip code feature attribute table to complete the zip code map layer. In this section, you will do the same task. The two inputs are: (1) the feature attribute table, called *zips.dbf* and (2) the consultant's data file, called *ziptags.csv* (where .csv is the file extension for **comma separated values**, a common file format for transferring data).

The first task is to open the feature attribute table and to add a sequence number attribute, so you can be sure to maintain its original row order in the finished product. Table joining requires sorting each table by the primary key (in this case, the 5-digit zip code), which changes the order of rows in the feature attribute table. After joining the tables, you can sort the product table by the sequence number to re-establish the needed, original order of the feature attribute table.

One important note: The zip code column has some duplicates with more than one row having the same zip code. This is because some zip code areas have more than one polygon! So zip code is not *truly* a primary key; nevertheless, you will be able to work around this problem and make the join, as we will explain. We had no other choice but to use zip code as the basis of the join—real-world projects often confront us with complications that we must handle in creative ways!

1. Start **Excel** and click **File, Open...**, browse to **c:\LearningAndUsingGIS\Maps** (Win) or **/LearningAndUsingGIS/Maps** (Mac). In the resulting Open window, change the **Files of type** field (Win) or **Enable** field (Mac) to **All Files(*.*)**, scroll to the right, click **zips.dbf** *(and not zipcodes.dbf)*, and then click **Open**.
2. Click in the **gray column selector cell C** to highlight that column, and then click **Insert, Columns**. *(This creates a new column C.)*
3. In new cell C1, enter **SEQUENCE**, in cell C2 enter **1**, and in cell C3 enter **2**.
4. Click in cell **C2**, hold down your **Shift** key, click in cell **C3**, and release your mouse button. See Figure 6-21. *(This selects cells C2 and C3.)*

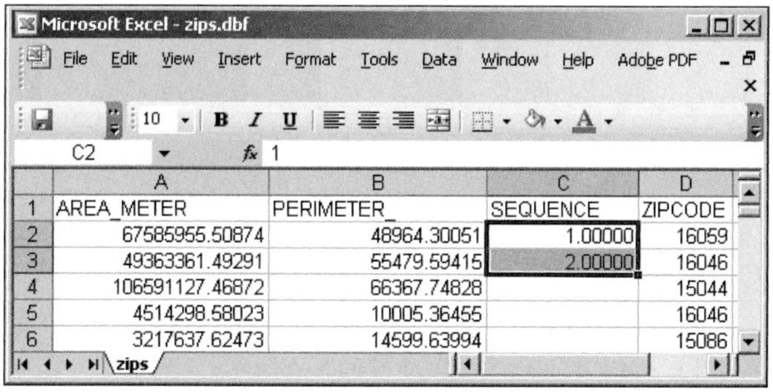

FIGURE 6-21 Creating a sequence number

5. Click and hold down your mouse button on the **grab handle** in the lower-right area of the two selected cells, drag your mouse all the way down to the bottom of the column (**row 118**), and release. *(If you overshoot and go down too far, just keep your mouse button down and reverse direction until you get to the correct cell. This creates a sequence number for rows with the original order of data rows.)*
6. Scroll to the right to the lower-right cell of the spreadsheet, click in cell **D118**, scroll to the top left corner of the spreadsheet, hold down your Shift key and click in cell **A1**. *(This selects the entire spreadsheet with data.)*

7. Click **Data**, click **Sort**, and in the resulting Sort window, click the **list arrow** in the Sort by field, scroll down, click **ZIPCODE**, and then click **OK**.
8. Scroll to the top of the spreadsheet. See Figure 6-22.

(Note that the next Practice exercise is needed to complete the remainder of the tutorial, so be sure to do it.)

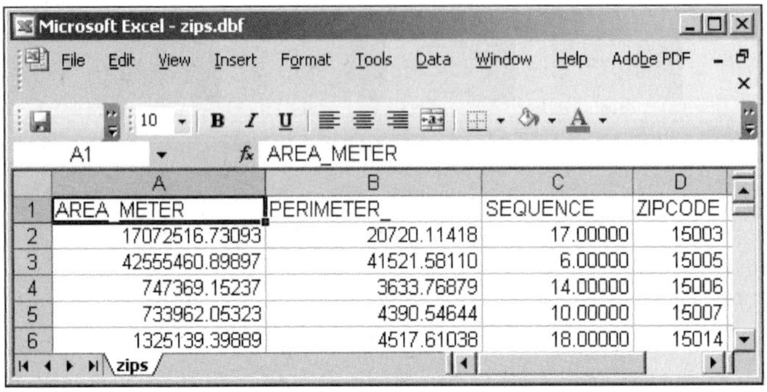

FIGURE 6-22   Data sorted by zip code

PRACTICE 6-5

Repeat Steps 1-8 for the data table *ziptags.csv*.
- In Excel, with *zips.dbf* still open, click File, Open..., navigate to *ziptags.csv*, and click Open.
- Sort by zip code, and leave Excel open.

The next task is to prepare *ziptags.csv* for joining. The major issue is zip codes that have two polygons in *zips.dbf* (there are none with three or more). Your first task is to create duplicate rows for the corresponding zip codes in *ziptags.csv* so the data table will match, row-by-row, with the zip code feature attribute table. You will simply enter the total number of pool tags in both rows that have duplicate zip codes. This practice results in a correct choropleth map: Both polygons of a single zip code show their combined number of pool tags.

1. Click the row selector for row **26** on the left of the *ziptags.csv* spreadsheet to select that row. *(This is a row that needs to be duplicated.)*
2. Click **Insert**, and then click **rows**. *(Excel inserts a new row above row 26.)*
3. Click the row selector for the same row again, now row **27**.
4. Click **Edit**, and then click **Copy**.
5. Click the row selector for row **26**, click **Edit**, and then click **Paste**. See Figure 6-23. *(That takes care of the first of nine such rows that need duplicates.)*

(Note that the next Practice exercise is needed to complete the remainder of the tutorial, so be sure to do it.)

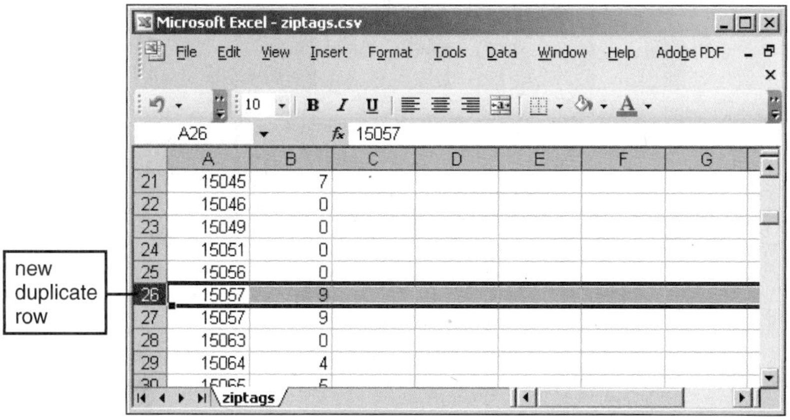

new
duplicate
row

FIGURE 6-23   Duplicating a row

PRACTICE 6-6

Repeat Steps 1 through 5 for the rows of the following zip codes: 15101, 15129, 15132, 15207, 15219, 15233, 15236, and 16046. Your finished table should have 118 rows. Leave Excel open when you are finished.

All preparation is complete. Next you will create the join, which you will accomplish by copying and pasting *ziptags.csv* into *zips.dbf*.

1. In Excel, click **Window**, and then click **zips.dbf**.
2. Click the column selector for column **D**, click **Insert**, click **Columns**, and then again click **Insert**, and then click **Columns**. *(This action inserts two new columns into the middle of* zips.dbf. *Recall that if you add new columns on to the end of the table, Excel will not save those columns.)*
3. Click **Window**, click **ziptags.csv**, scroll down to the bottom of the sheet (row **118**), click cell **B118**, scroll to the **top** of the spreadsheet, hold down your **Shift** key, and then click in cell **A1**. *(This selects all the data.)*
4. Click **Edit**, **Copy**.
5. Click **Window**, **zips.dbf**, click cell **D1**, **Edit**, **Paste**. *(That pastes and joins the data to the feature attribute table.)*
6. Scroll down the resulting table to check whether zip codes from both tables match. See Figure 6-24. *(If they do not match, see whether you can find the problem: Click Edit, Undo Paste, correct the problem in* ziptags.csv, *and repeat the paste process.)*

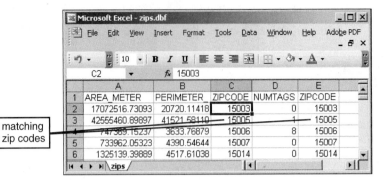

FIGURE 6-24 Matched-up zip code columns

7. Click the column selector for column **E** to select that column. *(This is an extra copy of zip codes, which you will next delete.)*
8. Click **Edit**, and then click **Delete**.
9. Scroll to the bottom of the *zips.dbf* (row **118**), click in the lower, right hand corner, cell **E118**, scroll to the top of the spreadsheet, hold down your **Shift** key, and then click in cell **A1**.
10. Click **Data**, click **Sort...**, choose **SEQUENCE** for the Sort by field, click the **Ascending** button, and then click **OK**. *(That places the feature attribute table in its original row sequence.)*
11. Click the column selector for column **C** to select the SEQUENCE column, click **Edit**, and then click **Delete**.
12. Click **File**, click **Save**, and click **Yes** to save the file.
13. Close Excel.

Chapter 6 Summary

Work on almost any significant computer project today requires using several programs, and GIS projects are no exception. Although GIS projects have GIS software at their core, you might need additional software for some analyses. Using ArcExplorer often entails adding additional software to extend ArcExplorer's capabilities. Because ArcExplorer is free, its capabilities are limited, especially when compared to a commercial GIS package, such as ArcView. This chapter demonstrated extending ArcExplorer by using Microsoft Excel, PowerPoint, and Paint.

A map layout is an arrangement of several graphic and text components yielding a stand-alone document suitable for interpretation and use by anyone who views it. Not only does a map layout have a map, but it also has a descriptive title, a legend for interpretation of symbols, and a graphic scale. You can use ArcExplorer to produce the map and legend, Paint or a similar image-processing package for some graphic clean-up work, and PowerPoint for assembling all the pieces and adding others. The end result is a pleasing and useful map layout.

Feature attribute tables generally include useful attributes for mapping and querying. Often-times, though, the map designer needs to create new attributes from existing ones. Generally, this involves adding some columns of data or dividing one column by another. Excel makes this task easy.

There are relatively few point-map layers available for downloading and use. Often, though, you can create your own point layer from data tables that have street addresses by using a street-centerline map layer, such as are available from the TIGER maps. Address matching takes an address, looks it up in the street feature attribute table, gets coordinates from the street map, and uses those coordinates to create a point. In a commercial GIS package, such as ArcView, address matching uses sophisticated matching programs that have built-in "intelligence," similar to that of your postal carrier (who can find an address written on an envelope, even if it has spelling errors and other problems). With ArcExplorer, you have to do the matching yourself and must use your common sense or knowledge of an area to do the matching.

One last extension for ArcExplorer is to join tables. For example, it is common to encounter tabular data that includes zip codes. To use such data in a GIS, you need to join them to a zip code map's feature attribute table. The join is one-to-one because we expect a single zip code data record for every zip code on the map. (We saw that zip codes are slightly more complicated but were able to handle the problem.) You were able to make a table join using Excel and its data sorting, copying, and pasting capabilities.

Key Terms

Address matching   The process of placing points in a new map layer by matching user-supplied addresses with street segments in street-centerline map layers. The process uses fuzzy matching to accommodate spelling, abbreviation, and address component placement variations between the user-supplied address and the street-centerline equivalent.

Block face   A level of resolution for street address data on block-long street segments. In TIGER/Line street-centerline maps, only the beginning and ending street numbers on the left and right sides of the segment are recorded.

Candidate keys   A column in a data table that has unique values and no missing or null values. If there are two or more such columns, just one is designated as the primary key.

Comma separated values A simple data format used to transfer data from one package or computer system to another. Each data value is separated, or delimited, with commas.

Concatenation A process in which two or more text values are combined to become a single value.

Map layout A composition of map, legend, title, graphic scale, and other components that allows anyone viewing it to be able to use and interpret the map correctly.

Neat line A rectangle drawn around the map in a map layout to make the map attractive and prominent.

Null value A cell in a data table that does not have a value. Often a special, non-printing symbol is used to denote such a cell.

Primary key A column in a data table that has unique and non-null values and that has been designated to be the primary identifier of rows.

Table join A process that combines two tables, row by row, to create a new table. Often rows are matched using a primary key.

Short-Answer Questions

1. When would it be important to use an overview map in a map layout? A north arrow?

2. Suppose that you need to create a new column in a feature attribute table: X=100*B+C/T where X is a percentage, B is the acres of farmland planted in corn, C is the number of acres planted in soybeans, and T is the total number of acres in production. What is the error in this expression, and how could it be fixed?

3. Suppose that you have a data table of male business owners and have attributes and values such as SALUTATION='Mr', LASTNAME='Smith', and FIRSTNAME='Al'. Write an expression to concatenate these attributes into an attribute called FULLNAME, including the salutation. Do the same for HOUSENUMBER=123, STREETNAME='Oak', STREET TYPE='Ave', STREETDIRECTION='E' to yield the attribute STREETADDRESS. *Hint:* To include blank spaces, you have to concatenate blanks explicitly; for example, SALUTATION & ' ' & concatenates a space after SALUTATION.

4. Suppose that you have addresses that include intersections, such as *Forbes Ave* and *Craig St.* How would you use ArcExplorer to address-match such data?

5. Suppose that you have address data, such as *333 Pine Ave*, and you are viewing the feature attribute table for a TIGER/Line, street-centerline map layer. Suppose further that there are six rows of data for *Pine Ave*, but a few of them are missing house numbers, including the 300 block. What might you do to approximately locate the address in spite of this problem?

6. Is it possible to have more than one point feature with the same coordinates? How could address matching lead to such an occurrence? *Hint:* Think about address-matching events such as deliveries of appliances to residences or crime incidents.

7. Suppose that you are joining a zip code data table that has a record with a zip code not in your feature attribute table. What happens to that record in the joined table?

8. If you change the order of rows in a map layer's feature attribute table, it scrambles the data on the map. Each mapped point will have the wrong data. Explain why this is the case for shapefiles.

9. Explain what block-face resolution is in TIGER/Line street maps and what consequences it has for address matching.

10. Suppose that you have a three-person team, and you want to address-match 250 retail stores, the addresses for which you got from *www.smartpages.com* for a city. Make a plan for all of the steps needed to produce the final *stores_shp* map layer.

Exercises

1. **Building a Map Layout for the Director of Pittsburgh Citiparks.** You may recall that the director of Citiparks wanted us to prepare some PowerPoint slides for him to convince officials from nearby municipalities to help pay for McBride Pool's operating expenses. Many pool tag holders reside in neighboring municipalities outside of Pittsburgh. Prepare a zoomed-in map layout that makes the director's point.

   a. Start with one of the ArcExplorer maps that we created for you, *Pools.axl* or *Queries.axl*. Save your map file as *McBride<YourName>.axl* in the Outputs folder.

   b. Be sure to think about what layers you should include, and use all of the guidelines included in this chapter for map layouts. Do not include a graphic scale.

   c. Query pool-tag-holder residences that indicated McBride as their intended pool, which will automatically highlight them with yellow point markers. Create a buffer around McBride Pool as a visual guide to emphasize pool tag holders near the pool.

   d. Save your map layout as the PowerPoint presentation called *Exercise1 <YourName>.ppt*.

2. **Create New Zip Code Attributes for Number of Tag Holders per Unit Area.** This exercise has you create two new variables for the ZipCodes map layer and then prepare a corresponding map in ArcExplorer.

   a. Create the two new variables in *ZipCodes.dbf* using Excel:

   ```
   AREA_MILE = 0.000000386091*AREA_METER

   TAGSNORM = NUMTAGS/AREA_MILE
   ```

   b. Start ArcExplorer and create a new map. Add two copies of the *ZipCodes.shp* map layer and create two choropleth maps: one for NUMTAGS and the other for TAGSNORM. Use cut points of 1000, 2000, 4000, and 6000 for NumTags; use 500, 1000, 1500, and 2000 for TagsNorm. Label both ZipCode layers with the zip code number.

   c. Add the Pittsburgh map layer, symbolize it to have transparent fill, and position it on top of the other layers. Zoom into Pittsburgh.

   d. Create a Word document called *Exercise2<YourName>.doc*, replacing *<YourName>* with your name. Save the file in the Outputs folder. At the top, include the title "Comparison of Choropleth Maps for Counts and Densities of Pool Tags" and include your name. Use the PrtSc key or other means to get screen captures of both choropleth maps and insert them into the Word document. Write a few lines stating any major differences in pool use patterns that you observe.

3. **Create New Block Centroid Attributes for Middle-Aged Population.** Create the following two new variables for *blockcentroids.dbf*:

```
AGE_30_49 = AGE_30_39+AGE_40_49
PAGE_30_49 = 100*AGE_30_49/POP2000
```

a. Convert error codes for dividing by *0* to *0*. Do not sort the data, but use the Replace function in Excel for this step.

b. Create a new ArcExplorer map composition for PAGE_30_49 that uses a color graduated scale, similar to that for youth population. Use equal interval scales with 5 classes. Add and symbolize Minor Civil Divisions and Rivers map layers.

c. Save your ArcExplorer file as *MiddleAge.axl* in the Outputs folder. Zoom into Pittsburgh (but show all of Pittsburgh), and make a map layout and turn it in as *Exercise3<YourName>.ppt*, replacing *<YourName>* with your name. Do not include a graphic scale in your layout.

Hint: After you create the column for PAGE_30_49, create another new blank column next to it. Select and copy the entire PAGE_30_49 column, click in the top cell of the new blank column, click Edit, Paste Special, click the Values option button, and then click OK. Delete the original PAGE_30_49 column, and use the Replace function on the copy you just pasted. The Replace function will work on the new column, but not the old, because the #DIV/0! codes for dividing by zero were not stored values in the original version but are in the pasted version.

4. **Address-Match Some Restaurants in Pittsburgh**. Go to *www.smartpages.com* and search by Business Type *restaurant*, and enter 15213 for the zip code. In the resulting response, click on the *Delicatessens* link. Then, on the next page, click the *Search only in 15213* link. This should yield about six delicatessens.

a. Create a spreadsheet in Excel with column headings in Row 1: Name, Address, City, Zipcode, X, and Y. Enter the corresponding delicatessens data to make a data table. Save your spreadsheet as *15213Delicatessens* with the DBF 4 file type in the Outputs folder.

b. Address-match the delicatessens and enter resulting x- and y- coordinates into your *15213Delicatessens.dbf* table.

c. Create a new map in ArcExplorer. Add *15213Delicatessens.dbf* as an event table, generating a shapefile called *15213Delicatessens _.shp*. Add Zipcodes and Streets map layers. Label the streets and delicatessens.

d. Create a map layout with the restaurants, saved as *Exercise4<YourName>.ppt*, replace *<YourName>* with your name, put the file in the Output folder. Include your map, legend, and table with delicatessen data.

5. **Join a Census Table to a County Map for Florida.** In Chapter 5, you downloaded a county map for Florida and STF 3 census data on income for these counties. This file, somewhat cleaned up, and the shapefile are in the Maps folder with file names *gct_dec_2000_sf3_ u_data0.xls* and *co12_d00.shp*, respectively. Table 6-1 contains the data dictionary for the census data and the attribute names that we created.

   a. Join the census data to the shapefile and produce maps for a new variable GENDER_ INC = INC_MALE / INC_FEMALE that shows the income disparity between females and males in Florida counties.

   b. Turn in an electronic copy of *co12_d00.dbf* but with your name included as *co12_ d00<YourName>.dbf*.

   c. Create a map layout of GENDER_INC, and turn it in as *Exercise5<YourName>.ppt*.

TABLE 6-1 Data Dictionary for Census Data

Attribute	Definition
MED_HH_INC	Median income in 1999 (dollars); households
MED_FAM_INC	Median income in 1999 (dollars); families
PCINC	Per capita income in 1999 (dollars)
INC_MALE	Median earnings in 1999 of full-time year-round workers (dollars); male
INC_FEMALE	Median earnings in 1999 of full-time year-round workers (dollars); female
PPOP_POV_ALL	Income in 1999 below poverty level; percent of population for whom poverty status is determined; all ages
PPOP_POV_18	Income in 1999 below poverty level; percent of population for whom poverty status is determined; related children under 18 years of age
PPOP_POV_65	Income in 1999 below poverty level; percent of population for whom poverty status is determined; 65 years of age and over
PPOP_POV_FAM	Income in 1999 below poverty level; percent of families

References

Clarke, K. C., *Getting Started with Geographic Information Systems*, 4th Ed. Upper Saddle River: Prentice Hall, 2003.

Heywood, I., S. Corneius, and S. Carver. *An Introduction to Geographical Information Systems*, 2nd Ed. Essex: Pearson Press, 2002.

Mapquest, Internet URL: www.mapquest.com (accessed March 10, 2005).

U.S. Postal Service, Zip Code Lookup. Internet URL: http://zip4.usps.com/zip4/welcome.jsp (accessed March 6, 2005).

CHAPTER 7

WORKING ON GIS PROJECTS

LEARNING OBJECTIVES

In this chapter, you will:

- Learn basic project management methods
- Understand how to structure projects
- Study two solved projects
- Finish the Swimming Pool Case Study, using the two solved projects as guides
- Use this chapter's solved projects as templates for your own advanced projects

Now you are getting the idea!

INTRODUCTION

You have studied GIS facts, concepts, and principles; worked through tutorial steps; and completed

practice and end-of-chapter exercises. Your introduction to GIS is almost complete! The final step is doing

a GIS project independently or as a member of a small team. Your GIS project is a capstone experience in which you will put all the pieces together. You will go through all the phases of building an analytical GIS, from initially defining the problem, to finding, downloading, and processing map layers and data; building map compositions and layouts; and reporting results.

To prepare you for independent project work, we begin by surveying the basics of project management. You will learn about project life cycles and project components.

After you've learned basic project structure, we will step you through two completed projects, which are written in first-person, as if presented by a student in the style of a GIS professional for a target audience. The first project centers on assessing the need for and utilization of public transportation in Phoenix, Arizona. The second project targets identifying environmental polluters in Minneapolis, Minnesota, and assesses their potential impact on specific at-risk groups. Solutions and implications for further study are given for both projects.

The Exercises section presents four projects, or exercises. The first exercise challenges you to complete the Swimming Pool Case Study. You will begin by assembling the information about the Case Study in Chapters 1 through 6. Then, you will put that information into project format, using the information in this chapter as a guide. For Exercises 2 and 3, you will resolve the public transportation and environmental pollution projects for cities of your choice. You'll use the Phoenix and Minneapolis projects' resources and structure as templates for carrying out your own projects. Exercise 4, your capstone project, is an independent project. You or your instructor will identify a new project that needs a GIS solution.

Let's begin.

PROJECT MANAGEMENT

Real-world projects are challenging! You must define the problem, decide which factors to ignore and which are important, deal with uncertainties (including whether the project outcome will be helpful), and on and on. Fortunately, the field of project management brings some structure to GIS project work. Of course, there are entire textbooks and courses devoted to studying project management, but through our many years of working on projects, we believe that learning just a few concepts will give you a good start on developing GIS projects. We translate these concepts directly into components of GIS projects you can build.

Project Life Cycle

Projects have phases organized in a **systems development life cycle**. The most widely used cycle is called the **waterfall model** because it assumes that a project has several phases and flows from one phase to the next, like water going over a waterfall. Ideally, as water does not reverse direction and flow upstream, project phases are sequential—once a phase is completed, it is not revisited. However, the reality is that most project phases do cycle back to earlier phases: Some phases repeat parts of earlier phases, with steps being revisited and modified as one learns from later phases or as conditions change. Nevertheless, the waterfall model is useful, even though it ignores the need to cycle back to earlier steps.

The major phases of any project are as follows (see Kendall and Kendall 1995). Each project phase is described in terms of what you must do.

- **Problem identification phase**: State the problem, opportunity, issue, or objective; provide an approach for a solution; and define the **scope** or limitations of the project. Include some background on the problem area and a few references for general information. The number of issues or concerns in a project can seem endless, so it is essential to restrict a project to only a few issues and to state them clearly. Generally, it is also a good idea to provide a rationale for why the parts of the larger problem are important. The **deliverable**, or product of this phase, is a memorandum or short report that is a project proposal. A client (or your instructor) must comment on and approve the proposal, and you should expect some helpful suggestions.
- **Analysis phase**: Determine the detailed needs for the solution, collect data, and represent the solution on paper. You should identify sources of data and collect the data, determine specific attributes (variables) that represent underlying performance measures, and provide a verbal or schematic representation of the finished system that can be discussed and easily modified before proceeding to building the solution. Early in this phase, if the project is a team effort, you should produce a **work-breakdown structure**, which is simply a list of tasks, who will do them, and due dates for completion of tasks.
- **Design phase**: Process data and build the system or models that provide a solution. Both problem identification and analysis focus on thought processes and the feasibility of carrying out the project. Most of the computer and other hands-on work occurs in the design phase. The deliverable for this phase is a working system, ready for use.

- **Implementation phase**: Provide access to the solution as an operating computer system or through reports. If others need to use the computer system, then documentation on use is another deliverable. Obviously, reports and other outputs are deliverables.

GIS Project Components

We envision simple projects for an introductory GIS experience, so we have developed an abbreviated systems development life cycle for use in this chapter. We have combined and streamlined project phases so we have only three components:

- *Project Proposal:* This project-phase deliverable combines the phases for Problem Identification and Analysis. The proposal states the problem or issue, limits the scope of the project to a geographic area and to specific purposes, lists map layers and data to be downloaded or otherwise obtained, provides a computer folder and file structure for all project components, and, if a team is involved, provides a work-breakdown structure. The project proposal is a Word document, a deliverable, that can be evaluated and commented upon by a client or an instructor. Some of the text and other material of the proposal can be recycled into the project's report.
- *Process Log:* The deliverable for this project phase lists each major step you've taken to build the analytical GIS. We have a well-developed and structured approach for building a GIS, so you already know how to design and build much of the solution. Thus, you can just list major steps. Also, if you have an instructor, he or she may want you to elaborate in more detail. A detailed log is useful if you have to revise parts of the project, so you do not have to reinvent steps. Include the process log as an appendix in your report. *Note*: A process log is especially valuable for student projects so instructors can assess and diagnose student work and provide feedback. Otherwise, many of the processing steps could remain hidden, and students would not get credit for them. For GIS professionals, a process log is also valuable, but it might be maintained only as an internal team document and be used as the basis for writing a report section on computer processing steps.
- *Report:* A report, along with the folders and files of your GIS, are the major deliverables of the project. Map layouts, such as were built in Chapter 6, are key parts of the report, which can be a Word document, PowerPoint presentation, or both. The report structure follows the lines of the systems development life cycle: problem identification, analysis, solution, and results. Also, include a "future work" section that notes implications for additional study: There is always more that could be done on a project, and it is important to summarize your ideas about what additional work might be done if time and resources are available.

Next, let's look at two projects and their solutions. You should also look at the Project1 and Project2 subfolders in the LearningAndUsingGIS folder. In addition to the input data files, finished map layers, and documents, you will also find ArcExplorer project files that you can open and study on your computer.

PROJECT 1: PUBLIC TRANSPORTATION

The material we present for this project is in the form of project deliverables—proposal, process log, and report—as if written by a student or GIS professional. The deliverables are "bare bones": We have not elaborated on points and have kept text to a minimum. Our comments to you are in square brackets.

Proposal

[You may find that preparing the proposal is the most difficult part of a GIS project. Finding a problem and structuring it into a feasible project is a challenge. The components that follow provide the components of a good GIS project proposal.]

Background

An efficient and well-designed public transit system is a vital component of a thriving and growing community. Although it is not the only force that influences neighborhood life, public transit is a significant force because it can add social, economic, and environmental value to a community.

Public transit yields numerous benefits, three of which are: (1) affordable mobility, (2) congestion management, and (3) economic growth. The Federal Transit Administration states that the fundamental reason for offering public transit is to provide low-cost mobility to those who cannot own or operate an automobile, such as the young, the aged, and the infirm. (See *www.fta.dot.gov*.) Public transportation provides a means for accessing employment, schools, medical services, shopping, entertainment, recreation, and other social opportunities. As such, effective public transportation helps promote equal opportunity across all income levels. See the Public Transportation Partnership for Tomorrow Web site at *www.publictransportation.org/pt2/* for reports on the many benefits of public transportation.

The Problem and an Approach to a Solution

The problem concerns public transportation and low-income areas of Phoenix, Arizona. I propose to compare maps displaying use of public transportation compared to the percent of female-headed households with children, all by 2000 Census tracts. Gaps in transportation coverage, if they exist, should be evident as areas having high percentages of female-headed households with children but relatively low public transportation use.

Scope

Statistically, the census description "female-headed households with children" designates one of the poorest segments of the total population. Of course, not every such household is poor, but a great many are. Federal policies are forcing the employable-but-unemployed segments of this population off of welfare and into employment. Often, there are jobs available but not in the distressed, low-rent areas in which many female-headed households with children are located. Public transportation is an important link, literally, between such households and jobs.

Data and Map Layer Sources

I need relatively few map layers: Minor Civil Divisions, Census Tracts, and Streets. They are for Maricopa County, Arizona, which includes the city of Phoenix.

I will download these map layers from the ESRI Tiger/Line 2000 Web site, *www.esri.com/data/download/census2000_tigerline/index.html*. This Web site also has tables of selected 2000 Census SF 1 variables, including the number of Female-Headed Households with Children and the Total Number of Households.

Additional data will come from the 2000 Census; namely, the Summary File 3 (SF 3) data found in table P30, Means of Transportation to Work for Workers 16+ Years. This data is available from *http://factfinder.census.gov/*. The main variables of interest are the total number of workers age 16 or older and the subset of them that take public transportation to work.

Note that there are additional SF 3 tables that could be used to expand this study; for example, P32 (Travel Time to Work by Means of Transportation to Work for Workers 16+ Years Who Did Not Work at Home), P52 (Household Income in 1999), and P87 (Poverty Status in 1999 by Age).

Folder and File Structure

The proposed folder and file structure for the project is as follows. The Project1<MyName> folder is a subfolder of the LearningAndUsingGIS folder. Mac users can reverse the direction of the slashes in the path names.

- ***Project1<MyName>*** : This will be the overall project folder. At this level, it will contain *PublicTransportationMaricopaCounty.axl*, the final GIS map composition.
- ***Project1<MyName>\\DownloadedFiles*** : This folder will contain original map and data files that have been downloaded. Some of the files expanded from zipped files will be moved to other folders.
- ***Project1<MyName>\\ProcessedFiles*** : This folder will contain files that were intermediate steps along the way to producing finished map layers. Any explanations needed from these files will be in *ReadMe.doc* files. This folder will also contain any images exported from ArcExplorer (or elsewhere) before they are inserted into the final report.
- ***Project1<MyName>\\Maps*** : This folder will have the finished map layers used in the GIS. They will have the original map layer names as downloaded. Again, *ReadMe.doc* files may be included for documentation.
- ***Project1<MyName>\\Documents*** *(Win)*: This folder will contain the final report or PowerPoint presentation. It will also contain the proposal and process log documents.

Process Log

This section has the list of major steps that I took to complete my project. Further details are in steps identified by lowercase letter (a, b, c, and so forth).

[*Note*: Normally you would not include the detailed steps unless required by your instructor. Some detailed steps, however, are important documentation, and you should include them. We have placed such steps in italics so you can identify them. Use your judgment and document steps that might be useful to you to explain your work. Also, we ask Mac users to convert folder and file notation from Windows to Macintosh in the Process Log (ignore the hard-drive letter and reverse the direction of slashes in PC path names). You will also need to refer to Chapter 5 for instructions to open *.dbf* files in Excel.]

Download Files

1. Start a **Web browser**, open **Fact Finder** at **http://factfinder.census.gov/**, and download the SF 3 table P30 for Maricopa County, Arizona.
   a. Click Data Sets and click **Census 2000 Summary File 3 (SF 3) - Sample Data**.
   b. Click **Detailed Tables**. (Mac users may have to use a browser other than Microsoft Explorer, such as Safari or Firefox, to access the Detailed Tables option.)
   c. Click **Census Tract** under Select a geographic type.
   d. Click **Arizona** under Select a state, and click **Maricopa County** under Select a county.
   e. Click **All Census Tracts** in Select one or more geographic areas.
   f. Click **Add**, click **Census Tract**, and then click **Next**.
   g. Click **P30** and then click **Add**.
   h. Click **Show Result** (and wait until data are retrieved).
   i. Point to **Print/Download** on the horizontal menu to drop a list, then click **Download**.
   j. Click **Microsoft Excel** (.xls) button, and make sure that the "Include descriptive data element names" check box is checked.
   k. Click **OK**, unzip the files and save them in the **c:\LearningAndUsingGIS\Project1\DownloadedFiles** folder.
2. Start the **ESRI Census 2000 TIGER/Line Data** Web site at **http://www.esri.com /data/download/census2000_tigerline/index.html**. You will download map layers for Maricopa County, Arizona, Census Tracts, SF 1 data, Municipalities, and Streets.
   a. Click **Download Data**.
   b. Click **Arizona**.
   c. Click the **Select a County** list arrow, click **Maricopa**, and click **Submit Selection**.
   d. Click **Census Tracts 2000, Line Features - Roads, Census Tract Demographics (SF1)**, and then click **County Census Divisions 2000** (Cities).
   e. Click **Proceed to Download**.
   f. Click **OK**, unzip the files and save them in the **c:\LearningAndUsingGIS\ Project1\DownloadedFiles** folder.

Prepare Files

1. Create column headings in *dt_dec_2000_sf3_u_data1.xls*. The downloaded table has two rows of column headings, one with code values, such as P030003, and the other with descriptions instead of data element names.

   a. Open **c:\LearningAndUsingGIS\Project1\DownloadedFiles\ dt_dec_2000_sf3_u_data1.xls** in Excel, and save it in **c:\LearningAndUsingGIS\Project1\ProcessedFiles**.

   b. Delete columns **SUMLEVEL, GEO_NAME, P030003, P030004, P030006, through P030012, P030015**.

   c. Click in **2nd row cells**, and read the full contents of the cell above in Excel's cell contents box.

   d. Change top-row column names:
      i. P030001 to **WORKER16P**
      ii. P030002 to **DRIVE**
      iii. P030005 to **PUBTRANS**
      iv. P030013 to **BIKE**
      v. P030014 to **WALK**
      vi. P030016 to **WORKHOME**

   e. Delete **row 2** that has the descriptive labels for columns.

   f. Click **File, Save as**, click **File Save as Type** (Win) or **Format** (Mac), click **DBF 4 (dBASE IV) (*.dbf)**, and then click **Save**. This yields *c:\LearningAndUsingGIS\Project1\ProcessedFiles\dt_dec_2000_sf3_u_ data1.dbf*.

2. Join *dt_dec_2000_sf3_u_data1.dbf* to *tgr04013trt00.dbf* .

   a. In Excel, open **c:\LearningAndUsingGIS\Project1\ProcessedFiles\ dt_dec_2000_sf3_u_data1.dbf** and **c:\LearningAndUsingGIS\Project1\ Maps\tgr04013trt00.dbf**.

   b. Windows users: Click **Window** and then click **Compare Side by Side**. Mac users: Click **Window**, click **Arrange**, click **Vertical** and then click **OK**.

   c. Check that the rows match up in both files.

   d. Insert **7 new columns** before **TRACTID** in *tgr04013trt00.dbf*.

   e. Scroll to the top of **dt_dec_2000_sf3_u_data1.dbf**.

   f. Click the **upper-left cell**, hold down your **Shift** key, scroll and click the **lower-right cell** of the *dt_dec_2000_sf3_u_data1.dbf* table.

   g. Click **Edit** and then click **Copy**.

   h. Click cell **E1** in *tgr04013trt00.dbf* and then click **Paste**.

   i. Windows users: Click **Window** and then close **Side by Side**. Mac users: Click **Window**, click **Arrange**, click **Vertical** and then click **OK**.

   j. Close **dt_dec_2000_Sf3_u_data1.dbf**.

3. Delete extra rows *tgr04000sf1trt.dbf*. This table has census tract data for all of Arizona. I deleted all but the Maricopa data rows.

   a. Open **c:\LearningAndUsingGIS\Project1\Maps\tgr04000sf1trt.dbf** in Excel.

   b. Delete rows **2–95** for counties 001 through 012.

   c. Delete rows **665 through the end of the sheet**, leaving rows just for county 013.

4. Join *tgr04000sf1trt.dbf* to *tgr04013trt00.dbf*.
   a. Insert **32 new columns** before TRACTID in *c:\LearningAndUsingGIS\Project1\Maps\tgr04013trt00.dbf*.
   b. Copy and paste **Pop2000 through RENTER_OCC columns** of *c:\LearningAndUsingGIS\Project1\Maps\tgr04000sf1trt.dbf* to the **new columns** in *c:\LearningAndUsingGIS\Project1\Maps\tgr04013trt00.dbf*.
   c. Add a **new column** to *tgr04013trt00.dbf,* key in **PPUBTRANS** in the first cell of the new column; enter the expression **100*PUBTRANS/WORKER16P** in cell 2 of the new column, and copy and paste that cell in the rest of the column.
   d. Replace all **#DIV/0** codes with **0** in the new column (be careful not to change the order of rows).
   e. Add another **new column**, enter **PFHH_CHILD** in the first cell of the new column, enter the expression **100*FHH_CHILD/HOUSEHOLDS** in cell 2 of the new column, and then copy and paste that cell in the rest of the column.
   f. Replace all **#DIV/0** codes with **0** in the new column (be careful not to change the order of rows).
   g. Save the file with the *.dbf* file extension type.

Build the ArcExplorer Map Composition

1. Start **ArcExplorer** and add two copies of **tgr04013trt00.shp**, one copy of **tgr04013lkA.shp**, and one copy of **tgr04013ccd00.shp**.
2. Symbolize **tgr04013lkA.shp** with a **gray color**, and change its name to **Streets**. Set a threshold scale so the layer shows up only when zoomed far in.
3. Symbolize a copy of **tgr04013trt00.shp**, using **PPUBTRANS** with manual break points of **5, 10, 15, 20** and a blue monochromatic scale. Change the layer name to **Percent Workers Using Public Transportation**.
4. Symbolize the other copy of **tgr04013trt00.shp** using **PFFHChild** with the same manual break points and a **red monochromatic scale**. Change the layer name to **Percent Female Headed Households with Children**.
5. Symbolize **tgr04013ccd00.shp** with no color fill and an **outline 3 pixels wide**. Change its name to **Cities**.
6. Save the map composition as **PublicTransportationMaricopaCounty.axl** in c:\LearningAndUsingGIS\Project1.

Build Map Layouts

1. Export two **full-extent map images**: one with **Percent Workers Using Public Transportation** turned on, and the other with **Percent Female Headed Households with Children** turned on. These files are **PubTran.jpg** and **FHH.jpg**.
2. Build a **legend** using Microsoft Paint (Win) or AppleWorks (Mac) for these maps and assemble the pieces in PowerPoint, in **MapLayouts.ppt**.
3. Export two versions of the same maps, zoomed in to an area with gaps in public transportation. These files are **PubTranZoom.jpg** and **FHHZoom.jpg**.

Report

[The report is the most visible and portable deliverable that you produce. It is a stand-alone document that covers all phases of the project and its results. It brings together several parts of the proposal and process log along with new materials such as map layouts.]

Introduction

[The report in *C:\LearningAndUsingGIS\Project1\Documents\FinalReport.doc* (Win) or *LearningAndUsingGIS/Project1/Documents/FinalReport.doc* (Mac) includes an introduction that restates material found in the proposal. We do not repeat that material here to save space. See the electronic version of the report, which is complete.]

Data Sources and Processing

I obtained map layers for this project from the ESRI TIGER/Line 2000 Web site at *http://www.esri.com/data/download/census2000_tigerline/index.html*. These consisted of three layers for Maricopa County, Arizona: first, Minor Civil Divisions or Cities, so I could display the boundary of Phoenix; second, 2000 Census tract boundaries, so I could prepare choropleth maps displaying variables representing the need for and utilization of public transportation; and third, Streets so I could provide a spatial context when zoomed in to problem areas that have potential gaps in providing public transportation.

Census data are from two sources. Variables from Census 2000 Summary File 1 (SF 1) are from the ESRI Web site and include FHH_CHILD = the number of female-headed households with children, and HOUSEHOLDS = the total number of households. I calculated a new variable, the percentage of female-headed households with children (PFHH_ CHILD = 100* FHH_CHILD/HOUSEHOLDS), to represent the need for public transportation for that group.

The second data source is the U.S. Census Bureau's American FactFinder Web site at *http://factfinder.census.gov/*. I downloaded table P30 from Census 2000 Summary File 3 (SF 3). The variables needed from this table are as follows:

- P030001 = Workers 16 years and over: Total, which I renamed WORKER16P, and
- P030005 = Workers 16 years and over: Means of transportation to work: Public transportation, which I renamed PUBTRANS.

I calculated a new variable, percentage of workers who use public transportation: PPUBTRANS=100*PUBTRANS/WORKER16P, which represents the supply of public transportation.

Results

Figures 7-1 and 7-2 are maps for Phoenix, Arizona, and they represent the need for and utilization of public transportation, respectively. Figure 7-1 shows the percentage of female-headed households with children by 2000 Census tract. There are several areas of Phoenix with high percentages of female-headed households, and I have drawn attention to two of them. The ellipse includes the largest area with high concentrations of this population, and the small rectangle within the ellipse is an area for which I later provide zoomed in maps.

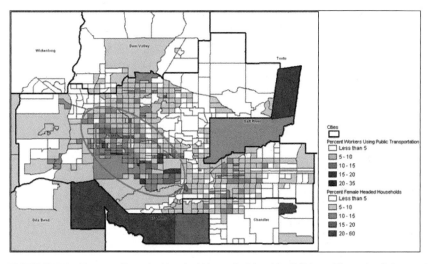

FIGURE 7-1 Percent Female-Headed Households with Children: Phoenix, Arizona, 2000 Census Tracts

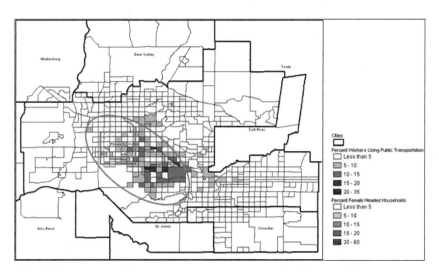

FIGURE 7-2 Percent Workers Using Public Transportation to Work: Phoenix, Arizona, 2000 Census Tracts

Figure 7-2 represents the general public's utilization of public transportation. You can see that the lower-right area of the ellipse has relatively good matches of need and utilization in several of its smaller areas, but there are still gaps with high percentages of female-headed households with children and low percentages of workers using public transportation. The rectangle inside the ellipse has even more gaps evident.

Figures 7-3 and 7-4 are zoomed in maps of the rectangular areas from Figures 7-1 and 7-2. In Figure 7-3, you can see a number of census tracts with 15% or more female-headed households with children. In Figure 7-4, which shows the percentage of workers using public transportation, I have drawn the outlines of the tracts with 15% or more female-headed households with children, so you can easily see the gaps in public transportation. In some cases, there are 20% or more female-headed households and less than 5% of the workers using public transportation to get to work.

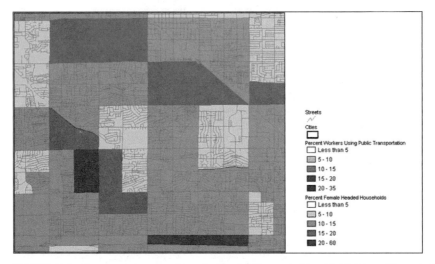

FIGURE 7-3 Zoomed in Percent Female-Headed Households with Children: Phoenix, Arizona, 2000 Census Tracts

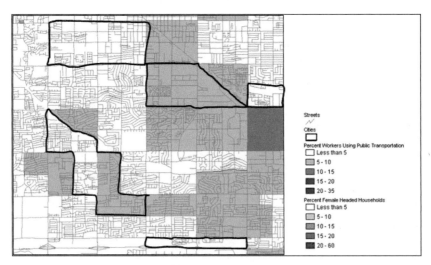

FIGURE 7-4 Zoomed in Percent Workers Using Public Transportation to Work: Phoenix, Arizona, 2000 Census Tracts

Conclusion

This report has analyzed the need for and utilization of public transportation in Phoenix, Arizona. To represent "need," I have used the percentage of households by census tract that have female-headed households with children. For the utilization of public transportation, I have used the percentage of workers who use public transportation to get to work. There are clear gaps, as shown on a series of four maps, with high percentages of female-headed households (at least 15%) and low percentages of workers using public transportation (5% or less).

There are two major extensions possible for future work. One is to use measures of poverty, such as the number of households that have poverty status, in addition to female-headed households with children. The second extension would be to obtain a map layer, if possible, with bus routes. Then I could start analyzing potential new bus routes in areas with supply gaps.

PROJECT 2: ENVIRONMENT

[The material we present on this project, like that of the first project, is in the form of project deliverables—a proposal, a process log, and a report—as if they were written by a student. This project is more advanced than the first project: It has more specialized map layers and more advanced spatial analyses.]

Proposal

The major issue on the feasibility of this project is data availability. The project needs data for point sources of pollution. Fortunately, environmental protection laws have led to the collection and public access of detailed pollution data.

Background

Air and water pollutants, toxic chemical releases, and other environmental hazards are of great interest to many people, ranging from homeland security experts to healthcare professionals and even to average citizens who want to learn more about the communities in which they live.

The Environmental Protection Agency (EPA), Environmental Defense (a leading non-profit organization representing more than 400,000 members), and other organizations track and make available pollution data across the U.S. For example, through its Enviro-facts Data Warehouse, the EPA provides access to several databases for air, water, and land pollution anywhere in the United States. The EPA also makes its Toxics Release Inventory database available, with data on toxic chemical releases and other waste management activities reported annually by various industry groups and federal facilities. You can learn more about the EPA at its Web site, *http://www.epa.gov*.

Environmental Defense is another great source of environmental data. Established in 1967, Environmental Defense has combined approaches from science, economics, and law to create innovative, equitable, and cost-effective solutions to society's most urgent environmental problems. You can learn more about the Environmental Defense at their Web site, *http://www.environmentaldefense.org/home.cfm*.

The Problem and Approach to Solution

The problem to be addressed concerns the proximity of environmental hazards to children and blacks in Minneapolis, Minnesota. I propose to compare maps displaying companies releasing the most pollutants in Minneapolis compared to locations of schools, K–12 school-age population, and blacks in that city. I will use buffers to identify schools and populations that are likely to be at risk because of their proximity to large-volume hazardous releases.

Scope

In general, children are highly susceptible to environmental health hazards, and minorities—including blacks—tend to live in communities with high levels of pollution. There are many reasons why minorities are situated near pollution sources, but the underlying causes are economic and political. Of course, not all people in minority groups are poor, but poverty is more concentrated in minority populations. The low-cost housing that poor people can afford is often located in polluted environments. On the political side, poor people generally have little political clout and historically have been under-represented in decisions impacting pollution in their areas. Similarly, if a school or playground is near a polluted environment, children are unlikely to know about or protest the danger. The field of environmental justice is concerned with redressing such inequities (see *www.epa. gov/compliance/environmentaljustice*). Clearly, school-age children and minorities are two groups that need increased protection from environmental pollution.

Generally, there are many polluters in an urban area, but for an exploratory study on environmental pollution in Minneapolis, I will restrict attention to the top 20 companies with toxic releases in Hennepin County, Minnesota, based on how many pounds per year of pollution they emit.

Data and Map Layer Sources

Data for this project includes census layers for Hennepin County, Minnesota, which has the city of Minneapolis within its boundaries. These layers are Minor Civil Divisions and Census Tracts. Also included are census tract data.

I will download these map layers from the ESRI TIGER/Line 2000 Web site, *http://www. esri.com/data/download/census2000_tigerline/index.html*. I will download Toxic Release Indicators from a Web site sponsored by the Environmental Defense organization, at *http://www.scorecard.org*. Included in the data are the latitude and longitude of polluters. Lastly, I will download latitude and longitude locations in Hennepin County, Minnesota, from *http://www.hometownlocator.com*.

Folder and File Structure

The proposed folder and file structure for the project is as follows. The Project2<MyName> folder is a subfolder of the LearningAndUsingGIS folder. Mac users should reverse the direction of the slashes in the path names.

- **Project2<MyName>**: This folder will be the overall project folder. It will contain *EnvironmentalHazardStudyHennepinCounty.axl*, the final ArcExplorer map composition.
- **Project2<MyName>\DownloadedFiles**: This folder will contain original map and data files as downloaded. Some of the files expanded from zipped files will be moved to other folders.
- **Project2<MyName>\ProcessedFiles**: This folder will contain files that were intermediate steps along the way to producing finished map layers. Any explanations needed about these files will be in *ReadMe.doc* files. This folder will also contain any images exported from ArcExplorer or elsewhere before they are inserted into the final report.
- **Project2<MyName>\Maps**: This folder will have the finished map layers used in the GIS. They will have the original map layer names as downloaded. Again, *ReadMe.Doc* files may be included for documentation.
- **Project2<MyName>\Documents**: This folder will contain the final report or PowerPoint presentation. It also will have the proposal and process log documents.

Process Log

This section has the list of major steps that I took to complete my project. Further details are in steps identified by lowercase letter (a, b, c, and so forth).

[*Note*: We ask Mac users to convert folder and file notation from Windows to Macintosh in the process log (ignore the hard-drive letter and reverse the direction of slashes in PC path names). Refer to Chapter 5 for instructions on opening *.dbf* files in Excel.]

Download Files

1. Start a browser and go to the ESRI Census 2000 TIGER/Line Data Web site at *http://www.esri.com/data/download/census2000_tigerline/index.html* and download map layers for Hennepin County, Minnesota census tracts, census SF1 data, and municipalities.
   a. Click **Download Data**.
   b. Click **Minnesota** and click **Submit Selection**.
   c. Click the **Select a County** list arrow and click **Hennepin**. Click **Submit Selection**.
   d. Click **Census Tracts 2000, Census Tract Demographics (SF1)**, and **County Census Divisions 2000**.
   e. Click **Proceed to Download**.
   f. Click **Download File**; the **File Download** window opens.
   g. Click **OK**, unzip the files and save them in the **c:\LearningAndUsingGIS\Project2\DownloadedFiles** folder.

2. Start the Scorecard.org Web site at *http://www.scorecard.org* and download data for the top 20 polluters in Hennepin County, Minnesota.

   a. From the **Pollution in Your Community** section, type in zip code **55401** and click **GET REPORT**. (The program uses any zip code in the county to identify the county.)

   b. Click on the link **the top polluters**. The top 20 polluters in your county will be listed.

   c. Click on the top polluter, **RITRAMA, INC.**, to see its location (the top polluter may change when data are revised on this Web site; just click the new top polluter).

   d. Towards the bottom of the list, click **Facility Information**. In addition to the address and contact information, it will list the latitude and longitude data for the site.

   e. Start Microsoft Excel and build a spreadsheet for variables Name, City, SIC_CODE, Latitude, Longitude, and Pounds that you will copy and paste from the Scorecard facility data site. City corresponds to 2002 Facility Name. Copy and paste data from the Web site into the spreadsheet. Include all companies that are the top 20 pollutants in Hennepin County.

   f. Before saving the file, select the cells in the latitude and longitude columns and change their format to **Number** and **5 Decimal places**.

   g. Repeat the cell format change for **Pounds**, but change the decimal places to **0**.

   h. Save the file as a DBF IV file called **HennepinCountyPolluters.dbf** in the **c:\LearningandusingGIS\Project2\Maps\ folder.**

3. Start the Hometown Locator Web site at *http://www.hometownlocator.com*, and download data for all of the schools in Hennepin County, Minnesota, that have latitude and longitude data.

   a. In the Search by County and State section, enter **Hennepin** as the county, click the list arrow, and click **Minnesota** as the state.

   b. Click the **County Search** button.

   c. Click **Hennepin County Physical Features & Cultural Features**.

   d. From the Hennepin County, Minnesota Physical & Cultural Features page, click **school**. A list for the school name, local area, latitude and longitude data, elevation, and map link will be displayed. There are multiple pages of school data so you will need to copy and paste one page at a time into an Excel spreadsheet.

   e. Using your mouse, select the row for the first school, and drag to the row for the last school so that you select **the rows for all the schools**.

   f. Right-click (Win) or control-click (Mac) the **selected rows** and click **Copy**.

   g. Open an Excel spreadsheet, right-click (Win) or control-click (Mac) in the **upper-left cell** in the spreadsheet, and click **Paste**. This will create rows for each school with separate columns for the school name, area, lat, long, elevation, and maps.

   h. You will need data only for the school name, area, lat, and long, so you can delete the other fields (elevation and maps).

   i. Repeat this process for the schools on the remaining pages.

j. Before saving the file, select the cells in the latitude column, and change their format to **Number** and **5 Decimal places**. Do the same for longitude.

k. Save the file as a DBF IV file called **HennepinCountySchools.dbf** in the *c:\LearningandusingGIS\Project2\Maps* folder.

Prepare Files

1. Join tgr27000sf1trt.dbf to tgr27053trt00.dbf.

    a. Open **c:\LearningAndUsingGIS\Project2\Maps\tgr27000sf1trt.dbf** in Excel.

    b. Delete rows **2–351** for counties 001 through 051 (*Note:* 052 is missing).

    c. Delete rows **650 through the end of the sheet**, leaving rows just for county 053.

    d. Delete all of the columns except for STFID, POP2000, WHITE, BLACK, AMERI_ES, ASIAN, HAWN_PI, OTHER, HISPANIC, AGE_UNDER5, AGE_5_17.

    e. Open **c:\LearningAndUsingGIS\Project2\Maps\tgr27053trt00.dbf** in Excel.

    f. Insert **11 new columns** before TRACTID in *tgr27053trt00.dbf*.

    g. Copy and paste **STFID through AGE5_17 columns** of *tgr27000sf1trt.dbf* to the **new columns** in *tgr27053trt00.dbf*.

    h. Save *tgr27053trt00.dbf* with the *.dbf* type.

Build the ArcExplorer Map Composition

1. Start ArcExplorer and add **tgr27053trt00.shp** twice and **tgr27053ccd00.shp** once and save the map composition as **EnvironmentalHazardStudyHennepinCounty.axl** in c:\LearningAndUsingGIS\Project2.

2. Symbolize one of the **tgr27053trt00.shp** layers using field **Age5_17** with manual break points of **500**, **1,000**, **1,500**, and **2,000** with a **gray monochromatic scale**. Change its name to **K–12 Population**.

3. Symbolize the other **tgr27053trt00.shp** layer using field **BLACK** and manual break points of **500**, **1,000**, **1,500**, and **2,000** with a **gray monochromatic scale**. Change its name to **Black Population**.

4. Symbolize **tgr27053ccd00.shp** with a **transparent fill** and an outline 3 pixels wide. Change its name to **Municipalities**, and label the **municipality** by name.

5. Add the **HennepinCountySchools.dbf** file as an event theme, using **X field = LONGITUDE** and **Y field = LATITUDE**, and symbolize it using **blue circles** size **5**. Change its name to **Schools**.

6. Add the **HennepinCountyPolluters.dbf** as an event theme using **X field = LONGITUDE** and **Y field = LATITUDE**, and symbolize it using **red graduated circles** sizes **5–20** with **3** manual classifications of **less than 25,000**, **25,000 to 50,000**, and **50,000 and greater**. Change its name to **Hazardous Emissions by Pounds**.

7. Select the **top 4 polluters in Hennepin County, Minnesota**, and create a **2-mile buffer** around these companies. When creating the buffer, select the schools that are within the buffer. From the selected records in the schools attribute table, export the school names as a *.dbf* file called *SchoolsWithin2MileBuffer.dbf* within **c:\LearningandUsingGIS\ProcessedFiles**.

8. Create another 2-mile buffer of the top 4 polluters, this time selecting the census tracts that are within this buffer. From the selected records in the census tracts attribute table, export the census tract records as a *.dbf* file called **c:\LearningandUsingGIS\Project2\ProcessedFiles**.

9. Open the exported *.dbf* files in Excel. Count or compute the number of schools in each area that are within 2 miles of the top polluters, and the total ages 5-17 population (representing the K–12 population) within this buffer.

Build Map Layouts

1. Export two full-extent map images of Hennepin County. One map should show the top polluters compared to K–12 Population as **PollutersvsK–12Population.jpg**, and the other map should show Black Population as **PollutersvsBlackPopulation.jpg**.

2. Build a legend for these maps and assemble pieces in PowerPoint, in *MapLayouts.ppt*.

3. Export two maps showing the 2-mile buffer around the top 4 polluters, one with the schools selected, and one with the K–12 population. These files are **2MileSchoolBuffer.jpg** and **2MileK–12PopulationBuffer.jpg**. Include the count of schools by area within the 2-mile buffer and count of K–12 Population within the 2-mile buffers. Build a legend for these maps and assemble pieces in PowerPoint, in *MapLayouts.ppt*.

4. Export two zoomed-in maps of the Minneapolis municipality. One map should show the top polluting companies labeled by company name, the school points, and the K–12 population. The other map should show the top polluting companies labeled by company name and the black population. These files are **MinneapolisPollutervsK–12Population.jpg** and **MinneapolisPollutervsBlackPopulation.jpg**. Build a legend for these maps and assemble the pieces in PowerPoint, in *MapLayouts.ppt*.

Report

The report draws attention to a potential environmental hazard: pollutant emissions emitted into the air near black populations and school children. The results show what is happening, but they cannot show effects of potentially related ill health.

Introduction

[The report in *c:\LearningAndUsingGIS\Project2\Documents\FinalReport.doc* (Win) or *LearningAndUsingGIS/Project2/Documents/FinalReport.doc* (Mac) includes an introduction that restates material found in the proposal's background, problem and approach to solution, and rationale for scope sections. To save space, we do not repeat that material here. See the electronic version of the report for the introduction.]

Data Sources and Processing

I obtained map layers for this project from the ESRI TIGER/Line 2000 Web site at *http://www.esri.com/data/download/census2000_tigerline/index.html*. These consisted of two map layers for Hennepin County, Minneapolis: Minor Civil Divisions so I could display the boundary of Minneapolis, and the 2000 Census Tract boundaries so I could prepare choropleth maps displaying variables representing the number of K–12 school-age children.

The second data source is the Environmental Defense Agency's Web site at *http://www.scorecard.org*. I downloaded data on the top 20 polluters in Hennepin County and compiled a data table describing the company name, type of company, latitude and longitude location, and the amount of toxic emissions in pounds per year.

The third data source is *http://www.hometownlocator.org*, which lists all of the schools in Hennepin County, Minnesota, with school name and latitude and longitude data. The primary source for this data is the U.S. Geological Survey.

Results

Figures 7-5 and 7-6 show the top 20 polluting companies in Hennepin County, Minnesota, by the amount of hazardous emissions in pounds per year compared to the K–12 school-age and black population. Both maps show populations near top pollution sources. Figures 7-7 and 7-8 provide further analysis for the case of school-age children.

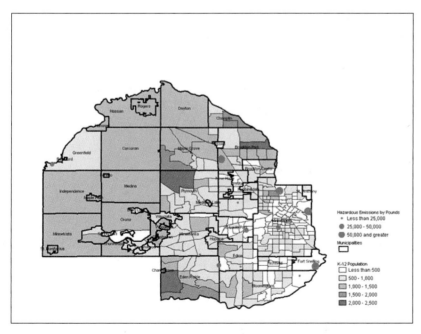

FIGURE 7-5   Hazardous Emissions by Pounds compared to K–12 Population: Hennepin County, Minnesota, 2000 Census Tracts

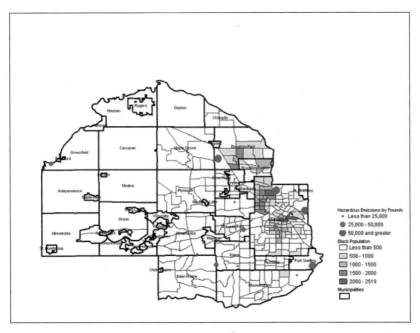

FIGURE 7-6   Hazardous Emissions by Pounds compared to Black Population: Hennepin County, Minnesota, 2000 Census Tracts

Figure 7-7 shows the number of schools within a two-mile buffer of the top four polluting companies in Hennepin County, Minnesota. There are 25 schools within those buffers. Figure 7-8 shows the K–12 school-age population that is within a two-mile buffer of same companies and census tracts within or crossing the buffer. There are over 27,000 school-age children within two miles of the top polluters. These results suggest that there is exposure of school-age children to pollutants while at school, but further study is needed to determine the actual risks involved.

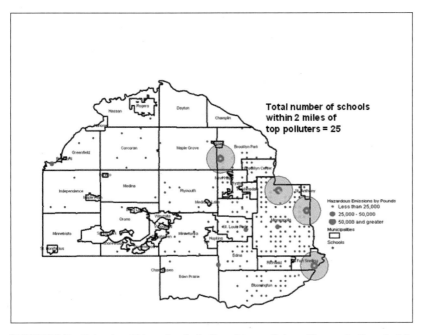

FIGURE 7-7 Schools within a 2-mile buffer of top polluters: Hennepin County, Minnesota, 2000 Census Tracts

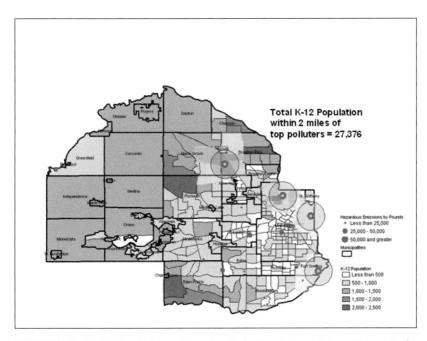

FIGURE 7-8 K–12 Population within a 2-mile buffer of top polluters: Hennepin County, Minnesota, 2000 Census Tracts

Conclusion

This report has analyzed populations in close proximity to environmental hazards in Minneapolis, Hennepin County, Minnesota. For data on environmental hazards, I have used the top 20 polluters in Hennepin County and the amount of toxic emissions by pound per year. For population statistics, I have used U.S. Census variables for K–12 children and black population as well as the number of schools. There appears to be potential for exposure to environmental hazards around the top polluters. Actual risks would need to be determined through in-depth studies.

There are two major extensions possible for future work. One would be to consider other at-risk populations, including very old and very young persons. Another would be to obtain data on prevailing wind directions and to study populations downwind of polluters.

Chapter 7 Summary

Project management is a field concerned with the phases, components, and deliverables of project work. Project phases are organized into systems development life cycles. The most common such cycle is called the waterfall model because of the assumption that after a phase is completed, the project flows on to the next stage, never to return to earlier phases. Real-life projects often violate this assumption because: (1) later phases uncover new information that impacts earlier decisions, (2) the nature of the problem changes because of external influences, such as enactment of a new law, or (3) the client—if there is one—changes his or her mind about some aspect of the project.

Project phases are problem identification, analysis, design, and implementation. For GIS projects, we combine analysis with problem identification and introduce some special components for GIS. In this chapter, the deliverable of problem identification and analysis is a project proposal that includes problem-area background, problem identification, project scope, and a rationale for the scope. For GIS project proposals, we also include identification of GIS resources and the design of a folder structure for all project files.

The process log records major steps and some detailed steps used to build the GIS. The deliverable for implementation is the folder structure with completed GIS and other files and a written report that includes an introduction, data sources and processing, and results sections.

We presented deliverables for two completed projects: one on public transportation done for Phoenix, Arizona, and the second on environmental pollution done for Minneapolis, Minnesota. Exercises 2 and 3 of this chapter have you use these projects as templates for your own county and city. If time permits, you could work on an entirely new project.

We obviously love GIS and project work. We hope that you will too. Bon voyage!

Key Terms

Analysis phase   A phase of project management that transforms a problem statement into a solution on paper. This is a phase that requires much creative work to forge a solution approach and results in a description, diagrams, or other paper-based representations of the end product.

Deliverable   Documents or computer-based components that are the result of a phase of project management. Generally, the client or instructor reviews and approves deliverables at the end of each project phase.

Design phase   A phase of project management during which the solution gets built. It is here that the ArcExplorer map composition gets built.

Implementation phase   A phase of project management in which the client or instructor starts using the completed system. Deliverables may be limited to reports and presentations, or in some cases may include interactive use of the completed GIS. Documentation, including instructions for use, is an additional deliverable for the latter.

Problem identification phase   The first phase of project management in which the problem is stated along with a solution approach that includes project scope and limitations.

Scope   A statement of what a project will and will not accomplish. Generally, some rationale is desirable for choices and limitations, such as limiting work to high priority, feasible, or important objectives.

Systems development life cycle   The collection of all project phases and deliverables.

Waterfall model   The most common systems development life cycle that a project's phases are linear rather than recursive. In reality, project development usually requires cycling back through previous phases, but the simplicity of this model makes it desirable.

Work-breakdown structure   A list of tasks, generally organized by project phase, showing who is assigned to do them and when the tasks are due.

Short-Answer Questions

1. What is the purpose of project management? Would a GIS staff person need project management for daily tasks, such as adding new points to a map layer for events that occur regularly (an example is a crime analyst who adds yesterday's crimes to a point map layer every day)? Why or why not?

2. Two options often taken for describing the problem to be addressed in a computer-based project are: (1) to state the solution, including appropriate use of information technologies, or (2) to state symptoms of a gap between current and desired states of affairs. One of these options is right and the other wrong. Which is which? Explain your answer.

3. The systems development life cycle has two major parts: conceptual work (problem identification and analysis) and hands-on work (design and implementation). What are the benefits of doing the conceptual work before starting the hands-on work?

4. Scope is a critical aspect of project management. What is scope and why is it important?

5. What purposes does the work-breakdown structure serve? If you were the manager of a project team, how would you go about creating the work-breakdown structure?

6. A simple option for storing the files of a computer project is to create a folder with a good, descriptive name and then place all files directly in that folder. Is this a good idea for GIS projects? Why or why not?

7. On a team project, it is desirable to store project files on a shared network server. Why? What rules would you establish for team members and their project work in regard to use of the shared storage site?

8. What is a process log? Why is it valuable to project members, the project manager (if there is one), and the client?

9. If you were to make a PowerPoint presentation of a GIS project, what would the major sections of the presentation be? State them in order of presentation.

10. Should project reports include a "future work" section? What is the value of such a section to team members? To the client?

Exercises

1. **Swimming Pool Case Study.** By reading the material and doing the exercises in Chapters 1 through 6 of this book, you have carried out much of the work for a project on the Pittsburgh Swimming Pool Case Study. In this exercise you will pull those materials, its GIS, and results into project form. Requirements and guidelines for the project follow. Your instructor may limit the exercise by reducing the number of components within various parts of the requirements. We indicate some of the options.

Proposal:

- Include Background and Problem-and-Approach sections with materials drawn from Chapter 1.

- Have the scope of the project focus on issues and analyses included in the following: a new map layout for the map produced in Exercise 1 of Chapter 4; the map layout produced in Chapter 6; and the spatial analyses conducted in Exercises 1, 2, and 4 of Chapter 3. Options for reducing work here is to skip the material in Exercise 1 of Chapter 4 and Exercise 4 of Chapter 4. If any of these materials is eliminated, there are obvious downstream reductions in work throughout the remaining project components.

- For the information in the Data and Map Layer Sources section, use the sources provided in Chapters 1 through 5.

- For the Folder and File Structure section, use c:\LearningAndUsingGIS\Maps for the map layers. Create a new folder called c:\LearningAndUsingGIS\ProjectPools<YourName>\ for the Documents, ProcessedFiles, DownloadedFiles section, and your *.axl* files.

Process Log:

Write only the major steps of building the layouts and conducting the spatial analyses.

Report:

- Produce figures with maps and tables with statistics from the exercises.
- Describe the patterns found in each figure and table.
- Draw some conclusions.
- State the potential for future study.

Place your results in your c:\LearningAndUsingGIS\ProjectPools<YourName>\ folder. Make arrangements to compress that folder and its subfolders and files to turn in to your instructor. Name your compressed file *ProjectPools<YourName>.zip*.

2. **Public Transportation Project.** Replicate the public transportation project of this chapter for the county or city of your choice. Create a folder called c:\LearningAndUsingGIS\ProjectPublicTransportation<YourName>\ that includes all subfolders and files comparable to c:\LearningAndUsingGIS\Project1\. You can simply reuse certain parts of the deliverables, if applicable, such as the background of the proposal. As an option, carry out one of the future work suggestions that we provided in the project's solution, or pursue an additional issue that you identify on your own. Make arrangements to compress c:\LearningAndUsingGIS\ProjectPublicTransportation<YourName>\ and its subfolders and files to turn in to your instructor. Name your compressed file *ProjectPublicTransportation<YourName>.zip*.

3. **Environmental Pollution Project.** Replicate the environmental pollution project of this chapter for the county of your choice. Create a folder called c:\LearningAndUsingGIS\ProjectEnvironmentalPollution<YourName>\ that includes all subfolders and files comparable to c:\LearningAndUsingGIS\Project2\. You can simply reuse certain parts of the deliverables if applicable, such as the background in the proposal. As an option, carry out one of the future work suggestions that we provided in the project's solution, or pursue an additional issue that you identify on your own. Make arrangements to

compress c:\LearningAndUsingGIS\ProjectEnvironmentalPollution<YourName>\ and its subfolders and files to turn in to your instructor. Name your compressed file *ProjectEnvironmentalPollution<YourName>.zip*.

4. **Independent Project.** Carry out a project that you or your instructor identify. If you have an instructor, write the proposal, turn it in, and get feedback from your instructor before proceeding to building the GIS. Quite often, the feedback includes suggestions to narrow the scope of your project so it is feasible within time limits. Finally, build the GIS and produce all the deliverables. Name your project folder c:\LearningAndUsingGIS\ProjectIdependent<YourName>\, compress it, and turn it in to your instructor.

References

ESRI Census 2000 Tiger/Line Data, Internet URL: http://www.esri.com/data/download/census2000_tigerline/index.html (accessed April 26, 2005).

Hometown Locator, Internet URL: http://www.hometownlocator.com/ (accessed April 26, 2005).

Kendall, K. E. and J. E. Kendall (1995). *Systems Analysis and Design*, 3rd Ed. Englewood Cliffs: Prentice Hall, pp. 7-11.

Public Transportation Partnership for Tomorrow, Internet URL: http://www.publictransportation.org/pt2/ (accessed April 26, 2005).

Scorecard, The Pollution Information Site, Internet URL: http://www.scorecard.org/ (accessed April 26, 2005).

U.S. Census Bureau American FactFinder: Internet URL: http://factfinder.census.gov/servlet/DatasetMainPageServlet?_program=DEC&_lang=en (accessed April 26, 2005).

U.S. Environmental Protection Agency, Internet URL: http://www.epa.gov/ (accessed April 25, 2005).

DOWNLOADING AND INSTALLING ARCEXPLORER AND THE LEARNINGANDUSINGGIS DATA FILES

In order to work with this book, please download and install *ArcExplorer—Java Edition for Education* and the LearningAndUsingGIS data files.

Instructions follow for download and installation of ArcExplorer on Windows and MacIntosh computers as well as installation of the data files.

WINDOWS

You will need a total of 268 MB of free space on your c: drive for installation of ArcExplorer and data files. Of the total disk space needed, 91 MB are for ArcExplorer and 177 MB are for the data files.

Downloading and Installing ArcExplorer from the Internet

1. Go to *http://www.esri.com/software/arcexplorer/download.html*.
2. Go to Java Edition for Education and click on the link to download with instructions.
3. Follow the instructions for installation.

Installing ArcExplorer from CD

1. Insert the *Learning And Using GIS* CD into your CD-ROM drive.
2. If the CD does not automatically open in a My Computer window, open **My Computer** and double-click your **CD's drive** icon.
3. In the My Computer window for the CD, double-click the **ArcExplorerWindows** folder.
4. In the ArcExplorerWindows folder, double-click the **Install.exe InstallAnywhere Self Extractor** icon.
5. Follow the instructions for installation, using the default selections.

Installing Data Files

1. To install the data files, go to the ArcExplorerWindows folder on My Computer, and then click the **Up button** to go up a level so you can see the **LearningAndUsingGIS** folder.
2. Right-click the **LearningAndUsingGIS** folder icon and then click **Copy**.
3. Click the **Up button** in My Computer so you can see the icon for your c: drive.
4. Right-click the **c: drive** icon and then click **Paste**. This will create the c:\LearningAndUsingGIS\ folder.

It is critical that after installation you have exactly the path c:\LearningAndUsingGIS\ for this folder; otherwise, the map compositions we have prepared for ArcExplorer will not function.

MACINTOSH

You will need a total of 268 MB of free space on your hard drive for installation of ArcExplorer and data files. Of the total disk space needed, 91 MB are for ArcExplorer and 177 MB are for the data files.

Downloading and Installing ArcExplorer from the Internet

1. Go to *http://www.esri.com/software/arcexplorer/download.html*.
2. Go to Java Edition for Education and click on the link to download with instructions.
3. Follow the instructions for installation.

Installing ArcExplorer from CD

1. Insert the ***Learning and Using GIS*** CD into your CD-ROM drive.
2. When the CD icon appears on your desktop, double-click it.
3. In the resulting Finder window, double-click the **ArcExplorerMacintosh** folder.
4. Double-click the **install** icon that appears on your desktop.
5. Follow installation instructions. The default install location for ArcExplorer should be "inside AEJEE in folder ESRI on the disk Macintosh HD." If this is not the default location on your computer, navigate to your hard drive and select it. *Do not install this application in your "Applications" folder!*
6. Finish the installation process by following the directions on the screen.

Installing Data Files

1. Double-click the **CD** icon again.
2. Open another Finder window and navigate to the ESRI folder.
3. Click the **LearningAndUsingGIS** folder and drag it to the ESRI folder. This will create the /ESRI/LearningAndUsingGIS/ folder.

It is critical that after installation you have exactly the path /ESRI/LearningAndUsingGIS/ for this folder; otherwise, the map compositions we have prepared for ArcExplorer will not function.

B

C